Killing the
Rising Sun

Also by Bill O'Reilly and Martin Dugard

Killing the Rising Sun

HOW AMERICA VANQUISHED WORLD WAR II JAPAN

BILL O'REILLY

AND MARTIN DUGARD

St. Martin's Paperbacks

Published in the United States by St. Martin's Paperbacks, an imprint of St. Martin's Publishing Group.

KILLING THE RISING SUN

For information, address St. Martin's Publishing Group, 120 Broadway, New York, NY 10271.

www.stmartins.com

Library of Congress Catalog Card Number: 2016018160

ISBN: 978-1-250-75561-2

Our books may be purchased in bulk for promotional, educational, or business use. Please contact your local bookseller or the Macmillan Corporate and Premium Sales Department at 1-800-221-7945, ext. 5442, or by email at MacmillanSpecialMarkets@macmillan.com.

Printed in the United States of America

10 9 8 7 6 5 4 3 2 1

This book is dedicated to all World War II veterans.

Freedom rings because of you.

The land of the rising sun

> —ANCIENT CHINESE
> DESCRIPTION OF JAPAN,
> REFERRING TO THE MORNING
> SUN'S REACHING THE ISLANDS
> OF JAPAN BEFORE THE ASIAN
> MAINLAND

Map Legend

Allied   Japan

→   Advance   ←

◄-----   Retreat   ----►

🯇   Infantry   🯇

Military features

〰   Front line

✺   Clash/event

Combatant nationalities

 United States

     Soviet Union

●   Japan

Physical features

〰   Major road

〰   Minor road

〰   Railroad

〰   River

     Terrain

     Forest

○   City/town with urban area

☂   Nuclear detonation

Killing the
Rising Sun

On September 16, 2001, five days after the savage attack launched by Al Qaeda terrorists on the United States, Barack Obama's longtime Chicago pastor, Reverend Jeremiah Wright Jr., delivered a stunning anti-American diatribe in his church. Listing what he believed to be atrocities America had committed in the past that would explain or perhaps justify the 9/11 mass murder, Wright got around to condemning his country for dropping two atomic bombs on Japan in 1945.

"We bombed Hiroshima. We bombed Nagasaki. And we nuked far more than the thousands in New York and the Pentagon. . . . America's chickens are coming home to roost."

Seven years later, Wright's explosive statements were uncovered by the media. Senator Obama, then campaigning to become president, quickly repudiated his pastor's assessment, distancing himself from the militant minister who officiated at his wedding and with whom he had a close relationship for about twenty years.

It is safe to say that many people around the world had little or no idea what Wright was talking about. Sure, most folks know that A-bombs were dropped and the carnage caused was catastrophic. But, sad to say, the events leading up to the end of World War II are not that widely known anymore. Thus, statements like the one Wright made sometimes go unchallenged.

Every person on this planet lives with a common threat: nuclear annihilation. The nuclear weapons of today dwarf the first A-bombs in destructive power. Currently, the Iranian nuclear treaty has raised awareness of the threat, but still, the nuclear bomb's origins and the brutal world of the mid-1940s are no longer common knowledge.

Enter this book. It comes with a warning: the following pages contain some extremely troubling material. The violence the world witnessed in 1945 is unprecedented in history and will be chronicled on the following pages in detail.

What Martin Dugard and I are about to tell you is true and stark. The way the United States defeated the Japanese empire is vital to understand because the issues of that war are still being processed throughout the world today.

Killing the Rising Sun is the sixth in our series of history books. We believe you will know far more about America by the book's end. We also believe you will be very able to put the comments of people like Reverend Wright in their proper context.

We live in a time of spin and deception. It is important to know the truth.

Here it is.

BILL O'REILLY
LONG ISLAND, NEW YORK
MARCH 2016

INTRODUCTION

———•———

OVAL OFFICE, THE WHITE HOUSE
WASHINGTON, DC
OCTOBER 12, 1939
10:00 A.M.

The age of mass destruction is about to dawn.

"What bright idea do you have now?" an up-
beat Franklin Delano Roosevelt asks Wall Street
financier Alexander Sachs, one of his key advisers on
the New Deal that lifted America out of the Great Depression. The forty-six-year-old economist sits on the
opposite side of the president's massive wooden desk.
FDR was up past midnight, as is his custom. The deep
circles under his eyes and his pale skin, resulting from
constant exhaustion and too little time spent outdoors,
make the president look far older than his fifty-seven
years. His health is not enhanced by the Camel cigarette he now holds, one of the more than twenty he will
smoke today.

Sachs chooses his reply carefully. This meeting is so
top secret that it will not appear in the official daily log
of presidential appointments. Sachs can only hope that
it will go better than the hour he spent with Roosevelt

yesterday, when he labored unsuccessfully to find the right words to describe what could possibly be the greatest single threat to mankind.

It has been six weeks since Nazi Germany invaded Poland, beginning what will become known as the Second World War. One month prior, on August 2, theoretical physicist Albert Einstein wrote an urgent letter to President Roosevelt warning "that it may become possible to set up a nuclear chain reaction in a large mass of uranium . . . extremely powerful bombs of a new type may thus be constructed."

Einstein is a longtime friend of Roosevelt's, but he felt that sending Alexander Sachs to deliver the letter in person would be the most effective way of getting his point across. Yet when Sachs finally managed to get an audience with Roosevelt yesterday morning, the pompous financier was unable to articulate his case.

Rather than simply reading Einstein's two-page letter aloud, he appeared in the Oval Office with a stack of technical papers detailing America's uranium output and then read from an eight-hundred-word summary he had written. Sachs never mentioned that Einstein and other top American scientists believe that the new bombs could obliterate entire cities—or that Nazi Germany is currently racing to build such weapons. Roosevelt grew bored as Sachs droned on. With pressing business to address, the president dismissed Sachs, telling him to come back the next day.

That time is now. Realizing his mistake, Sachs gets right down to business. As Roosevelt listens attentively, the Wall Street leader reads Einstein's letter aloud. The president may not have appeared to be listening yesterday, but some of the discussion seems to have sunk in. Roosevelt probes Sachs with questions about uranium, the Nazis, and this new bomb. Einstein's letter makes it clear that the Germans have already taken control of a key uranium mine in Czechoslovakia and that scientists at the Kaiser Wilhelm Institute in Berlin are attempting to use this uranium to set up a nuclear chain reaction that could lead to the most lethal bomb in history.

Roosevelt has finally heard enough. "Alex," he summarizes for the financier, "what you are after is to see that the Nazis don't blow us up."

"Precisely," a relieved Sachs answers.

Roosevelt immediately summons his personal secretary, retired US Army general Edwin "Pa" Watson, into the Oval Office.

"Pa," Roosevelt orders, "this requires action."

1

Peleliu, Caroline Islands
Pacific Ocean
September 15, 1944
0832 Hours

Destruction is near for the empire.

The morning heat is so unbearable that Corporal Lewis Kenneth Bausell, USMC, has trouble breathing. He is huddled inside an amphibious landing vehicle with a dozen other marines of the First Battalion, headed for the section of Japanese-held beach code-named Orange One. Even this early in the morning, the temperature hovers at 100 degrees. The Americans are sweating profusely as their armored craft brings them ever closer to the sand. But heat is not the only factor—some of the perspiration is from nerves. These marines understand that they may soon die or be maimed for life and few will ever know what happened to them.

Unlike in the much more publicized war in Europe, where reporters like Ernie Pyle and Edward R. Murrow are making names for themselves by covering every aspect of the fighting, there are no journalists

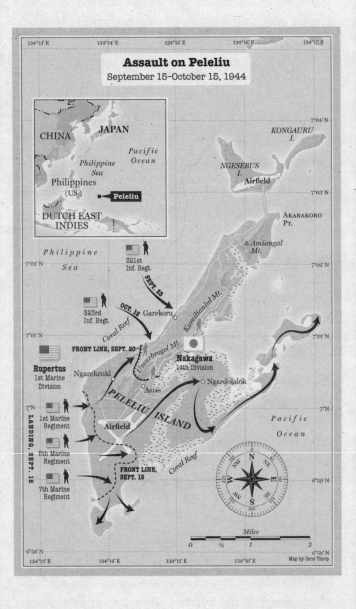

Assault on Peleliu
September 15–October 15, 1944

CHINA
JAPAN

Philippine Sea

Pacific Ocean

Philippines (US)

Peleliu

DUTCH EAST INDIES

7°04' N
KONGAURU I.

NGESEBUS I.
Airfield

AKARAKORO Pt.

△ Amiangal Mt.

7°03' N

Philippine Sea

7°02' N   7°02' N

321st Inf. Regt.

SEPT. 23

323rd Inf. Regt.

OCT. 15   Garekoru

Coral Reef

Kamilianlul Mt.

7°01' N   7°01' N

FRONT LINE, SEPT. 20

Umurbrogol Mt.

Nakagawa
14th Division

Rupertus
1st Marine Division

Ngarekeukl

Asias

Ngardololok

PELELIU ISLAND

7° N   7° N

1st Marine Regiment

Airfield

5th Marine Regiment

Pacific Ocean

7th Marine Regiment

FRONT LINE, SEPT. 15

Coral Reef

6°59' N   6°59' N

LANDING, SEPT. 15

N
NW   NE
W   E
SW   SE
S

Miles

0   ½   1   2

6°58' N   6°58' N

Map by Gene Thorp

or photographers hitting this remote beach today. The crucial upcoming battle against the Japanese will be waged in near anonymity.

Peleliu is important because of its airstrip, a hard-surfaced field capable of launching long-range fighter-bombers. The island is just six miles long and two miles wide, but the terrain is exceptionally rugged, a film of thin soil laid atop coral and limestone. A thousand yards off the beach rise the jungle-covered Umurbrogol ridges, a series of low, jagged peaks forming the island's spine. The Japanese have long coveted tiny, remote Peleliu, first taking possession of the empty island in 1914. For two decades it remained basically unused, but with the war came renewed awareness of its tactical importance. Since this past summer, knowing that the Americans would soon attack, the Japanese have labored to transform Peleliu into a fortress.

Most American marines could not care less about the history of Peleliu. Each man approaches the coming battle in his own way. Some smoke to calm their fears, some vomit onto the steel deck, and others worry about wetting their pants. But there is one belief that every man shares: no matter what happens when they hit the beach, surrendering to the enemy will not be an option.

Lewis Bausell has been through this before. Only twenty years old, the apprentice bookbinder from Washington, DC, has an easy smile and a wide boxer's nose. His hair is cropped close to his skull. Bausell had a semester left at McKinley Technical High School when the Japanese bombed Pearl Harbor in December 1941. He immediately dropped out of school and tried to enlist in the navy but was rejected. So instead, he enlisted in the Marine Corps. During his more than two years serving his country, Bausell has earned the respect of his peers, and although his rank is not yet official, just one month ago Bausell was selected for promotion to the rank of sergeant because of his heroic performance and leadership during invasions on Tulagi, Gavutu, Guadalcanal, and Cape Gloucester.*

Now, as the amtrac churns forward through the flat surf toward Peleliu, Bausell buckles the chin strap of his steel helmet. The landing craft stalls momentarily on the coral reef one hundred yards offshore, then continues churning toward the landing zone. Bausell is tempted to peer up and over the side to glimpse the battlefield, but he keeps his head down. Japanese snipers are known to target the curious.

All at once, geysers of water erupt around the landing craft. Incoming Japanese 141-mm mortar rounds fill the air. Many find their mark, killing Bausell's fellow marines on other landing craft. The explosions and the roar of artillery are so loud that Bausell and his squadmates cannot hear one another without yelling. The smoke of battle has turned the blue morning sky

---

*The American military campaign in the Pacific followed a strategy known as "island hopping." The US Navy, Army, and Marine Corps invaded Japanese island strongholds in the Pacific, slowly working their way north toward an eventual invasion of Japan. Islands not deemed vital to the advance were bypassed.

Final moments before landing on Peleliu

black. On any other day, Peleliu is a tropical island paradise. Today it is a living hell.

"Hit the beach," yells a sergeant as the amtrac's steel treads reach the shore. Bausell vaults up and over the side, landing hard on the bone-white sand and coral. The staccato chatter of hidden Japanese machine guns forces Bausell to press his body flat against the earth. All around him, explosions bring flashes of light. The palm trees lining the beach are in flames. Crimson pools of American blood mingle with the yellow phosphorus of Japanese incendiary devices.

"All any man could do was sweat it out and pray for survival," one marine will later write of his first moments on Peleliu. "It would have been sure suicide to stand up during that firestorm."

Everything Bausell sees and hears gives the lie to what he and his fellow marines had been told about this tactically vital Japanese stronghold. In preparation for Operation Stalemate, the United States Navy bombarded Peleliu with ten days of aerial raids and two more days of naval shelling. It seemed impossible that anyone could have lived through such an intense barrage of napalm and artillery; "we have run out of targets," a top naval officer complained. American intelligence supported this notion, suggesting that the enemy response would be minimal. The Marine Corps officer commanding the invasion, Major General William Rupertus, predicted a quick and easy battle— "a hard fought 'quickie' that will last for four days, five days at most."

But as Corporal Lewis Bausell and his squad can now attest, Peleliu will not be taken easily. Its defenders have had months to prepare. Mortar launchers and artillery are concealed behind the 2,200-yard beachfront, targeted to strike the precise spots at which the Americans now race ashore. In addition, the Japanese have constructed antitank barriers, laid hundreds of mines, and lined the beach with every coil of barbed wire in the Caroline Islands. "Spider traps"—machine-gun nests made of coconut-tree logs—are camouflaged so well that they are almost invisible in the swampy landscape where jungle meets the sand.

Yet Japanese commander Colonel Kunio Nakagawa is a realist. He knows the Americans will eventually work their way ashore. The US force is huge. So the wily colonel is employing a strategy tried just once before in the war.* Despite the horrific welcome the Americans are now receiving, it is not his goal to win this battle on the beaches. Just a fraction of his army now fights the marines, but thousands of other elite troops wait inland, in a network of five hundred hidden caves in the nearby Umurbrogol highlands.

These *fukkaku* defenses will allow Nakagawa and his men to counter the Americans, "bleeding them white" by coming out of hiding to attack when the marines least expect it.

The attacking Japanese soldiers' ability to swarm out of nowhere led top British general William Slim to refer to them as "the most formidable fighting insect in history." The men of Nakagawa's Fourteenth Imperial Division embody that sentiment. Almost all are veteran warriors, hardened by years of battle. They have been living five stories underground, subsisting on a simple diet of rice and fish and enduring the beatings and harsh discipline from their officers that are

---

*The concept of endurance engagements, as opposed to decisive engagements, as a means of fighting a protracted defensive battle to wear down the Americans was initially used on the small island of Biak, off the western coast of New Guinea. It was unsuccessful there; the Japanese were annihilated during the battle, losing 6,100 soldiers. The soldiers of the US Army's Forty-First Division, most of whom hailed from Oregon and Montana, earned the nickname "The Jungleers" for their success in the dense rain forests. They lost fewer than five hundred men.

typical of the Japanese army. "You could be beaten for anything," one Japanese soldier later remembered. "Being too short or being too tall, even because somebody didn't like the way you drank coffee. This was done to make each man respond instantly to orders, and it produced results. If you want soldiers who fight hard, they must train hard."

These soldiers have been taught another crucial lesson: that the Japanese race is superior to all others, and that triumph over the inferior Americans is inevitable.

That is a lie.

But to soldiers of the Imperial Japanese Army, it doesn't matter. Their strongest belief of all is in the samurai code of Bushido, which stipulates that surrender is a form of dishonor. "The man who would not disgrace himself must be strong," reads a line from the Japanese army's *Senjinkun*, a pocket-size code of behavior issued to all servicemen. "Do not survive in shame as a prisoner. Die, to ensure that you do not leave ignominy behind you."

Therein lies the basis for Colonel Nakagawa's trap.

There is no escape route for the Japanese, no evacuation plan. The forty-six-year-old Nakagawa, who was decorated nine times for his heroism during Japan's earlier war with China, has already informed his wife that he will never see her again.

Soon, very soon, he will lure the unsuspecting Americans into the Umurbrogol highlands and slaughter them.

But in turn, he and his men will also be slaughtered. Surrender is not an option.

⋆　⋆　⋆

Corporal Lewis Bausell rises up off the sand and sprints in a low crouch. His goal is the protective shelter of a small coral ridge a hundred yards inland. All around him as he runs, shouts of "Get the hell off the beach!" mingle with desperate pleas of "Corpsman!" Bausell has never seen such destruction. Two hundred marines will die today; hundreds more will be wounded. Terrified corporals and privates now watch the bodies of their brother marines torn apart as fire from Japanese heavy artillery crashes down.

"One figure seemed to fly to pieces," a marine will recall of a particularly grisly death. "With terrible clarity I saw the head and one leg fly into the air."

"I saw a wounded Marine near me staggering," another American will remember. "His face was half bloody pulp and the mangled shreds of what was left of an arm hung down like a stick . . . he fell behind me, in a red puddle on the white sand."

Every man here knows what the Japanese army does to prisoners of war. Rather than hold men captive, the Japanese murder them in the most heinous fashion. Veterans of previous battles with this enemy have seen the corpses of marines unlucky enough to be taken alive. Some had their bodies roped to a tree and used for live bayonet practice. Some had their heads, arms, and legs chopped off; scores of

US Marines were emasculated with bayonets as they lay dying on the ground.

"It was kill or be killed," Marine Corps private Dan Lawler will later remember. "The Japs didn't take prisoners so we didn't take prisoners either."

Or, as Marine Corps colonel Lewis "Chesty" Puller ordered his men before the Peleliu invasion: "You will take no prisoners. You will kill every yellow son-of-a-bitch, and that's it."

⋆ ⋆ ⋆

It seems an eternity, but it is only an hour before Corporal Bausell and a few of his fellow marines manage to get off the sand. Bausell's smile has been replaced by a tight-lipped glare. His instincts sharpened by his many previous landings, Bausell searches the tree line for signs of hidden enemy machine-gun emplacements targeting the invasion force. Suddenly, a burst of light gets Corporal Bausell's attention. The Japanese machine guns fire tracer bullets to help them zero in on a target, but these illuminated rounds can also help the marines pinpoint the shooter's precise location. Bausell sees a stream of tracers emerging from a small cave with a commanding view of the beach. The entrance is concealed by scrub plants and thick brush.

Taking charge of the squad, he motions for his men to follow him toward the cave's location. Reaching the cave first, he fires into a small opening. Lieutenant Jack Kimble of Greenville, Mississippi, arrives with a two-man flamethrower team; a stream of fire is launched into the Japanese position in the hope of forcing the enemy to come out. Corporal Bausell, meanwhile, stands ready to shoot them as they emerge.

The first Japanese to run screaming from the cave is carrying a grenade. He pulls the pin before Bausell can fire his M1 carbine. Not only does the explosion kill the Japanese soldier but shrapnel slices into several nearby marines.

More flame is shot into the cave. Another Japanese soldier emerges.

This time, Bausell shoots him dead.

Yet another Japanese soldier runs out of the cave, choosing the sure death by rifle fire to being roasted alive. He too carries a grenade, hurling it at the Americans as Bausell raises his weapon.

The grenade is launched before Bausell shoots; it lands near him and several other marines. The blast may kill them all.

Without hesitation, Corporal Bausell throws his body onto the grenade. His torso rises off the ground as it explodes, smothering the blast. None of his fellow marines is hurt.

"Get that Jap," Bausell shouts. Somehow, he is still alive.

The flamethrower team shoots off a burst of flame, turning the Japanese soldier into a human torch.

Less than two hours after landing on Peleliu, Corporal Lewis Bausell is put on a stretcher and carried back down the beach. He is loaded aboard an amtrac, then ferried out to the hospital ship *Bountiful*, where he is immediately taken into surgery.

But doctors cannot stop the bleeding. The Japanese

grenade has sent deadly shards of metal deep into Bausell's internal organs. On September 18, 1944, three days after the invasion of Peleliu, Corporal Lewis Bausell dies.

Unlike those of soldiers fighting on World War II's European front, his body will not be lowered into the ground and marked with a monument so that his family might someday visit. Instead, his corpse is wrapped in sailcloth, tethered to a spent artillery shell, and dropped at sea.

Corporal Lewis Bausell is the first United States Marine at the Battle of Peleliu whose death will see him awarded America's highest award for valor, the Medal of Honor, for actions above and beyond the call of duty in combat.

He is not the last.

2

---◆---

General Douglas MacArthur is grinning. "As Ripley says, believe it or not, we're here," he boasts to his chief of staff.

Seven hundred miles west of Peleliu, where marines are now mired in their fifth bloody week of combat, the sixty-four-year-old commander of American forces in the Pacific leans over the rail of the USS *Nashville*.* He gazes into the distance at his beloved Philippines, which were invaded by more than a hundred thousand US Army troops under his command less than four hours ago. His counterpart in Europe, General Dwight Eisenhower, became famous for the D-Day invasion of France this past June. So MacArthur, well known

---

*Two months after MacArthur's landing, Japanese kamikaze aircraft flew into the *Nashville*. The light cruiser remained afloat but suffered the loss of 133 sailors and an additional 190 wounded in the fiery explosions.

for his ego, has chosen to call the date of this invasion "A-Day," for "Attack Day."*

As on Peleliu, intelligence reports predicting minimal enemy resistance have proven very wrong. The Japanese are putting up a fierce fight for the Philippines. Even miles out to sea, MacArthur can hear the chatter of automatic-weapons fire coming from groves of palm trees and see the billowing plumes of black smoke from the jungle. Just overhead, American fighter-bombers buzz toward entrenched enemy positions, keeping a sharp eye out for Japanese Zero fighter planes.

Two years ago, after the fall of the Philippines to the Japanese, the most humiliating defeat of MacArthur's storied career, the general promised the world that he would one day come back in glory to retake the islands. Now, he is setting out to make good on that vow.

Douglas MacArthur, who likes to refer to himself in the third person as simply "MacArthur," is a shade over six feet tall, the son of a Medal of Honor–winning general through whom he has a lifelong connection to the Philippines. Arthur MacArthur Jr. fought in the American Civil War as a teenager and, after the Spanish-American War, served as military governor

---

* At the time, the invasion of Leyte was the second-largest amphibious landing of the Second World War, next to that of Normandy. Leyte was unique in that the American soldiers had to travel four thousand miles by ship—a distance greater than the width of the United States—in order to launch their invasion. The distance from England to Normandy was roughly twenty miles.

of the Philippines.* Douglas graduated at the top of his class at West Point, and to this day is as narrow-waisted and fit as on his commissioning day in 1903.

MacArthur clambers down a ladder hanging over the *Nashville*'s side and into a waiting landing craft. As he does every day, the general wears a freshly pressed khaki uniform that bears no insignia or ribbons. He fastidiously maintains the creases on his shirtsleeves and trousers by changing clothes frequently, and has just donned a fresh uniform for the landing. In case the landing goes horribly wrong and MacArthur is at risk of being taken prisoner, a loaded derringer that once belonged to his father rests in his hip pocket.

Sweat stains seep into the gold braid encircling MacArthur's weathered field marshal's cap; his dark brown eyes are shielded from the ocean's glare by wire-rimmed Ray-Ban sunglasses. Completing these trademark aspects of his appearance, all of which have made the general an iconic figure worldwide, is the un-lit corncob pipe clenched firmly between his teeth.[†]

---

* Arthur MacArthur Jr. was just eighteen when he rallied Union troops during the pivotal battle of Missionary Ridge, outside of Chattanooga, on November 25, 1863. The son of a former Wisconsin governor, MacArthur rushed to the top of the hill during thick fighting, planting the regimental colors of the 24th Wisconsin Volunteer Infantry Regiment on the summit and shouting "On Wisconsin!" as he did so.

[†] MacArthur's pipes were made to his precise specifications by the Missouri Meerschaum Company, which continues to sell a replica of his deep-bowled, long-stemmed pipe. Similarly, Ray-Ban named a line of sunglasses in the general's honor in 1987.

Chief of Staff Richard Sutherland, a lieutenant general, follows MacArthur down the ladder. After the remainder of MacArthur's "Bataan Gang" descend into the landing craft, a select group of war correspondents joins them. Douglas MacArthur knows the value of good publicity and has carefully choreographed his landing so that images of this great moment will soon be splashed across front pages around the world. The plan is to land not on the beach but at a dock. The photographers will step out of the boat first, then turn around to capture the immaculately starched and pressed general once again setting foot on Philippine soil.

Like many a scripted moment, however, the actual event will unfold in a quite different fashion.

Almost one thousand days after fleeing the Philippines, General Douglas MacArthur orders the landing craft to sail for shore.

He has returned.

☆ ☆ ☆

Douglas MacArthur well knows that this landing in the Philippines is a vital step toward the eventual invasion of Japan. Though plans are still in the conceptual phase, and such an assault is at least a year away, it promises to be the greatest amphibious landing in history. It is expected that hundreds of thousands of American soldiers, marines, pilots, and sailors will take part, on a scale dwarfing that of the D-Day landings in Normandy. The cost will be extreme—loss of life is expected to approach one million on both sides. As the most revered general in the Pacific, MacArthur will most assuredly be called upon to lead this devastating invasion.

Yet were it not for a direct order four years ago from President Franklin Delano Roosevelt, a man whom MacArthur tolerates rather than admires, the general wouldn't be under consideration for such a glorious command.* Indeed, he would most likely be starving to death in a prisoner-of-war camp.

It was December 7, 1941, when the Japanese launched a surprise attack on the American fleet moored at Pearl Harbor, Hawaii. Blindsided by violence on this "date which will live in infamy," America declared war on Japan and its ally, Germany.

Following the sneak attack, the Japanese quickly struck again one day later and more than five thousand miles west across the open Pacific. Shortly after noon, a flight of Japanese fighter-bombers from the Eleventh Air Fleet destroyed the American air base at Clark Field in the Philippines. Two days later, two more waves of Japanese aircraft flew unopposed over the Cavite Navy Yard, laying waste to the docks. The US destroyers *Pillsbury* and *Peary* barely escaped, and the submarine *Sealion* was bombed in her berth. As with the attack on Clark Field, the Japanese chose to drop their bombs on Cavite just after noon. Incredibly, two short days after the shock of Pearl Harbor, many of America's defenders were still not on full alert and were at lunch as the raids began.

---

* MacArthur is a right-wing Republican whose political philosophy does not line up with that of the liberal Roosevelt.

But the Philippine Islands were different than Pearl Harbor. Their location is much closer to Japan, making possession of them a much more urgent tactical necessity. Capturing the Philippines would effectively give Japan control of the western Pacific. Rather than conduct a savage aerial bombardment, the forces of Dai Nippon—or "Great Japan"—aimed to seize control of the entire country.* The invasion was planned for almost a decade, beginning with an influx of Japanese soldiers disguised as immigrants, a systematic mapping of the Philippines' more than seven thousand islands, and spying on Philippine coastal defenses. "Only later," Filipino president Manuel Quezon will remember, "did I discover that my gardener was a Japanese major and my masseur a Japanese colonel."

At the apex of American leadership in the Philippines at the time was Douglas MacArthur. He and his wife, Jean, lived with their three-year-old son, Arthur, in an opulent penthouse atop the Manila Hotel. MacArthur had left the US Army in 1937 after a brilliant career, then accepted a high-paying position as a field marshal in the Philippine Army. But he was recalled in July 1941, as war began to appear imminent, and named commander of American forces in the Far East. He was the obvious choice for the position: not only had he lived in the strategically vital Philippines during the

---

* "Dai Nippon" refers to the assemblage of islands and colonies under Japanese control at the outset of World War II. The usage is similar to the term "Great Britain," the name of another island nation dependent on colonies and conquests as a source of empire.

1920s and 1930s, he had overseen the creation of the Philippine Army.*

Within a matter of months, after Japanese bombing destroyed his air force on the ground, MacArthur's small army was powerless against invasion. Fleeing Manila, MacArthur retreated to fortified positions on the Bataan Peninsula, where he assured his men that reinforcements were on the way.

But this was not true. American and British policy dictated that most resources be spent on defeating Germany before Japan.† Even if that were not the case, the remote location of the Philippines and the Japanese naval domination of the Pacific meant that reinforcements wouldn't get through in time. President Roosevelt, upon hearing MacArthur's promise, called his words "criminal."

For the next two months, the Japanese continued their advance. The small American and Filipino forces under MacArthur's command were pushed back to the

---

*In addition, MacArthur's list of accomplishments and battle commands during his long military career would have made it ludicrous for any other general to assume this post. His passion for the Pacific way of life extended to the Orient—he often relaxed wearing a Japanese kimono.

†The Arcadia Conference, a summit between British and American leaders in Washington, DC, during December 1941 and January 1942, led to the "Europe first" strategy. While the United States and Britain worked closely together to defeat Germany, the British role in the Pacific theater was focused on General William Slim's victories in Burma. The battle against Japan in the last year of the war was largely an American enterprise.

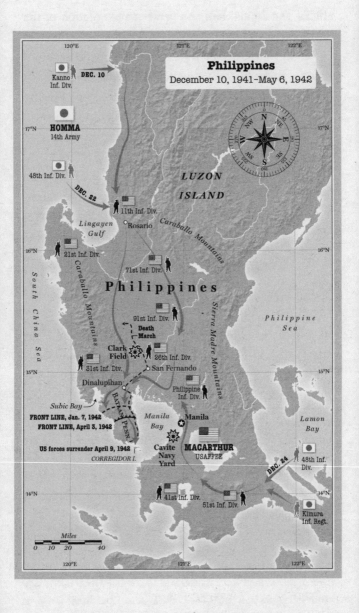

Philippines
December 10, 1941–May 6, 1942

Kanno Inf. Div.

DEC. 10

HOMMA
14th Army

48th Inf. Div.

DEC. 22

11th Inf. Div.

Lingayen Gulf

Rosario

Caraballo Mountains

LUZON ISLAND

71st Inf. Div.

Philippines

Caraballo Mountains

91st Inf. Div.

Death March

Clark Field

26th Inf. Div.

31st Inf. Div.

San Fernando

Dinalupihan

South China Sea

Sierra Madre Mountains

Philippine Sea

Philippine Inf. Div.

Subic Bay

FRONT LINE, Jan. 7, 1942
FRONT LINE, April 3, 1942

BATAAN PENIN.

Manila Bay

Manila

US forces surrender April 9, 1942

CORREGIDOR I.

Cavite Navy Yard

MACARTHUR
USAFFE

Lamon Bay

DEC. 24

48th Inf. Div.

41st Inf. Div.

51st Inf. Div.

Kimura Inf. Regt.

Miles

0 10 20 40

tip of the Bataan Peninsula, where many took refuge in a fortress on an island known as Corregidor. Even when it became clear that Bataan and Corregidor would soon fall, MacArthur directed the resistance from the safety of his underground bunker in the bombproof Malinta Tunnel. His desperate battle became a symbol of resistance to the Japanese onslaught throughout the Pacific, and MacArthur was largely portrayed as a hero in the media, making him world famous.

It soon became clear to President Roosevelt that he had to rescue MacArthur. He had no choice: America was stunned by its sudden immersion into war. The Japanese seemed unbeatable. Allowing Douglas MacArthur to become a prisoner of war would have devastated national morale.

On February 22, Roosevelt ordered MacArthur to flee. The navy spirited his family and twenty of his staff, along with his son's Chinese nanny, out of the Philippines on swift patrol torpedo (PT) boats. Some felt that the nanny, with the unlikely name of Ah Cheu, should be replaced by an army nurse, but MacArthur was adamant that she come along. All told, the group, allowed one suitcase each, would undertake a six-hundred-mile voyage in four PT boats, traveling over the open ocean in hopes of making it to the island of Mindanao.

The remainder of MacArthur's American and Filipino soldiers on Bataan and Corregidor were left behind under the command of Lieutenant General Jonathan "Skinny" Wainwright.

Thus two parallel odysseys began. The defenders

of Bataan and Corregidor endured a descent into hell. Bataan fell first, in April 1942. In what would become known as the Bataan Death March, seventy-six thousand captured American and Filipino soldiers were stripped of their valuables and force-marched sixty-five miles to a prison camp. Their hands were bound the entire way; those unable to keep pace in the brutal heat and humidity were shot, bayoneted, or beheaded by their captors. Japanese trucks rolled right over those who collapsed. In all, more than seven thousand men perished.

Corregidor fell one month later. General Wainwright and his remaining men were placed in prison camps, where the ritual abuse and murder of Americans by the Japanese army would continue for the next three and a half years. Throughout the war, the forces of the emperor would turn their American prisoners into slaves. Living conditions in their concentration camps were deplorable, and men died from dysentery, beriberi, and starvation. General Wainwright, already a very thin man at the outset of the war, became skeletal during his captivity. He was nominated for the Medal of Honor while still in a Japanese prison camp, but Douglas MacArthur objected to the request, stating that Wainwright should never have surrendered.*

---

* General George C. Marshall put forth Wainwright's name for the Medal of Honor on July 30, 1942. MacArthur, still stinging from the surrender of Corregidor, openly opposed the nomination, an act unheard of in the history of the award. In a letter to Marshall, MacArthur wrote: "As a relative matter, award of the Medal of

Meanwhile, MacArthur's journey eventually led him to Australia, where he assumed command of all forces in the Pacific. Many Americans saw his escape from Corregidor as an act of daring, but some considered the desertion of his men an act of cowardice. MacArthur explained his actions to reporters while in Australia: "The President of the United States ordered me to break through the Japanese lines and proceed from Corregidor to Australia for the purpose, as I understand it, of organizing the American offensive against Japan, a primary objective of which is the relief of the Philippines. I came through and I shall return."

On April 1, 1942, Douglas MacArthur was awarded the Medal of Honor for "conspicuous leadership" in his heroic defense of the Philippines, making MacArthur

---

Honor to General Wainwright would be a grave injustice to a number of general officers of practically equally responsible positions who not only distinguished themselves by fully as great personal gallantry thereby earning the DSC but exhibited powers of leadership and inspiration to a degree greatly superior to that of General Wainwright thereby contributing much more to the stability of the command and to the successful conduct of the campaign. It would be a grave mistake which later on might well lead to embarrassing repercussions to make this award." Marshall rescinded the nomination. Wainwright never held a grudge toward MacArthur, whom he considered a dear friend and great general. Upon his release from a Japanese prisoner-of-war camp at war's end, Wainwright was treated like a national hero and honored with a ticker-tape parade in New York. On September 10, 1945, he was finally awarded the Medal of Honor.

and General Arthur MacArthur Jr. the first father-son Medal of Honor winners in American history.*

So it is that island by island, men under MacArthur's command are retaking control of the Pacific as the general works his way back to the Philippines. His desire to redeem himself trumps all other motives and has drawn critique from navy commanders.[†] The devastating battle for Peleliu, which has already incurred four thousand American casualties, is taking place only because MacArthur fears that Japanese planes will launch from its runways and harass his Philippine invasion force. In truth, the American navy now controls the sea and the skies and would have little trouble stopping an aerial attack.

☆　☆　☆

It has taken MacArthur almost three years, but his landing craft finally arrives at Red Beach on Leyte. The general's face hardens as he steps off the boat into

---

*Teddy Roosevelt (awarded posthumously in 2001) and his son Theodore III were the second such pair.

[†] Admirals Ernest King and Chester Nimitz believed retaking the islands was not a priority, and that they could be bypassed altogether. They felt MacArthur was too emotionally attached to the Philippines to view them with a critical strategic eye. Even General George Marshall, MacArthur's superior in Washington, cautioned him, "We must be careful not to allow our personal feeling . . . to override our great objective, which is the early conclusion of the war with Japan. . . . 'Bypassing' is not synonymous with 'abandonment.'" MacArthur refused to change his pro-invasion stance, and ultimately won the argument in the summer of 1944.

knee-deep ocean water, the razor-sharp creases in his pants disappearing in an instant.

"Let 'em walk," barked the navy officer in charge of directing the traffic of landing barges moving on and off of Red Beach when he heard that MacArthur wanted a special dock on which to land. A "beachmaster," as this officer is known, enjoys supreme authority over the landing zone; not even the great Douglas Mac-Arthur receives special treatment.

It is forty paces from the landing craft to shore. Mac-Arthur glares at the impertinent young officer as he wades through the flat surf. His personal photographer, Captain Gaetano Faillace, captures the moment for posterity, even as the Japanese snipers roped high up in the palm trees could very well be taking aim at the sixty-four-year-old general standing tall on the white sand.

General Douglas MacArthur wading ashore on Leyte, fulfilling his promise to return

Once on land, MacArthur is handed a microphone.

"People of the Philippines," he proclaims, "I have returned!"

In his excitement, the normally imperturbable general's hands shake.

Soon after, General Douglas MacArthur turns around and wades back to his landing craft, which quickly returns him to the shelter and safety of the USS *Nashville*.

3

———————

have long since become immune to mudslinging and find the best tactics are to ignore it," Harry Truman writes in a letter to his friend J. L. Naylor as his campaign train pulls into Kansas City. The sixty-year-old Truman drains his glass of Old Grand-Dad bourbon and sets it on the writing table. The great locomotive that has pulled him around America glides into the city's Union Station, bringing the Democratic vice presidential candidate's monthlong barnstorming tour to an end.

Despite Truman's hard work, the war has garnered more front-page news than his speeches and rallies—and with good reason. Almost eight thousand miles away in the Pacific, Peleliu has become a ghastly mess, with thousands of marines killed and wounded. In the Philippines, General Douglas MacArthur's hopes for an easy victory have been dashed by a determined enemy, poor strategic planning, and something new: the kamikaze—Japanese suicide pilots dropping out of the sky to sink American ships by deliberately flying their planes into the hulls.

Tonight, Harry Truman will sleep in a luxury hotel rather than the train's cramped berth, knowing that he has done all he can to help elect President Franklin Roosevelt to a fourth term in office. In the morning, as he sometimes prefers, Truman may toast the journey's end with a breakfast shot of Old Grand-Dad.

The night air is chill and smells of rain. Truman, his wife, Bess, and their daughter, Margaret, step down onto the platform. The vice presidential candidate adores Bess and proves it by writing long love letters to her when he is away. On June 28, they celebrated twenty-five years of marriage.

Margaret Truman is a student at George Washington University who aspires to a singing career. She is the couple's only child. Margaret is not exceptionally beautiful but possesses an honesty and intelligence common among those secure in their own skin. In these ways, she is much like her father.

A car waits for the Truman family. The driver watches as their luggage is loaded. The potential vice president is glad to finally be back in Kansas City; since Truman was first elected to the Senate, in 1934, his family has divided their time between Washington and his home state of Missouri. This is where his political career began more than twenty years ago, so it is fitting that his campaign should end here. There will be one final speech tomorrow evening here in town, and then Truman can do little but wait for Election Day, when he may be elected vice president of the United States, replacing Henry Wallace.*

Truman is confident of victory—Franklin Roosevelt's overwhelming popularity and steely leadership during the Second World War has seen him elected a record three times. Now, with the war in Europe seemingly won and the battles in the Pacific slowly turning against the Japanese, the public continues in its support of the patrician Democrat. FDR's opponent in the election of 1944 is the Republican Thomas Dewey, the diminutive governor of New York with the Fuller Brush mustache. Dewey likes to attack Roosevelt as a Communist with unsound domestic policies. Although simplistic, Dewey's assertions elicit resounding ovations wherever he campaigns.

In truth, America loves Franklin Roosevelt like a trusted rich uncle. Dewey and his running mate, Ohio governor John W. Bricker, have campaigned with an underdog's zeal, but they have no chance at victory[†]—support for Roosevelt is just too strong.

---

*While he was popular with the Far Left, Wallace's Communist sympathies were well known. Roosevelt publicly endorsed him as his vice president before the 1944 Democratic Convention but was pressed to see a replacement by party leaders who worried that he might die in office. Truman, the dark horse choice due to his outspoken nature, was seen as a better successor to lead America into the postwar world. In the end, FDR acceded to the demands of some Democratic power brokers who wanted Wallace off the ticket.

[†] The Roosevelt-Truman ticket won the election in a landslide over the Republican ticket of Thomas Dewey and John W. Bricker; the final Electoral College tally was 432 to 99.

The same cannot be said of Harry Truman. America knows nothing about him. The Republicans have made his anonymity a campaign issue, warning that the untested Truman would lead the nation if Roosevelt were to die. Even the media agree. "The hind half of the ticket is a storm center, exciting almost as much debate as the standard bearer himself," wrote the *New York Times* in early October. "The competence of Mr. Roosevelt's current running mate is the nearest thing this country has to a burning issue."

The *Chicago Tribune* is just as direct, stating that "Senator Truman . . . is a newcomer. We ought to know more about him, and the best way to learn is from his own lips." But Harry S. Truman* is nothing if not discreet. Stoicism in the face of controversy requires the same chin-up attitude that made him successful as an artillery officer in France during World War I and allowed him to rise through the political ranks. The polio that has put the president in a wheelchair, combined with his passion for gin and cigarettes, is hardening his arteries and dulling his thoughts. But Harry Truman

---

*The S stands for nothing. Truman's parents were torn between using the family names of Solomon or Shipp as a middle name; in the end, they could not decide and simply used the S. Common in Roman times, middle names fell out of favor for more than a thousand years. In America, middle names made a resurgence after the Civil War but were not standard practice until after World War I. Many of America's founding fathers, including George Washington, John Adams, Thomas Jefferson, and Benjamin Franklin, had no middle name.

does not know FDR well enough to comment on the president's condition.

Presidential politics are a ruthless business. So Truman volunteers little about himself during his four-week train campaign from Atlantic to Pacific and back again. Even an oversight can be blown up by the media. Three weeks ago at a speech at the Shrine Auditorium in Los Angeles, Truman unknowingly endorsed a former member of the Ku Klux Klan for Congress. Republicans immediately pounced. Rumors arose that Truman himself was a member of the white supremacist group. "Of course I'm not a member of the Klan," Truman barked when a Chicago reporter questioned him two weeks later. And still the innuendo would not disappear: on October 30, one night before Truman greeted a crowd of twenty thousand at New York's Madison Square Garden, fabled actress Gloria Swanson spoke on the radio in an address paid for by the Republican National Committee, making accusations about "Mr. Truman's membership in the Ku Klux Klan."

Although he was furious, Harry Truman offered no response.

It was not until leading members of the black community stated, "Mr. Truman is a friend of the Negro people . . . a true progressive," that the baseless rumors slowly abated.*

---

* Truman had long been a public proponent of civil rights for black Americans. The quote comes from an editorial in the *People's Voice*, a Harlem, New York, newspaper founded by civil rights

★ ★ ★

Harry Truman's driver drops the Truman family at the Muehlebach Hotel at the intersection of Twelfth and Baltimore. Ernest Hemingway once stayed here; so did Bob Hope, Babe Ruth, and Helen Keller. In time, the Beatles will party in its corridors. At this point in his life, Harry S. Truman knows no such celebrity.

Bellmen scramble for the Trumans' luggage. Unlike General Douglas MacArthur, who hasn't opened a door for himself or carried his own suitcase for years, the ever-practical Truman is self-sufficient. During his train ride around America, he washed his socks between stops and hung them outside the window to dry. Stepping into the lobby of the Muehlebach, he is quick to thank the doorman.

Now, Bess and Margaret at his side, Harry Truman can finally rest.

Or so he thinks.

leader Adam Clayton Powell Jr. In addition, the National Association for the Advancement of Colored People (NAACP) came to Truman's defense.

4

Colonel Kunio Nakagawa kneels in the cave that has served as his command post for more than two months. The short, razor-sharp blade of a *tantōç* is clutched in his right fist. Nakagawa has inflicted more than ten thousand casualties on the Americans, more than any other Japanese officer in the war. His strategy of retreating into an underground fortress to fight a defensive battle has terrified the Americans. Unable to dig deep foxholes in the coral that covers so much of the island, the marines lie exposed, easy targets for sniper fire or nighttime stealth attacks. Often, Nakagawa's men will quietly leave their cave networks to kill any American who makes the cardinal error of falling asleep while on watch. Nakagawa's soldiers can often smell their victims before actually laying eyes on them: the Americans are unable to bury their excrement or take a simple shower, resulting in a stench of human waste and tang of sweat-soaked uniforms that has only been intensified by the searing island heat. Even more aromatic is the smell of Japanese and American corpses left to rot in the sun, the bloated skin of the dead men covered in giant blowflies.

All of this is the handiwork of Colonel Nakagawa. Almost all of his soldiers are dead now; the Americans have pressed their attack despite the enormous loss of life. They have aimed flamethrowers into the caves to burn men alive and exploded the caves with artillery and hand grenades, entombing Nakagawa's warriors forever. Once upon a time, Nakagawa commanded the entire island. Now his redoubt is just a few hundred meters wide. The time has come to do what he needs to do so as not to disgrace himself. Already, Nakagawa has set fire to his regimental colors so that they will never fall into American hands. He has proclaimed to his remaining fifty-six emaciated soldiers that "our sword is broken and we have run out of spears" as he divided them into small groups. He then ordered the men to fan out deep in the caves and attack the Americans—fighting to the very end.*

If necessary, Nakagawa was prepared to act as *kaishakunin* for his superior officer, Major General Kenjiro Murai. Unknown to the US Marines, Murai has been on Peleliu throughout the invasion. His job has been "to make sure Nakagawa does not make any mistakes," as one Japanese soldier will admit to the Americans when he is taken prisoner. Nakagawa has

---

* The last of Nakagawa's soldiers eluded capture until April 22, 1947.

now seen the tables turn. Where he was once watched over by Murai, now it has been his job to make sure that Murai did not lose heart when the moment to commit ritual suicide was upon him. As Murai's *kaishakunin*—or "second"—it would be Nakagawa's role to stand by and help Murai with his sword, prepared to assist in the general's death should Murai no longer be able to control the knife with which he is committing seppuku.

But Murai has completed the task. He lies dead, intestines spilling from his body onto the command post's coral floor.

Nakagawa watched as the general knelt, then plunged the *tantōç* into the left side of his abdomen. Murai then wrenched the blade sharply to the right, slicing through the soft belly skin. Blood and internal organs spilled from the gash in a torrent. Murai writhed in agony as he fell forward. Death came for him in less than thirty seconds.

The forty-six-year-old Colonel Nakagawa now kneels down beside his dead commander, praying for the same courage to end his life with honor.

★ ★ ★

The marines have fought gallantly on Peleliu for two months, displaying the depth of their training and their commitment to one another.

Corporal Lewis Bausell was the first to give his life for his brother marines. Seven others will be awarded the Medal of Honor for conspicuous courage under fire, four of whom also threw themselves on live grenades to save the lives of their brothers.*

On September 18, the same day that saw the death of Corporal Bausell, Private First Class Arthur J. Jackson of Cleveland, Ohio, single-handedly attacks a thick cement pillbox containing thirty-five Japanese soldiers. Even as he takes heavy fire, Jackson pokes the barrel of his M1 into a narrow gun opening and squeezes off a round. He then hurls white phosphorus grenades inside the bunker, killing everyone inside.

Spotting two similar pillboxes nearby, Jackson storms them alone, with the same unlikely result.

But PFC Jackson is not finished. Identifying each and every one of the hidden Japanese machine-gun nests, the square-jawed nineteen-year-old dashes from emplacement to emplacement, killing each and every soldier who is shooting at him. "He stormed one gun position after another, dealing death and destruction to the savagely fighting enemy in his inexorable drive against the remaining defenses, and succeeded in wiping out a total of 12 pillboxes and 50 Japanese soldiers," Jackson's Medal of Honor citation will read.

When his one-man offensive comes to an end, the nineteen-year-old marine collapses from heat exhaustion. It is a moment Jackson will long remember: "I felt

---

* The other recipients of the Medal of Honor were First Lieutenant Carlton Robert Rouh, Private First Class Charles Howard Roan, Captain Everett Parker Pope, Private Wesley Phelps, Private First Class John Dury New, Private First Class Richard Edward Kraus, and Private First Class Arthur J. Jackson.

like I was a ballplayer that had just made the winning touchdown."*

☆ ☆ ☆

One day later, it is Captain Everett P. Pope who demonstrates the Corps's grit. Captain of the tennis team while at Bowdoin College, where he was elected to Phi Beta Kappa and graduated magna cum laude, the twenty-five-year-old Bostonian is also a fluent speaker of French, a loving husband, and the father of two young sons.

But that was before the war, in another life. Since first seeing action at Guadalcanal in June 1942, Pope has become a trained killer and leader of men. During the New Britain campaign earlier this year, he led a fourteen-man squad into thick jungle in search of Japanese positions. Not only did his men kill twenty of the enemy, but Pope performed the almost impossible feat of bringing back seven Japanese prisoners for interrogation.

Now, with Peleliu's airfield in American hands, the marines face the daunting task of moving inland to flush the enemy from their caves in the Umurbrogol ridges. Company commander Pope is ordered to take Hill 154, a sheer coral outcrop on a slope known as Suicide Ridge.

---

* Arthur J. Jackson received his Medal of Honor at a White House ceremony on October 5, 1945. In 1961, having attained the rank of captain, he fatally shot a Cuban spy at the Guantánamo Bay naval base in Cuba. Fearing an international incident due to the strained relations between Cuba and the United States, Jackson attempted to conceal the death by burying the body. Jackson was found out, however, and lost his commission.

Pope and his men are already exhausted. Since landing on Peleliu four days ago, his company has suffered 30 percent casualties; the loss of trained riflemen has forced Pope to utilize "cooks and bakers and company clerks" on the line. It is dawn as they prepare to attack, but few have slept, as the Japanese sent soldiers out in the night to infiltrate the American lines. They are thirsty, for the equatorial heat is relentless, never dipping below 100 degrees, even at night. Coral tears their clothing, cuts through their boots, and is heated by the sun, burning their skin on contact. The three-pound steel helmets protecting their heads from shrapnel also serve as pillow, cook pot, and latrine. Many choose not to wear underwear or a T-shirt due to the heat, and are not likely to change their socks for days at a time—if at all. The water with which they fill their canteens is rust-colored and tastes like gasoline because the navy has stored the water in fifty-five-gallon drums that once stored fuel. The marines desperately need to drink, but the water makes them nauseated.

And yet they must attack.

Pope gives the order to advance. The company approaches Hill 154 through a swamp, supported by mortar rounds and machine-gun fire. In addition to the packs on their backs, each man carries a rifle, pistol, canteen, and ammunition. Immediately, the Japanese pop up out of the ground to let loose a stream of bullets before disappearing into their caves once again. Many of the shots are fired at point-blank range from the other side of the swamp.

Pope and his marine assault unit fall back.

But Hill 154 must be taken.

Hours later, the afternoon sun beating down on them, Pope's company attacks once more. His marines are again overwhelmed by precise enemy fire and suffer horrific casualties. Pope's company numbered almost 235 men four days ago. By 1800 hours, as dusk falls on Hill 154, just 14 remain.

But those fourteen control the hill.

Pope must now hold this position at all costs. Those are his orders. But he immediately recognizes that his position is tenuous: Hill 154 is barren and exposed on three sides, leaving Pope and his men open to enemy fire. His only option is to spread the two officers and eleven enlisted men in strategic positions across the top of the hill. The weapons at their disposal are few: tommy guns, rifles, a light machine gun, and a small number of hand grenades. Pope's men are from Pennsylvania, Kentucky, Massachusetts, Texas, Maine, Michigan, Kansas, California, and New York City. Now, as the sun sets and the utter blackness of the island night is upon them, fate has brought them all to the peak of Hill 154, the place where they all might die.

A crescent moon rises, a mere sliver in the sky. Pope and his soldiers cannot see the faces of the Japanese who now creep forward to kill them, many clad in black pajama-like uniforms. Nor can the Americans hear their enemy, for the Japanese wear split-toed shoes with a rubber sole that allow them to walk without a sound. At first the Japanese are bold, attacking in ones and twos. But Pope's men's senses are heightened by the knowledge that any mistake will be their last.

The Americans easily fend off the first teams of Japanese killers.

Toward midnight, the strategy shifts. Twenty-five enemy soldiers at a time creep in toward the American positions. One of them comes close enough to bayonet Second Lieutenant Francis T. Burke in the leg. Unable to reach his gun, Burke beats his assailant to a pulp with his fists and then throws the Japanese soldier off the side of a cliff.

As the battle stretches into the early morning hours, many of Pope's men are wounded, but they still hold Hill 154. The Japanese begin shooting flares into the sky to light the American position, then let loose salvoes of small-arms fire. The Americans respond with precise grenade throws that keep the enemy at bay. When the grenade supply runs low, they substitute rocks. "The Japs didn't know which were which," one marine will later recall. "We would throw three or four rocks, then a grenade."

When the Japanese respond by hurling grenades of their own, the Americans pick them up and throw them right back.

With morning still hours away, the Americans run out of bullets and grenades. But they refuse to surrender. With no conventional weapons at their disposal, they fling empty ammunition boxes at the enemy. When the ammunition boxes are gone, the marines use their bare fists.

As sunrise limns the horizon, Pope is down to just nine able-bodied marines. Yet Hill 154 is still in American hands.

Dawn offers Captain Pope and his men the hope that reinforcements will soon strengthen their tenuous position. Japanese dead lie everywhere around them, many just a few feet from the American positions. Pope's group has exhibited outstanding bravery.

But it is all for naught. In the light of day, the Japanese are astonished to see just a handful of Americans, without guns or grenades, holding Hill 154. Within minutes they assemble to descend en masse upon the marines.

"We could clearly see the Japanese forming up for a very heavy attack, fifty or a hundred men," Pope will later remember. "At that point we were ordered to withdraw. So we came tumbling down the hill."

Captain Everett Pope will tell that story until the day he dies—sixty-five years later, at the age of ninety. He and his men retreated to safety after that perilous night, then waited in frustration for the moment when American forces would once again attempt to capture Hill 154. For Captain Pope, the return was more personal than tactical.

"The hill was not taken again for ten or eleven or twelve days," Pope will add as he tells of that horrific night. "And it took that long for my dead on that hill to be buried. A lot of brave Marines died on that hill. I can never forget it."

★ ★ ★

The battle for Hill 154 sets the tone for the next month of combat—the Americans attack, and the Japanese fight back from hidden fortifications. As Colonel Nakagawa envisioned when he oversaw the building of the Japanese cave network so many months ago, his strong defensive positions are almost impervious to the steady American assaults. After three weeks of battle, the Americans have seized almost all of Peleliu, including the all-important airfield, yet they still don't control Nakagawa's stronghold in the Umurbrogol Pocket. And until it is taken, the Japanese can launch artillery fire at any American position on the island.

Though just a quarter mile wide and three-quarters of a mile long, the mountain ridges of the Umurbrogol Pocket are a killing zone like no other. Marine casualties run as high as 60 percent. Names like Five Sisters, Dead Man's Curve, and Bloody Nose Ridge join Suicide Ridge in marine lore, never to be forgotten for the toll exacted by Nakagawa's soldiers. Death becomes so common that men have become calloused to the sight. "We passed several stacks of dead Marines," one American will later recall. "They were piled five one way and five the other way. The stacks were about five feet high."

American F4U Corsair fighter-bombers take off regularly from the nearby airfield to bomb the Umurbrogol Pocket with napalm, a liquid petroleum designed to burn the Japanese out of their caves. Its gelling agent sticks to the skin, making the fiery death it causes all the more painful. Once the pilots drop their payload, they return and strafe the ridgeline, their bullets igniting the napalm. The time from takeoff to when the Corsairs make their two passes and return to the airfield is just five minutes—so short that most pilots don't even retract their landing gear.

But the enemy remains defiant. "The Japs weren't *on* the island, they were *in* the island," one marine will marvel years later. "One cave was big enough to house about fifteen hundred Jap soldiers. This big cave started on one side of a ridge, went all the way under, and came out the other side. They had a dispensary set up there, a hospital. All kinds of stuff."

Americans kept their heads down at all times lest a Japanese sniper take aim. "Captain Haldane peeked over the top of this ridge. Bang. One shot was fired. He was shot right through the forehead. It killed him immediately," one marine will recall about the death of a beloved officer.

The island smells of decomposition as dead bodies turn black and bloat in the sun. Land crabs feed on the corpses at night. Blow-flies ingest so much flesh and blood that they become too heavy to fly. The stench of rotting food and diarrhea adds to the fetid odors. The heat is so great that artillery shells must be kept in the shade lest they explode. And merely killing Americans is not enough for the soldiers of the Imperial Japanese Army. As they did so often early in the war, they mutilate the bodies of dead marines whenever they can, cutting off their penises and stuffing them into mouths yawned open by rigor mortis.

Yet, cave by cave, the Americans slowly take control of the Umurbrogol Pocket. The tactics of conventional warfare are set aside; napalm and flamethrowers flush the Japanese from their hiding places. For those who refuse to come out, explosives are used to seal the cave entrances, forever burying the Japanese soldiers within. And while the island's eleven thousand defenders almost all perish, the cost in American lives is equally extraordinary—the First Marine Division suffers 6,500 casualties in one month of fighting. Midway through the Battle of Peleliu, they no longer constitute a vital fighting force. Despite having captured the island's most strategically important terrain, they are evacuated, replaced in combat by the Fifth Marines and elements of the US Army's 81st Infantry Division.

Finally, the Umurbrogol Pocket is declared secure. Peleliu has been captured. The battle that was supposed to last just four days has taken twelve weeks. In his underground command post, Colonel Nakagawa lies dead, his hand still clutching the short-bladed knife with which he committed ritual suicide. One day soon, his wife will learn that he has been posthumously promoted to lieutenant general for his genius and courage.*

It has taken the marines an average of 1,500 rounds of ammunition to kill just one Japanese soldier. More than 13 million bullets were fired by the Americans, along with 150,000 mortar rounds. The mental and physical toll on the Americans has been tremendous. "I was wiped out after thirty days of constant fighting. Exhausted—mentally and physically. We all were," Private R. V. Burgin will remember. "Everybody's

---

*The bodies of Colonel Nakagawa and Major General Murai would not be discovered for almost forty years, at which time they were transported to Japan for burial. Colonel Nakagawa's wife lived to see the day her husband finally made his return home.

clothes were ragged, frayed, torn. Shoes were just about gone. Everybody stunk. Nobody was changing his socks. . . . There was a lot of diarrhea going on. We were a bunch of raggedy-ass Marines."

★ ★ ★

For both American and Japanese military planners, Nakagawa's tactics provide the blueprint for all future island invasions. In all, his defensive style of battle has cost the Americans more than fifteen thousand casualties.

Back in Washington, war strategists begin to ask one vital question: If the Japanese will fight with such determination over a small, remote island of little tactical significance, how many Americans will die when the time comes to invade the Japanese homeland?

5

As Colonel Kunio Nakagawa commits ritual suicide in a dark Peleliu cave, the man to whom he prays for courage sits down for a lunch of dumpling soup and vegetables. In America, it is Thanksgiving, and President Franklin Roosevelt issues a special exhortation. He encourages citizens not just to give thanks but to read their own version of Scripture every day between now and Christmas to ensure "a renewed and strengthening contact with those eternal truths and majestic principles which have inspired such measure of true greatness as this nation has achieved."

In Japan, sipping his soup, Emperor Michinomiya Hirohito does not give thanks to a god—he *is* a god. This short, shy, nearsighted forty-three-year-old is considered to be a descendant of the sun goddess Amaterasu, a Shinto religious deity.

Hirohito's daily life, however, is far from transcendent. In fact, it is quite common. Though he lives in an enormous castle with its own forest and moat, he does not smoke or drink and a litany of worries keep him up at all hours of the night. If the emperor really believes he is a god, he surely now knows that thousands of mortal men are looking to destroy him.

The 124th emperor of Japan rises promptly at seven o'clock each morning, then starts his day with oatmeal and a slice of black bread. He parts his black hair on the left, has a passion for marine biology, and has fathered seven children with the distant cousin whom he married twenty years ago. Being absent-minded, Hirohito often strolls through the Imperial Palace with his pants undone. He is unbothered by the many visible moles on his face or the fact that he often has trouble seeing, even though he constantly wears thick spectacles.

At five feet five inches tall, Hirohito is the smallest of the world's wartime leaders, though he surpasses the five-feet-six-inch Winston Churchill on those ceremonial occasions when he dons his thick-soled cavalry boots. He continues to live in splendor as the war forces the Japanese people to endure enormous deprivation. But there is little resentment among his subjects, who celebrate him as their "cosmic life force." In turn, the citizens of Japan know themselves as the "*shido minzoku*"—the chosen people.

The irony is that Hirohito ventures out of the castle so infrequently that he considers his life to be that of "a bird in a cage." So great is his isolation that Hirohito has never actually addressed his subjects; instead, his proclamations are printed and then distributed throughout Japan.* Few of his subjects know the sound of his voice. Many of them have no idea what their emperor even looks like.

Still, the soldiers of the Imperial Japanese Army fight to the death in his name. Even though Hirohito publicly prefers to let his military leaders conduct the war, he plays a pivotal role. In 1937, when Japanese troops conquered the Chinese city of Nanking, slaughtering hundreds of thousands of civilians in the process, Hirohito pronounced himself "deeply satisfied." And while he worried that the Pearl Harbor attack would pull Japan into a "reckless war" with the United States, he did nothing to stop his generals and admirals from proceeding.

Now, as he eats lunch within his lavish Tokyo palace, Hirohito is paying particular attention to the battle for the Philippine island of Leyte, which he has ordered commanding Japanese general Tomoyuki Yamashita to hold at all costs. The emperor has allowed his prime minister, the former army intelligence officer Kuniaki Koiso, to publicly declare that Leyte will be Japan's greatest military victory since the long-ago Battle of Yamazaki in 1582, which began a period of Japanese reunification.†

---

* Japan is made up of 6,852 islands, of which just 430 are inhabited. The four largest and most populous are Honshu, Hokkaido, Shikoku, and Kyushu. The capital city of Tokyo is located on Honshu's eastern shores.

† Prior to this battle, Japan was ruled by daimyo (samurai lords) who established their own small kingdoms. Forces led by Toyo-

The emperor's public proclamations are bluster. He is aware that the Philippines may indeed fall, but he will do anything to prevent the Americans from conquering Japan. The United States would first have to take the key islands of Iwo Jima, Okinawa, and perhaps Formosa, so the Japanese have at least a year to prepare. For the past three months, a campaign has been under way to arm every citizen of Japan. Military training is now mandatory in all schools and places of employment. The nation's air defense network is being upgraded to prevent attack by American bombers. And Hirohito himself is involved in the development of "sure victory weapons," a form of unconventional warfare against which the Americans will be powerless.

Hirohito has approved the launching of these weapons. If all goes well, these hydrogen balloons carrying incendiary bombs and antipersonnel weapons will waft skyward from Japan five miles up into the jet stream, which will then whisk them five thousand miles across the Pacific to America. There, the explosives will detonate in cities and towns, surprising an American public that thinks it is safe from attack. In this way, the people of United States will see for themselves that Japan will never be defeated.

These firebombs will fall from the sky as if hurled

tomi Hideyoshi defeated those of the shogun (military dictator), Akechi Mitsuhide, thus beginning the reunification of Japan. Hideyoshi's brilliant generalship has been compared to that of Napoleon Bonaparte. Daimyo rule remained in effect in some areas of Japan, coming to an end in 1871.

down by the hand of a vengeful god. From his vast castle in the middle of Tokyo, Emperor Hirohito's divine power will shock the barbaric Americans. Of this, the emperor is certain.*

★ ★ ★

The Second World War officially began on September 1, 1939, with Germany's invasion of Poland. But that act of aggression took place two years after Japan sought to increase its sphere of influence by conquering the northeastern provinces of China, collectively known as Manchuria—a region the Japanese had renamed Manchukuo. The world's great powers were at a loss as to how to stop them.

Like Formosa, which Japan colonized in 1895, and Korea, colonized in 1910, Manchuria both enriched Dai Nippon and gave it enough power to compete with China and the Soviet Union as a leading power in Asia.

But Japanese military leaders did not stop there. In fact, they could not. As an island nation, Japan is lacking in many natural resources; chief among these are oil and rubber, two items vital to military mobility. The bulk of Japan's oil, steel, and iron throughout the 1930s was imported from the United States, while the planta-

---

*The so-called fire balloons were indeed launched. Most did not reach America, and those that did inflicted little damage. Yet the fire balloons were history's first intercontinental weapons. Not until 1982 and the Operation Black Buck raids of the Falklands War would they be surpassed as the longest-range attacks ever conducted.

tions of British Malaya provided Japan's rubber supply. These products continued to flow into Japan even after Japan invaded China in the summer of 1937.

But by that time, the world's powers had grown wary of Japan's increasing belligerence. The United States, the Soviet Union, and even Germany began providing military aid to the Chinese, but it did not matter. Fighting in the name of *hakkōç ichiu*, a belief that all of Asia must be united under one emperor, Japanese troops quickly overwhelmed China, their superior training and aggressive tactics devastating the forces of Chiang Kai-shek.

The Japanese did not limit their killing to Chinese soldiers. "At 10:00 on 29 November 1937 we left to clean out the enemy in Chang Chou and at noon we entered the town," Japanese army doctor Hosaka Akira wrote in his three-by-five-inch pocket journal. "An order was received to kill the residents and eighty of them, men and women of all ages, were shot to death. I hope this will be the last time I'll ever witness such a scene. The people were all gathered in one place. They were all praying, crying, and begging for help. I just couldn't bear watching such a pitiful spectacle. Soon the heavy machine guns opened fire and the sight of those people screaming and falling to the ground is one I could not face even if I had had the heart of a monster."

By December 1937, the Japanese had captured the capital city of Nanking. Prior to that, the battle for Shanghai during the autumn months of 1937 had cost the Japanese ninety-two thousand casualties; more than

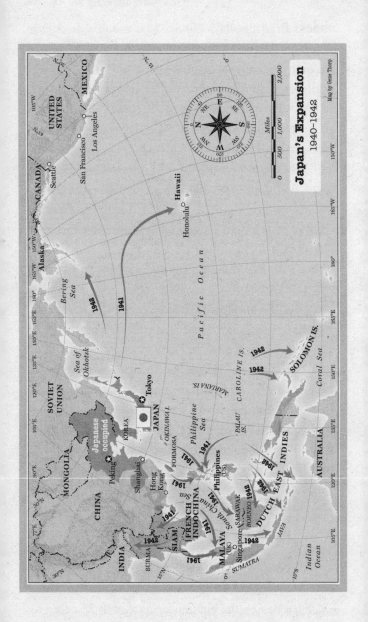

Japan's Expansion
1940-1942

Map by Gene Thorp

two hundred thousand Chinese also lost their lives. The Imperial Japanese Army immediately sought revenge for their Shanghai dead, inflicting horrifying atrocities on the civilian population.

The Japanese began their killing spree with the execution of ninety thousand captured Chinese soldiers. In a pattern of behavior that displayed Japan's contempt for the Geneva Conventions, which protect prisoners of war from torture, assault, or execution, these men were stabbed to death, hung by their tongues, attacked by dogs, set ablaze, machine-gunned, buried alive, and beheaded.*

Next, civilians in the city were shot at random, sometimes being forced to dig their own graves beforehand. Japanese soldiers held horrifying killing contests in which they strived to see who could behead the most Chinese.

Those barbarous acts were a mere prelude to what became of the women of Nanking, an estimated eighty thousand of whom were systematically raped. Japanese soldiers would recount for years to come how much they enjoyed these acts, often perpetrated against children and grandmothers. Teams of Japanese soldiers developed a routine for each assault: the group would hold a victim down while one man checked to ensure

_____

*The first Geneva Convention of 1864 was signed by Japan in 1886; subsequent agreements were produced in 1906 and 1929. Japan signed the 1929 treaty and verbally agreed to adhere to the terms of the 1906 treaty. The emperor obviously did not live up to his word.

that the woman did not have a sexually transmitted disease. Then the soldiers would cast lots to see who would go first. Victims were often bayoneted after the last man finished; if a woman was pregnant at the time, the baby might be cut from her womb with a knife.

If the soldiers who fought in the name of Emperor Hirohito came upon a family, it was common for them to force fathers to rape their daughters, brothers to rape their sisters, and even sons to rape their mothers. Those females who survived these horrors often went on to become "comfort women" for the Japanese soldiers who would occupy China until 1945. These sexual slaves had no choice but to endure many more years of rape.

In all, the Japanese systematically defiled and murdered half of Nanking's six hundred thousand citizens. Their behavior was hardly a secret. The people of Japan thrilled to news that the Chinese were being savagely tyrannized; in Tokyo, the *Japan Advertiser* ran a daily tally of the dead in a decapitation contest between two prominent Japanese soldiers.

★ ★ ★

Back in Washington, DC, President Roosevelt and Congress all but ignored the Japanese atrocities. When the *New York Times* printed a front-page story about the brutality in Nanking, the article was treated with skepticism—some Americans considered the "Rape of Nanking" too gruesome to be true. And the American leadership stayed silent.

When the Japanese continued their military expansion

with the invasion of French Indochina in 1940, President Roosevelt embargoed the sale of all oil to Japan. As an ally of America, Great Britain soon followed suit. On July 26, 1941, FDR went a step further and froze all Japanese assets in the United States.

On the surface, FDR's action was a simple attempt to stop Japanese aggression in Asia. Yet it sent shock waves through the Japanese military: without oil, their tanks and ships would be useless. Japan's navy had a six-month reserve of fuel, but no more. Japan's top generals began making plans to find new sources of oil. Japan began to see itself as a victim of American aggression. Unfortunately, rather than discouraging war in the Pacific, Roosevelt's embargo made it more likely.

As tensions rose between Japan and the United States, the Japanese military came up with a most audacious plan: it would invade every nation, island, and colony that could offer it natural resources. In a matter of days, Japanese forces would spill onto the beaches of the Philippines, Singapore, the Dutch East Indies, British Malaya, Sarawak, and British and Dutch Borneo, and into the jungles of Burma. Prisoners taken along the way would be put to work as slave labor—building infrastructure, harvesting on plantations, and digging in the mines.

The plan was horrifying but brilliant. While Japanese aggression was not unexpected, the scope of this outrageous design would catch the rest of the world flat-footed. Japanese generals hoped the element of surprise would guarantee total victory. The peace-loving prime minister at the time, Fumimaro Konoe, hoped for a diplomatic breakthrough with the United States, but by October 1941, it was quite clear this would not come to pass. Konoe then resigned, not having the stomach for a brutal world war.

His replacement was Hideki Tojo, a short, arrogant army general. Nicknamed "Razor" for his brusque demeanor and attention to detail, fifty-six-year-old Tojo distinguished himself on the field of battle in the early days of the war in China. He is descended from Japan's venerated samurai warrior class. Selected over others who thought him too militaristic, Tojo was handpicked by Emperor Hirohito to serve as the new prime minister, making him the second most powerful man in Japan. His pro-war stance made it very clear how he would wield that strength. "We have finally committed to war," a high-level Japanese official will write in his journal shortly after Tojo's selection. "And now we must do all we can to launch it powerfully."

For those who opposed his jingoistic attitude, Tojo had a simple argument: "Sometimes it is necessary to shut one's eyes and take the plunge."

Tojo had to manage two key elements if the plunge was to succeed. The first was Hirohito himself. For months, the emperor wavered on whether or not to expand Japan's war with China to include a continuation of its conquest of Asia and vital Pacific island nations within its sphere of influence. "Of course his majesty is a pacifist, and there is no doubt he wished to avoid war," former prime minister Konoe will write on the day he resigns from office in October 1941, knowing that his attempts to prevent war will be in vain.

"When I told him, that to initiate war is a mistake, he agreed. . . . Gradually, he began to lean toward war."

Through Tojo's careful ministrations, Hirohito became more hawkish. At first, the emperor was reluctant to give his final blessing to the attack plans. But on November 2, 1941, just two weeks after Tojo took office, his persuasion won the day: Hirohito agreed that it was time to complete the Japanese mission of conquest.

Which left one last stumbling block to Japanese victory in what the nation will come to call the Greater East Asia War: the United States Navy.

No other force was capable of stopping Japan's mighty fleet as it sailed forth through the Pacific, sending aloft its planes and delivering waves of soldiers to foreign beaches. As long as the US Navy loomed as a threat, Tojo could never be completely assured of Japanese success.

So in addition to overseeing the invasion plans that would place tiny Japan in a position of dominance no other Asian nation had ever known, Tojo also made Emperor Hirohito aware of plans to destroy America's Pacific Fleet.

All of it.

For years, the Japanese military had known its primary adversary might eventually be the United States. Although himself opposed to embroiling Japan in a dangerous and costly war, commander in chief of Japan's Combined Fleet Admiral Isoroku Yamamoto had long been in favor of an aerial bombardment that would destroy the "dagger being pointed at our throats," as he referred to the US fleet.

The attack would happen on a Sunday morning, a time when most sailors would be sleeping in after a night on the town. Waves of carrier-launched Japanese dive-bombers would drop from the skies, unloading torpedoes and bombs that would sink destroyers and demolish airplanes, forever ending America's naval presence in the Pacific.

Yamamoto knew just where to find these ships. They were anchored bow to stern and side by side at a balmy tropical naval base in Hawaii—a place known as Pearl Harbor.*

On November 8, 1941, Emperor Hirohito was provided with specific details about the surprise attack.

After very little deliberation, he approved the plan.

★   ★   ★

Since the start of the war, Hirohito has allowed his generals and admirals to be the military face of the nation. He has been content to let the world view him as a man of peace forced into the conflict by his military advisers. But now, well into 1944, as the American army and navy edge ever closer to Japan, Hirohito takes a more intentional stance to defend the land his predecessors have ruled since 660 BC.

Hirohito's first step was to oust the fanatical Tojo, the prime minister who often behaved like a dictator during the early days of the war. Indeed, Tojo has become as

---

*President Roosevelt had ordered the Pacific Fleet's headquarters moved from San Pedro, California, to Pearl Harbor in May 1940. This intended show of strength instead became a vulnerability.

synonymous with Japan as Hitler is with Germany and Mussolini with Italy. But unlike those Axis allies, Tojo has been serving at the pleasure of the emperor. In July, the pivotal island of Saipan fell to the Americans, and Tojo's fate was sealed.

Saipan's airfields are close enough to Tokyo that United States Army Air Forces B-29s can now bomb Japan at will. This fact has irreversibly changed how the war is waged, forcing Japan into a defensive stance; the days when a similar long-range bombing attack could be launched against the Americans are over. On July 18, 1944, two months before the battle for Peleliu, Hirohito withdrew his support for Tojo's government. The prime minister was immediately removed from office. It was a crushing humiliation for the ruthless Tojo, who had orchestrated Japan's war strategy since before Pearl Harbor and whom many had once thought invincible. So great was Tojo's loss of face that many called for him to commit ritual suicide. Instead, he retired to a farmhouse on the outskirts of Tokyo, longing for the day when the emperor might once again call him to public service.

Hirohito has become the consummate wartime sovereign, sharing responsibility for Japan's tactical maneuvers and supporting Tojo's strategy of slaughtering innocent civilians and executing prisoners of war. Since the days leading up to Pearl Harbor, and even after forcing Tojo from office, Hirohito has immersed himself in the smallest details of wartime planning. The emperor is fed daily reports from the army and navy, apprising him of their actions. Many Japanese military leaders refuse to publicly acknowledge the string of defeats that has all but sealed the nation's fate, but in his rare moments of pragmatism Hirohito knows that his fleet is almost completely destroyed, most of his airplanes have been shot down, and that the precious gas and steel that were the catalysts for this war can no longer be imported due to the ring of US submarines and warships now forming a tight blockade around Japan.

Yet, despite this knowledge, and all other indications that the war is lost, the emperor refuses to seek peace. His stated goal is to "remain in this divine land and fight to the death."

6

Eight hundred American servicemen cheer patriotically as Harry Truman pulls up a chair and takes his place at the keyboard of an upright piano. It is Saturday night. The air in this crowded ballroom smells of cigarette smoke and male perspiration. There is a microphone to Truman's left, allowing him to banter and play at the same time. The soldiers and sailors are here for the National Press Club's weekly canteen—a tradition that entitles them to a few hours of free beer, hot dogs, and a stage show. Celebrities, generals, and politicians often make an appearance to serve food and support the troops. On one occasion, the entire Supreme Court stopped by, which led to the amusing sight of Justice Felix Frankfurter passing out actual frankfurters.

Top billing tonight goes to the man from Missouri. The applause for Truman suggests a mixture of respect and curiosity, for few in the crowd know much about their new vice president. But if Harry Truman is willing to pound out a few standards and tell some jokes, he is okay with them.

Truman is not the only celebrity in the house tonight. Twenty-year-old sex symbol Lauren Bacall, star of the recently released film noir *To Have and Have Not*, is seated at a table right up front. She is the lupine focus of this all-male audience. Almost to a man, these soldiers and sailors have seen her performance opposite Humphrey Bogart, and can recite her character's famous come-on: "You know how to whistle, don't you, Steve? You just put your lips together and . . . blow."*

Harry Truman rests his fingertips atop the keyboard and jokes into the microphone, comfortable acting the part of the showman. In fact, playing piano to raise troop morale is one of many aspects of his new job that Truman enjoys very much. The "political eunuch," as

---

*Based on a 1937 Ernest Hemingway novel of the same name, *To Have and Have Not* tells the story of a down-on-his-luck charter boat captain in wartime Martinique. The character of Harry "Steve" Morgan, played by the forty-five-year-old Bogart, soon falls for the young American traveler, Marie "Slim" Browning, played by Bacall. The two generated a great deal of interpersonal chemistry on and off the set, leading director Howard Hawks to enlarge Bacall's role. Bogart's third wife, actress Mayo Methot, filed for divorce in May 1944. Bogart and Bacall married in May 1945 and would remain happily wed until his death from cancer in 1957. Their son, Stephen, born in 1949, is named for the character in *To Have and Have Not*.

the vice president likes to refer to himself, delights in a schedule that consists of ceremonial speeches, presiding over the Senate, and a standing appointment for a glass of bourbon with Speaker of the House Sam Rayburn each afternoon at 5:00 p.m. Truman is unbothered by the fact that since the inauguration three weeks ago, President Roosevelt has virtually ignored him. FDR has not even spoken to his new vice president in person. Despite the snub, Harry Truman is having a whole lot of fun.

The vice president has played piano since he was ten and can perform Beethoven or Mozart from memory. Alternatively, Truman can launch into the ragtime tune "Missouri Waltz," a song he despises but which will no doubt elicit cheers from any Missourians who might be in the audience.

Truman's song selection soon becomes inconsequential. In fact, as the sultry Lauren Bacall stands up and strides toward the vice president in high heels and a knee-length skirt, the lusty roars from the crowd make it clear that it doesn't matter whether Truman plays anything at all.

With the help of some very willing soldiers, the young siren is boosted atop the piano. Bacall provocatively crosses her legs and dangles them over the edge, showing off her well-toned calves. Despite their forty-year age difference, she flirts with Truman. The actress smiles seductively, then reclines, never taking her eyes off the vice president.

Truman is equally bold. Unflustered, he plays the

Lauren Bacall vamping with a bemused Vice President Harry Truman

moment for all it is worth, flirting right back with Bacall. Flashbulbs pop as photographers rush to take pictures of the unlikely scene and Bacall turns her body to strike a new pose. And then another.

"Anything can happen in this country," marvels one appreciative soldier to a *Washington Post* reporter.

Anything.

Of this, Harry Truman—a former small-town

haberdasher who has risen to the second-highest office in the land—is well aware.

✳ ✳ ✳

The man with sixty-two days to live is being steam-rolled.

President Franklin Roosevelt sits in the pale Russian sunlight, a black cape draped around his shoulders. His face is gray, his lips are slightly blue, and there is fluid pooling in his lungs—all symptoms of the congestive heart failure that is slowly killing him.

To FDR's left, also seated, is Soviet premier Joseph Stalin. To Roosevelt's right sits the portly, constantly chatting British prime minister Winston Churchill. A cigarette dangles from FDR's left hand, but he lets it burn, knowing that the photographers now capturing this meeting of the "Big Three" will see the palsy that has afflicted his hands for months if he lifts the tobacco to his mouth.

It is morning in Crimea and the Big Three are wrapping up a week of meetings at the Black Sea resort of Yalta. Clearly, it is Stalin who has emerged from this conference as the big winner. "It was not a question of what we would *let* the Russians do, but what we could *get* the Russians to do," diplomat James F. Byrnes later told a reporter.*

---

* Byrnes was one of Roosevelt's eight appointees to the Supreme Court, but he stepped down after less than a year, leaving the bench in 1942. The former US senator from South Carolina and good friend of FDR preferred helping the president run the war effort to

The end of the war in Europe is now in sight. American and British troops have just thwarted Nazi Germany's last great offensive at the Battle of the Bulge. Led by aggressive American general George S. Patton and his vainglorious British counterpart, Field Marshal Bernard Law Montgomery, Allied forces are now preparing to invade the German fatherland.

In the east, Russian troops have already captured vast swaths of former Nazi real estate, including the nations of Poland, Hungary, and Czechoslovakia. In this way, American, British, and Soviet troops are squeezing tight the vise that will soon crush Adolf Hitler's Third Reich. In fact, Russian troops are now just forty miles from Berlin.

The purpose of the Yalta Conference has been to define the shape of the postwar world. But even before the conference began on February 4, Joseph Stalin tilted the odds in his favor, beginning with the location. Claiming that his health did not permit travel, Stalin insisted upon meeting in this Soviet city. The truth is, Stalin feels fine—he is simply afraid to fly.

Meanwhile, a visibly declining Roosevelt travels six thousand miles by ship and aircraft, then endures an eight-hour car ride to attend the conference. His villa room is bugged, and the servants in his quarters are Soviet spies, meaning that FDR can never completely relax because he knows his every movement is being scrutinized.

That is as Stalin designed it.

---

the intellectual rigor of the Supreme Court. He would later go on to serve as secretary of state and governor of South Carolina.

For the brutal dictator well knows that if he gets what he wants from Roosevelt and Churchill at this conference, he will rule almost half the globe. Stalin's goal is straightforward: return the Soviet Union to the same size and shape as the nineteenth-century Russian empire. His forces now occupy most of the northern Baltic-to-the-Pacific expanse, and the ambitious dictator has no intention of giving up any captured territory.

Yet there is one significant part of the former empire that Russian troops do not yet occupy: Japanese-held Manchuria, in northern China. So when Roosevelt requests that Stalin enter the war against Japan, the president plays right into the dictator's hands. Stalin agrees to fight Japan, but only after demanding that Roosevelt acquiesce to Russian designs on Manchuria.

The Japanese and the Russians last waged war over this territory during a nineteen-month conflict beginning in 1904. Then, it was Japan that emerged triumphant, sowing the seeds for Emperor Hirohito's global expansion.

Soon, Stalin will have his revenge.*

---

*The reason for the Japanese invasion of Manchuria was its need for precious resources: coal, iron, salt, and arable land. The growing Japanese population meant that the nation was not self-sufficient. Manchuria offered the chance to gain access to those natural resources and relocate Japanese citizens to work the fields. The Soviet Union's intended invasion was fueled by a similar search for territory and mineral resources and also by desires to regain lands lost in the Russo-Japanese War, particularly the warm-water naval base at Port Arthur; install a pro-Soviet regime in Korea; and invade Japan itself.

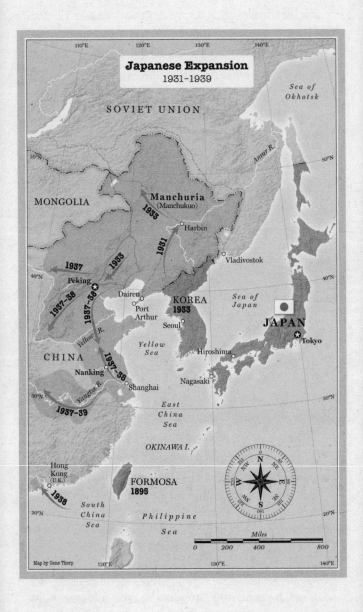

Japanese Expansion
1931–1939

SOVIET UNION

Sea of Okhotsk

MONGOLIA

Manchuria
(Manchukuo)

1933

1931

• Harbin

1937

1933

1937–38

1937–38

Peking ✪

• Vladivostok

Dairen •
Port Arthur •

KOREA
1933

Sea of Japan

JAPAN

Seoul ○

Tokyo ✪

CHINA

Yellow R.

Nanking •

1937–38

Yellow Sea

Hiroshima ○

1937–39

Yangtze R.

Shanghai •

Nagasaki ○

East China Sea

OKINAWA I.

Hong Kong (U.K.) ○

1938

FORMOSA
1895

South China Sea

Philippine Sea

Miles
0   200   400   800

Map by Gene Thorp

☆ ☆ ☆

Franklin Roosevelt waits patiently for the ceremonial photographs to be completed as Yalta finally concludes. Churchill's Great Britain is the biggest loser of the conference and is emerging as a nation impoverished by war; Britain's former colonies are sure to seek independence at war's end. Roosevelt is content in the knowledge that the United States will remain a superpower and the world will be divided principally between America and the Soviet Union. Roosevelt has no problem with this; he likes Joseph Stalin and believes he can trust him. There is no reason the two great nations shouldn't work well together.

Hands shaking, Roosevelt finally takes a long drag on his unfiltered Camel. He smokes at least a pack a day. Doctors have suggested that just six cigarettes should be his daily limit, but he ignores that order. Doctors have also advised the president to get ten hours of sleep each night, limit his drinking to just one cocktail at dinner, minimize his salt intake, and relax for two hours each afternoon.

He refuses. Franklin Delano Roosevelt is president of the United States. Medical advice that makes sense for ordinary men does not apply to him.

But the stress and strain of Yalta are taking an enormous physical toll on him. Though younger than Joseph Stalin by a little more than three years, FDR looks a decade older. The photographers capture the shadows beneath the president's eyes and the tight set of his jaw. He came into the week tired and will return to the White House exhausted. After an arduous seven days of haggling with Stalin, the president knows that the six-thousand-mile return journey will be painful.

Inside the sixty-three-year-old Roosevelt's chest, his enlarged heart labors to beat.

☆ ☆ ☆

As Yalta ends, Franklin Roosevelt has unwittingly consigned millions of Eastern Europeans to decades of Soviet occupation. They will be deprived of basic freedoms such as unfettered speech and the ability to come and go as they please. All but forgotten is the fact that several years earlier, on February 19, 1942, Franklin Roosevelt himself decreed that tens of thousands of American citizens would suffer similar indignities.

Under Executive Order 9066, authorities were ordered to intern Japanese-Americans simply for being of Japanese heritage. They were incarcerated against their will, having committed no crime other than having ancestors from Japan.

Thousands of Japanese-Americans are placed in camps, one of the most prominent being located on the eastern slopes of the Sierra Nevada mountains, where the Manzanar War Relocation Center rises from the barren soil of California's high desert. In summer, temperatures routinely rise past 100 degrees. In winter, brutal, freezing winds sweep down from the snowy peaks above, bending trees sideways and sending clouds of sand and dust through the air.

Entire families have been rounded up and sent to live in these prisons for the duration of the war. They sleep side by side in barracks, surrounded by barbed-wire fences. Armed guards look down from high sentry towers, scrutinizing their every movement. Until Emperor Hirohito surrenders, they must remain here, in a place with no such thing as privacy: showers are communal, as are the latrines, which lack the decency of a simple partition.

These Americans are unsure of what their lives will be once the war ends—where they will go, where they will work, how they will rebuild.

Yet, as the people of Eastern Europe will soon learn, they have no choice but to endure the hardships.*

★ ★ ★

Nine hundred miles southeast of Manzanar, in another windswept American desert, a team of scientists work feverishly on a device designed to cause mass death and destruction. Utilizing a revolutionary new technology, the team is locking down the final design of a brand-new bomb. Shortly before World War II began, scientists discovered how to split the nucleus of an atom; the "fission" that occurs results in an enormous release of energy. Once news of this development leaked, weapons designers from around the world rushed to find a way to translate the research into a devastating implement of war.

---

* Approximately 127,000 Japanese-Americans were interned during World War II.

Since April 1939, the Nazis have also tried to build what scientists are calling an "atom bomb." The Japanese too have been seeking such a weapon. Both have had no luck. Yet here in the New Mexican desert, after years of top secret research, the American effort has finally moved from research to production. Now that Hitler is almost defeated, it is certain that this new bomb will not be used against Germany. Instead, Japan will be the target. The new device is still untested, but if all goes according to plan, B-29 bombers launching from captured Pacific islands will soon drop it on Japan. Estimates are that the explosive force could be equal to as many as ten kilotons of dynamite, even though the bomb will detonate almost two thousand feet above its target, never actually reaching the ground.

But those estimates are merely a guess. No one knows the exact power of this theoretical weapon.

It is not yet known which city or cities will be bombed, but a short list has been drawn up by Brigadier General Leslie Groves, leader of the Manhattan Project, as this deadly undertaking is known. To measure the full power of the blast, Groves wants each bombing target to be previously unscathed. This means that the people of Kokura, Kyoto, Hiroshima, Yokohama, and Niigata, who have largely been left alone by the American bombers up to now, may soon be in grave danger.

In a historical coincidence, Lauren Bacall's appearance on stage with Harry Truman unwittingly foreshadows an aspect of the new atomic bomb.

Taking inspiration from her soon-to-be husband's

film *The Maltese Falcon*, scientists code-name this bomb "Little Boy."*

---

* *The Maltese Falcon* was a 1941 film noir that marked the directorial debut of John Huston. Humphrey Bogart played private detective Sam Spade; he was complemented by a stellar supporting cast that included Sydney Greenstreet, Peter Lorre, Mary Astor, and Elisha Cook Jr. Robert Serber, the Los Alamos scientist in charge of code-naming the bombs, chose "Fat Man" from Spade's nickname for Greenstreet's character. The naming of "Little Boy" is more complicated. *The Maltese Falcon* was originally written by Dashiell Hammett. A third atomic bomb prototype, code-named "Thin Man" after a separate Hammett story, was abandoned in July 1944. "Little Boy's" shape was smaller and more bulbous than that of "Thin Man," which is how it earned its code name. At the time of the atomic bomb's development, Hammett was serving as an enlisted soldier in the Aleutian Islands, soon to be discharged at the rank of sergeant. Hammett would be called before Congress in 1953, suspected of harboring Communist sympathies. He refused to cooperate and was blacklisted, making it impossible for him to find work as a writer. Ironically, as a veteran who served in World War I and World War II, Hammett is now buried at Arlington National Cemetery.

7

---◆---

Douglas MacArthur's own little boy has been residing safely in Australian exile but is soon to return to the liberated Philippines with his mother. The Japanese army's brutal three-year reign over the islands is not yet over, but the capital city of Manila is now under attack by the United States Army.

Jean MacArthur and seven-year-old Arthur will not be going back to the lavish penthouse the family once called home. For as Douglas MacArthur now sees with his own eyes, this cherished site of so many fond memories has been burned to a husk.

The general smokes his favorite pipe as he steps over the blood-soaked corpse of a Japanese colonel. The ruins of the apartment still smolder; the Japanese used it as a command post, then set it ablaze in a final act of vengeance as the Americans fought their way up the stairs. On the shelves, MacArthur's vaunted collection of military-history books is now ashes. In the sitting room, the family's grand piano is charred and smoking. Valuable silverware has been stolen, and next to the dead colonel's body, the fragments of a precious set of ornamental vases given to MacArthur by none other than Emperor Hirohito, many years before the war, litter the carpet.

"They had fired it," MacArthur will later write of his former home. "I watched, with indescribable feelings, the destruction of my fine military library, my souvenirs, my personal belongings of a lifetime."

Just yesterday his wife and son boarded the refrigerator ship *British Columbia Express* in Brisbane. The voyage to Manila will take two weeks. In that time, the general must secure a new place for his family to live.

It is highly unusual to have his wife and child stay with him in a war zone, but MacArthur is a warrior who lives by the motto that it is better to seek forgiveness than to ask permission—although he mostly does neither. In almost all circumstances, even when answering to the president, Douglas MacArthur does exactly as he pleases.

⋆ ⋆ ⋆

More than a thousand miles away from MacArthur's scorched apartment and the ferocious battle for the control of the Philippine capital, "Manila John" Basilone paces the black sand of a deadly beach. Codenamed "Island X," this barren speck of volcanic rock is known to the world as Iwo Jima. It is here that Basilone and his fellow warriors of the Fifth Marine Division are pinned down. The twenty-eight-year-old sergeant

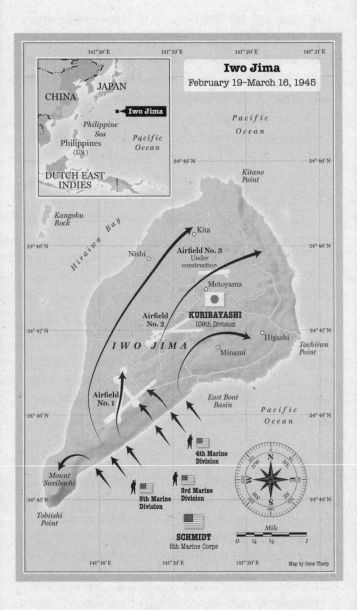

is a light heavyweight boxer and consummate marine. After being awarded the Medal of Honor three years ago, the hardened veteran was sent back to the United States, where he toured the country selling war bonds. He was the very image of what many Americans thought a marine should look like: trim, square-jawed, and handsome. But Basilone chafed at his non-combat role and successfully petitioned to return to the Pacific battlefield. Fittingly, the tattoo on Basilone's left arm reads "Death before dishonor."*

Now, as marines press their bodies into the black sand lining the beaches, Japanese bullets fly unabated. Yet Sergeant Basilone stands upright, surveying the situation.

The terrain slopes steeply forward from his position to a high bank directly behind the beach. Mortar shells rain down, throwing up great clouds of sand as they explode. Japanese artillery launched from a mile away, atop the flat peak of Mount Suribachi, pounds the Americans. Destroyed landing craft litter the beach, yet Basilone disregards the destruction. He has come ashore in the third wave of marines this morning and

---

* Basilone joined the army in 1934, at the age of seventeen. He was posted to the Philippines for three years, enjoying it so much that he talked about it continuously, which earned him the nickname "Manila John." He left the army in 1937 but joined the marines in 1940 when war appeared imminent. Basilone earned his Medal of Honor at the Battle of Guadalcanal in 1942, at one point battling his way through hostile positions in order to resupply men under his command. Basilone would also go on to be awarded the Navy Cross for his heroism on Iwo Jima.

now screams for his men to move forward. "Get your butts off the beach," he bawls in his best parade-ground voice. "Move out."

But some men don't move—they can't. Dead or mortally wounded, their bodies lie still, soaking the sand with blood.

Soon Basilone is leading some of the surviving marines forward, away from the extreme danger of the landing zone. Machine-gun fire peppers them as they labor to crest the bank. The Japanese have built elaborate concrete pillboxes and covered them with sand, not only camouflaging their positions but also dampening the blow of any incoming artillery. Quickly surveying his position, Basilone knows he will need a machine gun to knock out the bunker whose bullets are now killing his men. Spotting a gun crew amid the chaos and deafening noise of the explosions, he scrambles over and smacks the gunner on the back of the helmet to get his attention. "Fire on that target," he demands.

But Private First Class Chuck Tatum's gun barrel is full of sand. It will not fire. Quickly, the marine cleans his weapon as Basilone looks on, frustrated. In less than thirty seconds, the job is done. Tatum opens fire on the bunker, his illuminated tracer bullets showing the path.

To a man, Basilone and the marines are tired of war. They are exhausted by intense fighting and the six-week voyages needed to reach the next island to be captured. Yet Iwo Jima must be taken before they will finally reach the island that matters most: Kyushu, at the southernmost tip of Japan. One of its major cities is a port known for shipbuilding called Nagasaki.

The question for most marines is not how many more invasions will take place between now and the war's end but whether they will survive to ever see their families again.

Gunnery Sergeant "Manila John" Basilone is newly married, with everything to live for. Yet he conducts himself as a man with nothing to lose. As Chuck Tatum lays down covering fire, the sergeant moves down the line, desperate to destroy the pillbox and save the lives of his men.

★   ★   ★

Back in Manila, Douglas MacArthur turns to leave his former apartment, escorted by soldiers from the army's Thirty-Seventh Division. Their machine-gun barrels are still hot after the firefight that cleared the Japanese from the Manila Hotel. Beyond the hotel walls, the raging battle for this once-beautiful city has turned into urban combat, a rarity in the Pacific theater. Three American army divisions comprising thirty-five thousand men battle a combined group of seventeen thousand Japanese sailors, marines, and soldiers. For MacArthur, who has long known the transient life of a military man, Manila is as close to a hometown as any place he has ever lived. He considers the city a "citadel of democracy in the East" and has been reluctant to wage all-out war to recapture it. In fact, the general initially refused to allow the aerial bombardment and bruising artillery barrages needed to dislodge the Japanese occupiers.

MacArthur is cautiously optimistic. His material possessions are gone, but Jean and Arthur are on the way, and he still commands the largest army in the Pacific. Perhaps most important, MacArthur knows his military legacy remains untarnished, despite the many months it has taken to capture the Philippines.

The same cannot be said for the people of Manila. They have lost not just their homes but in many cases also their dignity.

The battle for Manila began two weeks ago, on February 3, 1945. By February 6, MacArthur had prematurely declared the fighting over, proclaiming to the press that "Manila had fallen."

That was false. Even though General Tomoyuki Yamashita had ordered Japanese forces to evacuate the city, rogue elements under his command refused to obey, successfully encouraging a large group of Japanese sailors and marines to join them in fighting the Americans to the last man.

These Japanese holdouts have mined the streets. Concealed snipers shoot Americans on sight. The fighting takes place from house to house, room to room. No place is safe. Even after American troops burn the Japanese alive with flamethrowers and demolish the buildings in which they are hiding, the Japanese still find a way to attack; one American patrol is suddenly assaulted by a sword-wielding Japanese soldier who slices open the point man's skull before the Americans shoot him and his six companions dead.

Knowing they will never win, some Japanese soldiers get drunk and then blow themselves up with hand grenades. But many more have become obsessed with brutalizing the citizens of Manila before they die. The Japanese believe their race is superior to the Filipinos. After three years of absolute authority over the city of Manila, they are unable to bear the thought that these lesser people will triumph.*

So even as they fight MacArthur's army for control of Manila, the Japanese are systematically murdering as many innocent local residents as possible. A formal order has been issued to Japanese troops detailing how this is to be accomplished: "When Filipinos are to be killed, they must be gathered into one place and disposed of in such a manner that does not demand excessive amounts of ammunition or manpower. Given the difficulties of disposing of bodies, they should be collected in houses scheduled for burning, demolished, or thrown into the river."†

---

*The army inspector general will formally conclude that General Yamashita never intended to completely evacuate Manila. Thus, the slaughter was "the consequence of a preconceived plan executed by the commander of Japanese Armed Forces in the Philippines, under orders from higher military command in Tokyo." The inspector general will go on to state that "the reason and purpose of the Japanese in committing these many atrocities against primarily the Filipino people was because of their partiality, cooperation and friendliness toward America and Americans."

†That order was issued at the battalion level to the renegade soldiers, sailors, and marines under the command of Admiral Sanji Iwabuchi, who had defied orders to leave Manila and instead chose

Douglas MacArthur's rationale for not allowing aerial bombardment of Manila is that the lives of innocent civilians will be endangered, yet the horrors being inflicted upon the Filipino people defy description. Instant death from a bomb might be preferable to the agonizing murders being perpetrated by the Japanese. These war crimes are heinous even by the imperial army's own gruesome standards.

In the weeks to come, from February 25 to April 9, US Army war crimes investigators will interrogate eyewitnesses and report on these barbaric acts in detail. Witnesses will be interviewed in hospitals, refugee camps, and their own homes. Claims of injury and dismemberment will be verified with photographs taken in the presence of US Army nurses and doctors; cases of rape are always verified by two eyewitnesses. With bureaucratic efficiency and matter-of-fact detail, these reports will permanently document the barbarity of the Japanese military during the Battle of Manila.

One report recounts: "On 11 February 1945, at about 6:00 PM, just after Mr. Lim Kinnog Tiang, Chinese, age 23, a grocer, had closed his store, the Japanese came and brought over one hundred Filipinos and Chinese who were all tied up. The Japanese covered

---

to fight to the last man. However, such a formal order was a rarity for the ill-disciplined troops under Iwabuchi's command, and the majority of the killings of Filipino citizens were undertaken by small packs of men under no central authority. Iwabuchi committed suicide by hand grenade on February 26, 1945, leaving the Japanese troops without any leadership for the last week of the fighting. This only encouraged more slaughter.

the eyes of the men by taking strips of cloth and blind-folding them. The victims were then taken in groups of ten upstairs and had their heads cut off."

And another: "In the early part of February 1945, at about 7:00 PM, a group of Japanese, most of them officers, came to the house, of Miss Asuncion Marvas, 239 San Marcellino [*sic*], Manila. Miss Marvas, and the members of her family were taken to the German Club. There were an estimated five hundred people as-sembled there. When anyone attempted to leave the building they were shot or hand grenades were thrown at them. Most of the people were killed because the place was burned. Miss Marvas wanted to go away, but the Japanese stabbed her in the buttocks. She was lying on her face or stomach at the time they stabbed her."

Other war crimes reports detail what the Japanese did to Filipino children. Soldiers gouged their eyes from their skulls and threw the innocent kids against walls until their bodies broke apart. Annoyed by the children's screams, some Japanese soldiers murdered them by swinging their heads against trees.

As the official United States Army investigators will soon document, every day brings brutal new terrors to the Filipino people.

★ ★ ★

On Iwo Jima, American marines are experiencing Japa-nese terror as well. Nippon fighters are deadly effective with their bayonets. Sergeant John Basilone, however, finds the flamethrower to be a suitable antidote. He di-rects Corporal William Pegg to pour fire on the besieged

Japanese pillbox. Pegg is a mountain of a man, well over two hundred pounds, and wields the flamethrower with ease. As napalm enters the small gun openings in the concrete, setting the men inside ablaze, Basilone unhooks PFC Tatum's machine gun from its tripod and runs toward the bunker. Tatum sprints at his side, clutching the ammo belt. "Basilone's eyes had a fury I had never seen before," Tatum will later write. "Rigid, hard clenched jaw, sweat glistening on his forehead. He was not an executioner but a soldier performing his duty."

Basilone and Tatum make it to the bunker. Then they wait, even as distant Japanese gunners now focus their aim on the two Americans exposed atop the pillbox.

But Basilone and Tatum don't wait for long. Eight Japanese soldiers, their bodies on fire, rush out the back entrance. Firing from the hip, Basilone mows them down. "Mercy killing," Tatum thinks to himself, noting that the Japanese bodies were already coated in fiery napalm.

Fearing for his life, Tatum turns to race back to the safety of the marine lines. But Basilone stops him. The sergeant can see a distant bunker's location on the edge of Iwo Jima's airstrip and is convinced it is a perfect strategic position.

"You're staying here come hell or high water," he coolly tells Tatum. "I'm going back to get more marines and we're going to fight our way across this island."

Then John Basilone hands Chuck Tatum the machine

gun and sprints back to the lines, ignoring the bullets whizzing all around him.

✳ ✳ ✳

In the meantime, US Navy vessels are firing from offshore, pounding the Japanese artillery atop Mount Suribachi. This allows the men under John Basilone's command to move forward.

But suddenly some of the Japanese naval ordnance descends on them. The marines hit the dirt.

Throughout the war, marines and army soldiers who fight on the ground grouse about how good life is for their naval peers, with their hot meals and clean living conditions aboard ships. Even some sailors are sheepish about their way of life in comparison to the fighting men on the islands. From the safety of their ships offshore of Iwo Jima, in the words of one young naval officer, the sailors "could just watch the war going on. Through the glasses I could see the tanks trying to get through the sand and not having a whole lot of luck, and see Marines diving into foxholes."

But life at sea can also be very dangerous. Japanese kamikaze pilots have proven adept at weaving through antiaircraft fire to fly their bomb-laden planes into American vessels.* The escort carrier *Bismarck Sea*

---

* Faced with growing American military superiority in the Pacific and a lack of aircraft carriers and experienced pilots, the Japanese began utilizing suicide missions in the fall of 1944. There was no lack of Japanese personnel willing to volunteer. A plane piercing a ship's hull not only tore open a gaping hole but spread fire and

and the Lexington-class aircraft carrier *Saratoga* will both be targeted during the fight for Iwo Jima. While *Saratoga* will suffer damage and stay afloat, *Bismarck Sea* will sink. The first kamikaze that strikes plows through the hangar deck and explodes the ship's ordnance. The second kamikaze hits the *Bismarck Sea*'s elevator shaft, destroying its firefighting system in the process. Three hundred and eighteen men are burned to death, scalded by exploding boilers, or set ablaze in oily waters as *Bismarck Sea* settles to the bottom of the Pacific. Six hundred more sailors agonize in the water for up to twelve long hours, repeatedly attacked by sharks, before being picked up by other nearby vessels.

Before the marine landing, the navy bombarded Iwo Jima for three days. More than 450 ships are massed offshore, including the battleships USS *Texas*, USS *Tennessee*, USS *Nevada*, and USS *Idaho*, each of which now shells the island. *Tennessee* alone has twelve fourteen-inch guns, sixteen five-inch guns, forty

---

explosions that killed American sailors and destroyed aircraft. Official numbers vary, but at least forty-seven ships were sunk by kamikazes, including fourteen destroyers and three aircraft-carrier escorts. Almost five thousand American and British sailors were killed in the attacks and another five thousand wounded. The number of dead Japanese pilots stands at almost four thousand. Coming so close to the end of the war, the attacks promoted a genuine hatred for the enemy among the newly endangered sailors, many of whom were already dreaming of returning home. The attacks largely came to an end when a lack of pilots and airplanes made it impossible to continue, though they did not cease altogether: the last kamikaze attack took place on August 15, 1945.

antiaircraft guns, and forty-one cannons. She will fire more than eight thousand rounds of artillery over the course of the three-week battle for Iwo Jima.

But it is not sailors who choose the targets during battle. Instead, marines known as forward observers radio back to the ships with precise firing instructions. Sometimes the enemy is so close that the men on board the ship can hear Japanese soldiers yelling in the background. "I've lost his name, unfortunately," young naval officer Ben Bradlee will later remember of the marine lieutenant calling in the naval bombardment. One day he will become famous as the editor of the *Washington Post*, but for now he is just another young American trying to survive the war. "He would ask for gunfire in such and such place—often within a few yards of his foxhole—and I would relay the coordinates he gave me to the gunnery officer. First 'fire,' then deafening explosion. Then, pause, while the 57-pound shells streaked toward their target, followed by comments from our unseen buddy. 'Fan-fucking-tastic' or 'Bullseye,' maybe. Often, even. And sometimes, 'that was a little close friends. Back off a blond one.'"*

As John Basilone moves his men into position, they are actually in front of the forward observers. This places them in extreme danger. "Bring back the men on this side," Basilone yells to one squad as he scrambles to keep his fighting force in the most ideal strategic location. The machine guns, flamethrowers, and carbines carried by his unit are no match for the Japa-

---

* A slang term for an artillery coordinate.

nese big guns high atop the mountain. "You're too far out front. I'm going back to get a tank or something to see if we can get some artillery in here."

As if bulletproof, Basilone sprints away under the fusillade of shells raining down from both directions. Beneath him, the ground rises and falls as mortars and artillery explode.

★ ★ ★

Back in Manila, inhumane acts against civilians continue and war crimes investigators gather testimonies. Mrs. Esther Garcia Moras reports in horrific detail:

On 9 February 1945, at 7:00 PM, fires were started in the Ermita section near our home. We went out of our houses. The Japanese separated the men from the women and children. I estimate that there were about 6,000 women and children in Plaza Ferguson near the Bayview Hotel. They separated the Filipinas from the Mestizas and the young girls from the older women and took the Mestizas in to the hotel. About twenty-five girls ranging in age from thirteen to twenty-seven years were placed in one room and given food, whiskey and cigarettes. They were allowed to eat and drink in the room, and for about twenty minutes there was nobody else present. Afterwards a group of three or four soldiers came into the room, and each took a girl from the room, including one of my two sisters, age 14, who was returned to the room by the soldiers when they found she was having a menstrual period. Afterwards they took my other sister who later came back and said the Japanese had attacked her by having her take off all her clothes and making her lie on the floor and then raping her. One of the girls tried to resist but she was slapped. Each soldier did it only once, but there were an average of four different soldiers per girl. My sister did her best to resist, but she and others could do nothing. She told all to everyone in the room. The Japanese soldiers would come in with candies and choose the girl they wanted. There were similar groups of girls in other rooms. I estimated at least five or six, making a total of about one hundred girls. Nothing was done to Luey Tani, age 24, as the soldiers found that she had a defect on her—that she was so small that they could not do anything to her. Gloria Gelzi was another girl, age 15, but the names of others are not known. After taking my sister, one Japanese returned and took me. He took me to a room and locked the door. He tore my dress and my pants. He threw me on the floor and did it. It hurt me. I screamed and shouted and tried to push him off, but in vain. He was about five feet, six inches tall. About twelve or fifteen different ones took me. The last one was so large that he hurt me. I actually bled. He took all of my clothes and put me on a bed. He kept me there about a half hour, raping me several times.

One girl was pregnant about eight months or more and they started to take her out. They did nothing to her because she kicked them. We stayed in the Bayview Hotel three days without food or water, but they only raped us that one night. When the building was on fire they told us to go away. We could not go home because our house was burned. We kept running about in Arquisa Street. No medical attention was given any of the girls. My sister was very badly hurt because she started to bleed as it was the first time anyone did that to her. They did it to her four times. We tried to take her to a doctor, but we couldn't. However, I saw a Filipino doctor about four days ago. He examined me and told me that I had a venereal disease. My sister also has a venereal disease from the raping. I would like to have my name and address and that I testified not told to anyone. The name of Mrs. Mora's [sic] sister who was also raped is Priscilla Garcia and the sister who was not raped because she was having a menstrual period was Evangeline Garcia.*

✸ ✸ ✸

Sergeant John Basilone surely has seen his share of Japanese atrocities on the battlefield. It is ten thirty in the morning as the sergeant runs back to where Chuck Tatum has been ordered to hold his position at the edge of the Iwo Jima airfield. Unable to find a large number of reinforcements, Basilone has just three men at his side.

But they will be enough.

Basilone's heroism is his final statement on earth.

---

* *Report of Investigation of Alleged Atrocities by Members of the Japanese Imperial Forces in Manila and Other Parts of Luzon, Philippine Islands.* The report is reproduced here complete with grammatical and punctuation errors. The Bayview and Manila Hotels are still in business.

He can clearly see Tatum near the Japanese bunker. As he and his three men run toward the bunker, all hell breaks loose.

"He was seventy-five yards from me, less than a football field," Chuck Tatum will later remember. "I heard the incoming mortar shell come in. That mortar shell hit right by Basilone and the other Marines."

Tatum, who will be promoted to lead the company in Basilone's absence later that day, will describe the sergeant's demise vividly. "I didn't see anyone moving. I knew they were all dead.*

"That's when I realized we had lost Basilone. Word went down the line from hole to hole: They got Basilone."

The date is February 19, 1945. The Battle of Iwo Jima will continue for five more weeks. In addition to "Manila John" Basilone, 6,820 other Americans will die.

Almost twenty-one thousand Japanese soldiers also die or go missing in action. This is virtually their entire garrison, yet Japan is no closer to surrender.

★ ★ ★

The SS *British Columbia Express* chugs into Manila's harbor just two days after the city is finally liberated from the Japanese. The date is March 6, a Tuesday. General Douglas MacArthur rides out to meet the ship

---

*While eyewitnesses have testified that Basilone was killed by a mortar round, the official Marine Corps cause of death was small-arms fire.

United States Marines raising the flag on Iwo Jima's Mount Suribachi.
The moment later become iconic when it was staged a second time for
the benefit of photographers.

in a small boat. His landing craft is an unusual choice
of launch; the utilitarian barge is normally meant to deliver men and matériel into combat, not ferry a five-star
general to reunite with his long-absent wife and son.*

---

*Designed by New Orleans boatbuilder Andrew Higgins, these
landing craft featured a shallow draft and a ramp at the bow that

The warm tropical air smells of diesel fuel from the 225-horsepower engine, which musters a speed of just twelve knots. MacArthur is emotional. He has not seen Jean or young Arthur in five months. The tough sixty-five-year-old general's devotion to his family can often bring him to the edge of tears. He knows that the Manila his family will soon see is not the city from which they fled three years ago. They will be shocked.

Yet Manila is free.

Jean awaits her husband on deck, clutching a set of clean bedsheets, not knowing if the family will need them. Arthur stands at her side, immaculately dressed.

Douglas MacArthur scrambles up a ladder and is piped aboard. He wraps his arms around his wife and son, in full view of his three aides and the sailors on deck crowding to get a view of this famous general.

Having witnessed the devastation of Manila and

---

was lowered once the boat reached dry land, allowing troops to run straight onto a beachhead. No less a military strategist than Adolf Hitler recognized the value of the Higgins boats utilized at the D-Day invasion, calling Higgins the "new Noah." The LCVP (Landing Craft, Vehicles and Personnel) was able to deliver thirty-six men plus eight thousand pounds of cargo and vehicles into a combat zone. Though used by American troops in amphibious landings in both the European and Pacific theaters of war, its plywood sides and rear gave it little defensive capability. There is a legend that when Higgins first developed the eponymous boat, years before the war, they were intended to help bootleggers land their cargoes of illicit liquor.

knowing the horrors endured by its people, Douglas MacArthur is more grateful than ever that his family is safe.

He pulls Jean and Arthur tight against his chest.

And he does not let go for a very long time.

8

TOKYO, JAPAN
MARCH 10, 1945
12:08 A.M.

Annihilation approaches as a hard northwesterly gale lashes Tokyo. An attacking wave of B-29 bombers flies low over the city. The *"bikko,"* as the Japanese have nicknamed America's most powerful aircraft, drop a small number of conventional bombs, then make the long turn south toward the Bōçsōç Peninsula. It has been almost three hours since the first air-raid sirens wailed over the blacked-out city. Tokyo has been largely untouched since the Americans began bombing Japan four months ago, so few citizens have bothered to leave their wood-and-paper homes for the safety of air-raid shelters on this clear and cold night. As the B-29s drone into the distance, the nervous people of Tokyo feel confident enough to settle down to sleep.

Seven minutes later, that confidence is shattered. The mournful yowl of the sirens once again floats over the city. This time, Tokyo's residents race for concrete shelters, all too aware that a second air-raid siren is confirmation that a brutal bombardment is imminent. The shelters hold just five thousand people, but hundreds of thousands desperately run through the streets—fathers, wives, children, grandparents, pregnant women. Many wear packs strapped to their backs that contain their vital possessions. Worried that they may not make it to the shelters in time, fathers instruct their families to take refuge in any place that offers concealment. They throw their bodies into trenches, canals, and hastily dug holes in the ground. Some gape at the sky, where spotlights sweep back and forth to illuminate the sky for antiaircraft gunners.

The moon is a crescent as the B-29s approach the heavily populated Joto district, home to forty thousand people per square mile. The observant among them realize that the planes are flying thousands of feet lower than usual. American planes typically attack from an altitude of more than five miles high; these B-29s are just a mile above the city.

Inside the American aircraft, an adrenaline rush wipes out the monotony of the long flight to Tokyo; it has been seven hours since the Americans took off from bases on Saipan, Tinian, and Guam. Three hundred and thirty-four aircraft of the XXI Bomber Command have flown fifteen hundred miles over open ocean to drop their payloads. To make room for an extra ton of bombs, each plane has been stripped of machine guns and ammunition, leaving these Superfortresses vulnerable to Japanese fighter aircraft. The pilots and navigators were shocked when informed of

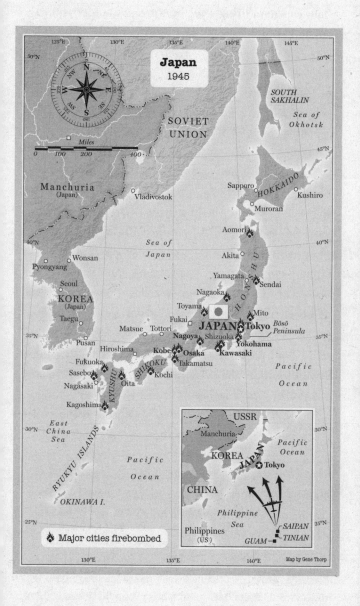

Japan
1945

SOVIET UNION

Manchuria
(Japan)

KOREA
(Japan)

HONSHU

HOKKAIDO

SOUTH SAKHALIN

Sea of
Okhotsk

Sea of
Japan

East
China
Sea

Vladivostok

Pyongyang

Wonsan

Seoul

Taegu

Pusan

Fukuoka

Sasebo

Nagasaki

Kagoshima

RYUKYU ISLANDS

OKINAWA I.

KYUSHU

Hiroshima

Oita

Kochi

SHIKOKU

Matsue   Tottori

Takamatsu

Kobe

Osaka

Nagoya

Fukai

Toyama

Nagaoka

Yamagata

Akita

Aomori

Sapporo

Muroran

Kushiro

Sendai

Mito

Tokyo

JAPAN

Shizuoka

Yokohama

Kawasaki

Bōsō
Peninsula

Pacific
Ocean

Pacific
Ocean

Miles
0 100 200   400

❀ Major cities firebombed

USSR

Manchuria

KOREA

CHINA

JAPAN ✪ Tokyo

Pacific
Ocean

Philippine
Sea

Philippines
(US)

SAIPAN

GUAM   TINIAN

Map by Gene Thorp

this decision during their briefing. The order is a calculated gamble on the part of American commander General Curtis LeMay, a thirty-eight-year-old career aviator considered "belligerent" and "brutal" by some, but widely revered for his tactical brilliance. With the deadly battle for Iwo Jima still raging, he believes that crushing the will of the Japanese people is now more important than simply bombing military targets.*

LeMay's gamble pays off. Few Japanese pilots can be scrambled to confront the air invaders, leaving the B-29s free to drop their ordnance with patient precision. Some Japanese aviators are afraid, unaware that the formidable armada has been stripped of the machine guns that might shoot them down. Harsh winds also give the American bombers an unexpected form of cover, distorting radio and radar signals. The Imperial Japanese Navy picked up the incoming flights more than a thousand miles out to sea, but due to a combination of the winds and a lack of communication between the navy and army, their warnings never make it to the Japanese night fighter squadrons stationed on the Kanto Plain outside Tokyo.

---

* Known as "Big Cigar" by the men under his command, LeMay instituted many bombing strategies that would be used for decades to come. The Ohioan was known for subjecting aircrews to intense training but never asked them to do something he would not do himself. While flying B-17s in the European theater of operations early in the war, LeMay insisted on piloting the lead plane over dangerous targets, subjecting his aircraft to the most intense enemy antiaircraft fire. Men who chose to abort the missions out of fear were subject to court-martial.

At precisely 1:00 a.m., the bomb bay doors open. Fourteen minutes later, Tokyo is ablaze.

★   ★   ★

It is a holocaust. The B-29s drop special M-69 fire-bombs from the belly of each fuselage. These are quite different from the atomic fission bombs being developed in Los Alamos, New Mexico, but on this night they are far more deadly.

This firebombing of Tokyo, known as Operation Meetinghouse, is the most horrific bombing in history, far deadlier than the recent Dresden attacks—or any other bombing of the Second World War.*

The use of mass aerial bombardment in World War II forever alters how future conflicts will be waged. The atomic device, which will use elements like uranium in order to create a single explosion of extraordinary intensity, has yet to be tested. The M-69 used on the people of Tokyo is a twenty-inch steel pipe packed with the jellied gasoline known as napalm, which

---

*The Dresden bombings in Germany on February 13–15, 1945, were a catastrophic slaughter of civilians. Allied bombers dropped 3,900 tons of bombs, killing somewhere between thirty-five thousand and one hundred thousand people and leveling four square miles of the city. The firebombing of Tokyo killed four times as many and destroyed a much larger swath of the city. The most well-known among civilian bombings during the war, the German "Blitz" of London from September 1940 to May 1941, saw forty-five thousand tons of bombs dropped on the city, with the loss of one million homes and forty-five thousand civilian casualties.

constitutes the Esso Corporation's most important contribution to the American war effort. The M-69s are bundled into clusters of thirty-eight, which are then loaded inside a finned casing and dropped from the aircraft. Two thousand feet above the ground, the casing opens, releasing the bombs and allowing them to plummet to the earth separately. Nothing happens immediately upon impact, but three seconds later a timed fuse ignites a white phosphorous charge, which forces the napalm to shoot out of the three-inch-wide pipe. Slow-burning and sticky, the napalm affixes itself to clothing, hair, and skin, burning straight down to the bone.

One M-69 is capable of starting a massive fire. One ton of M-69s will ensure complete destruction.

On the morning of March 10, 1945, American B-29 bombers drop *two thousand tons* of M-69 napalm bombs on Tokyo.

Driven by winds of nearly hurricane force, fire envelops entire city blocks. Mobs of Japanese citizens race for their lives, only to be surrounded by the inferno and summarily asphyxiated as the flames suck all the oxygen from the air. Water mains are destroyed by the blaze, rendering fire hoses useless. Crews armed with water buckets are helpless to stop the carnage. Eighty firefighters and more than five hundred volunteers refuse to leave their posts and burn to death where they stand. Flames destroy ninety-six fire engines. Orange tongues of fire shoot so high from the ground that they reflect off the underbellies of the silver bombers overhead.

As the heat rises, updrafts reach thousands of feet high, actually bringing the smell of burning human flesh into the nostrils of the American pilots. Many planes return to their home base with their fuselages coated in soot.

Soon fire consumes sixteen square miles of Tokyo. The entire geisha district is turned to ash. Hospitals, homes, temples, train stations, bus depots, convents, theaters, fire stations, workers' hostels, and schools are destroyed. From the safety of the Imperial Palace, which the Americans have specifically chosen not to bomb, Emperor Hirohito beholds a red glow across the horizon, turning darkest night into day.

Trapped inside walls of flame that throw off unimaginably high temperatures, citizens spontaneously burst into flames. Debris flies through the air, striking people dead at random. City canals boil. Dead bodies bob in the icy rivers. Charred corpses litter the ground, many still burning due to body oils. The heat takes its toll on the living as well, melting faces, fingers, and toes. Skin literally peels off bodies, hanging in great flaps from torsos.

At 3:20 a.m. the bombing stops.

As dawn rises over Tokyo, one-fourth of the city has been destroyed. One hundred thousand people are dead; forty thousand people are badly burned but alive. One million Japanese are homeless. Of the 324 B-29s that carried out the bombings, just 12 planes were lost, mainly due to engine failures.

General Curtis LeMay's stated goal for this mission

was that Tokyo be "burned down and wiped off the map to shorten the war."

Emperor Hirohito tours the burned-out portions of Tokyo on March 18. His caravan of vehicles and his own maroon Rolls-Royce carry the official chrysanthemum crest, signifying that a *gyoko*—a blessed visitation—is taking place. He comes upon exhausted citizens pawing through rubble, searching for some fragment of their former lives. Upon seeing his vehicles, instead of adopting a subservient stance, the people glare. Hirohito does not stop the cars to engage his subjects, nor does his facial expression display sorrow or regret. Despite the war weariness so evident among Tokyo's citizens, Japan's elite will send an emissary to Hirohito two days later, imploring him not to surrender. It is their belief that the Japanese people will become used to the bombings and grow closer together in the process.

In the weeks that follow, Japanese citizens lose sleep, as staying up late to prepare for yet another bombing attack leaves them exhausted and distraught. There is a rise in absenteeism in factories and a slowing of the nation's war production.

Yet the Japanese still will not surrender. Not even when General LeMay repeats the same firebombing in Nagoya, Yokohama, Osaka, Kobe, and Kawasaki.

Instead, schools in Japan close. As a sign that the nation will fight to the bitter end, all children are put to work producing food or munitions; some are even taught how to operate antiaircraft guns.

But that won't be necessary. After two weeks of "burn jobs," the firebombing of Japan comes to an end. There are two reasons: First, LeMay's pilots are exhausted. And second, after dropping five million M-69s on Japan, the XXI Command has run out of firebombs.

9

A light rain falls on the nation's capital as Harry Truman strides into a high-ceilinged room, thirsty for a drink. The vice president wears a gray suit with a white handkerchief folded in his breast pocket. Even after a long day presiding over the Senate, Truman appears dapper and polished. As he enters room H-128, on the ground floor of the Capitol, to enjoy Speaker of the House Sam Rayburn's nightly happy hour, Truman is content and at ease. Tomorrow, as he wrote to his mother just a few moments ago during a particularly long speech by a "windy Senator from Wisconsin," he will deliver a national radio address on Thomas Jefferson Day, the anniversary of the third president's birth. Other than that, he doesn't have much on his mind.

"Harry, Steve Early wants you to call him right away," Congressman Rayburn says the instant Truman steps through the door. The large room housed the Committee on Territories back in the nineteenth century, and the ceiling is painted with a mural celebrating America's expansion. At Rayburn's urging, the lone star of Texas was recently added to the collection of painted birds and plants. Otherwise, the room resembles a very comfortable men's club.

The sixty-three-year-old Rayburn has been Speaker for five years and often uses these nightly booze meetings he has dubbed the "Board of Education" as a means of building coalitions to support bills or simply to strategize. Invitations are extended according to Rayburn's political needs. Attending the Board of Education once or twice in a term is considered to be a status symbol. Some, however, like Truman and Texas congressman Lyndon B. Johnson, can stop by for two fingers of bourbon and branch water any time they like.

Truman picks up the phone and dials National 1414, the phone number for President Roosevelt's longtime press secretary Steve Early. Calls from the White House are rare, and Truman still has not been vice president long enough to have penetrated FDR's inner circle. So even though the president is at his Warm Springs, Georgia, hideaway, recuperating from the long journey back from Yalta, Truman is quick to answer Early's message in case something important is required of him. So far in his term, that has not been the case.

"This is the V.P.," Truman says at the sound of Early's voice.

Early gets to the point. "Come to the White House as quickly and quietly as you can."

"Jesus Christ and General Jackson," Truman exclaims, replacing the phone.

"I'm wanted at the White House right away," he tells Rayburn.

As Truman steps out the door, he realizes he has left his hat behind in his office. He walks each day for exercise, maintaining a brisk pace of 120 steps per minute. But now, Harry Truman begins to run. He dashes the length of the Capitol Building, his footsteps echoing off the marble floor. He wonders if Roosevelt has decided to cut short his trip to Georgia, or if there is some special errand pertaining to the Congress that the president requires of him. The two men have met in person just twice, so any summons from the president has a tone of urgency. Truman senses that Roosevelt is angry with him, though he does not know why. This only increases his desire to get to the White House as soon as possible.

By 5:25 p.m., the vice president's car is parked beneath the North Portico of the White House. Truman steps out and is escorted inside by two ushers. One of them guides him to a small oak-paneled elevator. Nothing is said. Truman still has no idea why he has been summoned. Stepping out from the elevator on the second floor, he is surprised to see Eleanor Roosevelt and her daughter, Anna, wearing black dresses. Truman's relationship with the First Lady has been wary and strained, so she would never summon him for social reasons, let alone invite him up to her personal study.*

---

*Eleanor Roosevelt had been very fond of Truman's predecessor, Henry Wallace, and was firmly against his removal from the ticket. Truman first met Eleanor at a White House reception in

Quickly, Truman realizes why he has been summoned.

"Harry," the now former First Lady tells him, "the president is dead."

Her voice is calm, for she has known for more than an hour. The marriage between Eleanor and Franklin Roosevelt has lasted forty years, but it is largely one of political convenience. FDR was known to stray—indeed, the cerebral hemorrhage that finally killed him in Georgia took place in the presence of his mistress, Lucy Mercer Rutherfurd.

"Is there anything I can do for you?" Truman asks Eleanor as the truth sinks in.

The First Lady looks directly at the new president. "Is there anything *we* can do for *you*? For you are the one in trouble now."

★　★　★

The time is 7:09 p.m.

A stunned Harry S. Truman places his left hand on a red-edged Bible and raises his right. His wife and daughter, nine cabinet members, six congressional leaders, several members of the White House staff, and a handful of reporters are crammed into the Cabinet Room. Everyone is standing. A portrait of Woodrow Wilson, Truman's favorite president, overlooks the pro-

---

1935, shortly after he was elected to the Senate; he thought her to be condescending. Between then and 1945 Truman had criticized her to family members, saying that she was too fond of the public eye and the sound of her own voice.

ceedings as Chief Justice Harlan Fiske Stone of the Supreme Court recites the oath of office. "I, Harry Shipp Truman," begins Stone.

Truman has the presence of mind to correct him. "I, Harry S. Truman," he replies.*

The oath continues.

Outside the Cabinet Room, a small army of reporters and photographers has gathered in the West Wing. News of Roosevelt's death has already flashed around the world, drawing a crowd of thousands to now stand vigil in front of the White House.

"So help me God," intones Stone, bringing the oath of office to an end.

"So help me God," replies President Harry S. Truman.†

The Bible on which Truman has sworn his oath is a cheap Gideon edition normally found in hotel rooms; it was all that could be found in the commotion. But now this common Bible has become a historical artifact. Outwardly, Truman shows no fear of what is to come, his face "taut," in the words of one report, but the new president concludes the oath impulsively,

---

* Shipp was the middle name of Harry Truman's grandfather, Anderson Shipp Truman. Margaret Truman later wrote of her father's inauguration, "Where Stone got the idea that Dad's middle name was Shipp no one has ever found out."

† Originally, the words "So help me God" were not part of the oath of office. Some historians believe George Washington added them when he was inaugurated in 1789, while others argue he did not say the words but they were later attributed to him. Either way, they have remained a presidential tradition.

suddenly pressing the Bible firmly to his lips in a sincere kiss.

✷   ✷   ✷

On April 24, President Truman is briefed on the top secret news that the United States will soon test an atomic bomb. "Within four months," begins the report brought to Truman in the Oval Office, "we shall in all probability have completed the most terrible weapon ever known in human history, one bomb of which could destroy a whole city."

If successful, this weapon could end the Pacific war, though at great loss of life to civilians. Hundreds of thousands, if not more than a million, Japanese citizens may die.

One day after that, Truman authorizes the wholesale invasion of Japan by American forces. Hundreds of thousands of soldiers are expected to perish if the attack is finally given the go.

The invasion of Japan, however, might be unnecessary if the A-bomb is ready.

The final decision about dropping the bomb will be made solely by Truman, though at this point he is not sure what the A-bomb really is.

But Truman knows that the bleeding of American lives needs to stop—Japan must be crushed.

10

LOS ALAMOS, NEW MEXICO
APRIL 22, 1945
5:00 P.M.

The most dangerous man in the world is celebrating his forty-first birthday. Sipping on a dry gin martini, the eccentric and brilliant physicist, J. Robert Oppenheimer, moves from conversation to conversation in the living room of his 1,200-square-foot stone-and-wood cottage. The air smells like pipe tobacco. His guests are physicists, chemists, and Nobel Prize winners, their accents British, American, and Eastern European.*

Everyone in the room has a top secret security clearance, allowing them to speak freely about a topic few in the world are aware of. With Germany all but defeated, these brilliant minds are divided between those

---

*The great Albert Einstein is not among them. The theoretical scientist's pacifist views have made him a security risk; with the exception of some minor work for the US Navy, Einstein has been virtually shut out of the war effort.

who want to see the atomic bomb dropped on Japan and those who believe it is morally wrong to destroy a country so near to surrender. Some believe that dropping the A-bomb will lead to a worldwide arms race. Indeed, the Hungarian physicist Leo Szilard is making secret plans to meet with President Truman to discuss this troubling matter in person.*

The altitude in Los Alamos is 7,300 feet atop a desert mesa. Newcomers often find themselves unable to handle their liquor because the thin air brings dizziness. But Oppenheimer's drinking stamina is legendary among his staff, surpassed only by his obsessive drive to create the world's first atomic weapon. Even after this Sunday night of celebration, Oppenheimer will rise well before the 7:30 a.m. factory whistle blows.

★　★　★

"My two great loves," Robert Oppenheimer wrote to a friend long before the war, "are physics and desert country. It's a pity they can't be combined."

Now, thanks to Brigadier General Leslie Groves and the top secret Manhattan Project, they have been. It has been six years since Franklin Roosevelt's Oval Office meeting with Alexander Sachs and its resulting call to action for America to pursue nuclear weapons. But

---

* Szilard will be thwarted in his efforts to speak to Harry Truman about what he perceives to be an impending arms race. Truman believed Szilard was misguided in wanting to share the A-bomb's technology with other Allied powers.

it has been less than three years since Oppenheimer was tasked by the overweight army bureaucrat with not only building a state-of-the-art laboratory in the middle of nowhere but also convincing some of the world's sharpest minds to put their lives on hold to spend the rest of the war here.

Oppenheimer was not the obvious choice to be in charge of the lab. His past indicated some trouble: the young professor from the University of California at Berkeley had a history of depression and eccentric behavior. In the late 1930s, Oppenheimer dated a woman known to be a member of the Communist Party, which concerned army counterintelligence and the Federal Bureau of Investigation. Also, Oppenheimer had no experience managing a large group of people, nor had he won a Nobel Prize. Many doubted that he had the experience required to build the world's first weapon of mass destruction.

Yet the outspoken Groves was determined to hire him. "Oppenheimer can talk to you about anything. He can talk to you about anything you bring up. Well, not exactly. . . . He doesn't know anything about sports," Groves would later tell an interviewer, referring to Oppenheimer as "a genius."

Word of a new laboratory devoted to splitting atoms eventually filtered into the scientific community. At the time of Oppenheimer's hiring, in October 1942, some were shocked at the "most improbable appointment." As one physicist noted: "I was astonished."

A twenty-five-year-old boys' school thirty-five miles northwest of Santa Fe with log dormitories and a stunning view of the Sangre de Cristo Mountains was soon purchased to build Oppenheimer's new lab. Included in the $440,000 price were 8,900 acres of land, sixty horses, fifty saddles, and one phone line. The school, named Los Alamos, was soon ringed with security fences topped with coils of razor wire and guarded by military personnel and attack dogs. Oppenheimer's scientists begin to feel so secure that many stop locking their front doors when they leave for work in the morning. That safety, however, comes at a cost: each employee at the Los Alamos National Laboratory is subject to constant monitoring of his or her personal life by security personnel. News of the atomic bomb research must be kept from reaching Germany and the Soviet Union.*

What began as a theoretical laboratory soon became a small town. A theater group was formed, with Oppenheimer himself making a cameo appearance as a corpse in *Arsenic and Old Lace*. A town council was elected. Parties were common and lasted late into the night, sometimes featuring the world's most learned minds playing piano or violin to entertain their friends.

---

*Even before the Manhattan Project got under way in 1942, the Soviets knew America was pursuing the bomb. Their code name for this effort was ENORMOZ—"enormous." German-born physicist Klaus Fuchs and American scientist Theodore Hall were both Los Alamos employees who also spied for the Russians. Fuchs was convicted as a spy in 1950 and sentenced to fourteen years in prison, of which he served nine; Hall was never charged. There were many more spies within Los Alamos. Though their code names are known, their identities have never been discovered.

Some found the remote location to be claustrophobic, while others thought it romantic, leading to an extraordinarily high birth rate.

As 1944 becomes 1945, and the testing of an actual A-bomb begins, the physical and emotional toll of transforming a weapon that once existed only in theory into a violent force that could end the largest war in history has been debilitating. Oppenheimer stands almost six feet tall but has wasted away to just 115 pounds. His teeth are rotting. He smokes five packs of Chesterfield cigarettes a day and is prone to long fits of smoker's cough that turn his face purple. He rarely eats, having abandoned his passion for spicy food in favor of a diet of gin, cigarettes, and coffee.

Worse, Oppenheimer's wife of five years, Kitty, a genius in her own right in the field of botany, has broken under the strain. She has gone home to live with her parents in Pittsburgh, taking their four-year-old son, Peter, with her. Strangely, Kitty leaves their four-month-old daughter, Toni, behind. Knowing that Oppenheimer will not be able to care for the baby, she has entrusted the child to Pat Sherr, a good friend who has just suffered a miscarriage. The truth is that Kitty has never been a good mother to Toni, whom she sees as an unwanted burden, frequently abandoning her to the company of friends for days at a time.

Robert Oppenheimer visits his daughter twice a week, though his own love for his daughter is just as precarious as that of his wife. Juggling parenting and the upcoming testing of the atomic bomb is too much

J. Robert Oppenheimer

for him. On one occasion he asks Sherr if she would like to adopt Toni, explaining that he "just can't love her." An appalled Sherr declines.

Robert Oppenheimer longs for Kitty's return. She is his sole confidante and one of the few people he can trust.*

---

* Known for her fiery, outspoken ways, Katherine Puening Oppenheimer returned to Los Alamos to be with her husband in July 1945. He was not her first spouse; in fact, she had been wed three times before marrying Robert Oppenheimer on November 1, 1940.

Yet in Kitty's absence, there are rumors. Despite his cadaverous look and the smell of stale tobacco that clings to him like a shroud, some women are drawn to Oppenheimer. He is not oblivious to their charms; talk of affairs follows him throughout his time at Los Alamos. Among the rumors (although it appears to have been nothing more than that) is one of a liaison with a pretty blond twenty-year-old secretary, Anne T. Wilson, whom Oppenheimer handpicked for the job upon meeting her in Washington.

Oppenheimer's relations with other women, however, go far beyond rumor. In June 1943, he rekindled an old romance with pediatric psychologist Jean Tatlock while on a business trip to Berkeley. Army intelligence agents, who were spying on Oppenheimer's every move due to the high security surrounding the Manhattan Project, reported that he had dinner and drinks with Tatlock before spending the night in her apartment. Years before, in the midst of a torrid relationship, Tatlock had turned down Oppenheimer on three separate occasions when he asked her to marry him. It was a decision she would come to regret by

---

Among her past husbands was a known Communist Party member who died while fighting in the Spanish Civil War. This led FBI director J. Edgar Hoover to investigate her loyalty to the United States in 1944. She was cleared of all charges. Kitty and Robert Oppenheimer remained married for the rest of his life, years that included frequent marital fighting and her downward spiral into alcoholism.

1943. Six months after Oppenheimer spent the night, Jean Tatlock drew a bath, swallowed a bottle of sleeping pills, and died.

✳ ✳ ✳

Another of Oppenheimer's affairs is with Ruth Tolman, a psychologist for the Office of Strategic Services who is ten years older than Oppenheimer. This affair will continue long after the war's end. Tolman's husband is also employed at Los Alamos and soon learns of his wife's infidelity. When Ruth's husband, Richard, dies of a heart attack in 1948, some will claim that despondence over his wife's love of Oppenheimer was a primary cause.

Right now, however, Robert Oppenheimer has little energy to stray. His "gadget," as he calls the A-bomb, is almost ready for testing. The detonation, when it occurs, will take place in the nearby desert, the Jornada del Muerto—or "Journey of the Dead Man," as this barren, windswept landscape is appropriately known. The site has been chosen because it is remote, unpopulated, and flat.

Robert Oppenheimer graduated from Harvard with honors in just three years and has a PhD in physics from Germany's University of Göttingen. He is a natural leader who enjoys the spotlight but rarely shows his true emotions.

Among his varied interests, Oppenheimer is a believer in Eastern philosophy. His code name for the upcoming A-bomb test is "Trinity," after the three

Hindu gods Brahma, Vishnu, and Shiva.* Oppenheimer can quote the Hindu scripture, the Bhagavad Gita, at will: "If the radiance of a thousand suns were to burst into the sky, that would be like the splendor of the mighty one. . . . Now I am become death, the shatterer of worlds."†

As his birthday party progresses, Oppenheimer shakes another martini with great flair. The cocktail is one of his personal trademarks. Although he drinks constantly, the scientist prefers to sip his libation slowly and rarely becomes inebriated.

Robert Oppenheimer's life is full of contradiction. But as his favorite selection from the Bhagavad Gita suggests, this man who chose to play a corpse onstage, and whose body now wastes away as he deprives it of simple nourishment, is a real-life Grim Reaper.

And he knows it.

---

*The gods are collectively known as "Trimurti" in Sanskrit, meaning "having three forms." This is coincidentally close to Trinity. Later in life, Oppenheimer will also state that the name came from the sonnets of John Donne and the line "Batter my heart, three person'd God."

†Hindu scholars say the passage refers to the god Vishnu, who is trying to persuade a prince to do his duty. Vishnu quotes the line about being a destroyer of worlds while trying to impress the prince with his power by transforming himself into a being with several arms.

11

---◆---

Five thousand miles away from Los Alamos, and just four hundred miles from Tokyo, the American marines know nothing about the A-bomb. "The Germans have surrendered," they are told as the battle for Okinawa enters its sixth miserable week. The news quickly passes up and down the line, from foxhole to foxhole.

To a man, the response is the same: "So what?"

Adolf Hitler is dead. The marines are trying to survive. The worldwide war that the German führer started six years ago still rages in this corner of the globe. The American military is moving ever closer to the Japanese mainland, but there is a high price to pay for that progress—and the marines know it.

The American island-hopping strategy began with the capture of the island of Guadalcanal in 1942, which put American forces within 3,000 miles of Tokyo. Capturing Peleliu in late 1944 put the Americans within

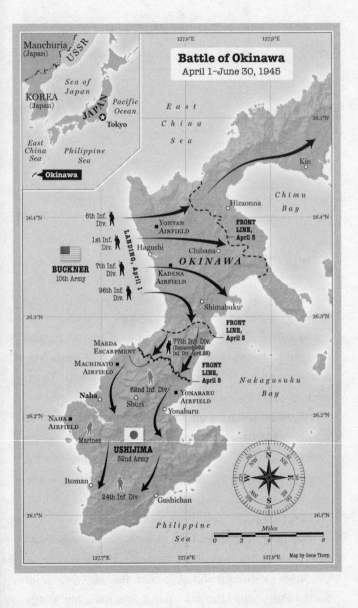

Battle of Okinawa
April 1–June 30, 1945

Manchuria
(Japan)

USSR

KOREA
(Japan)

Sea of
Japan

JAPAN

Pacific
Ocean

Tokyo

East
China
Sea

Philippine
Sea

Okinawa

E a s t
C h i n a
S e a

Kin

Chimu
Bay

Hizaonna

6th Inf.
Div.

YONTAN
AIRFIELD

FRONT
LINE,
April 3

1st Inf.
Div.

Hagushi

Chibana

OKINAWA

BUCKNER
10th Army

7th Inf.
Div.

KADENA
AIRFIELD

96th Inf.
Div.

Shimabuku

FRONT
LINE,
April 3

MAEDA
ESCARPMENT

77th Inf. Div.
(Replaced 96th
Inf. Div. April 29)

MACHINATO
AIRFIELD

FRONT
LINE,
April 8

N a k a g u s u k u
B a y

Naha

62nd Inf.
Div.

YONABARU
AIRFIELD

Shuri

Yonabaru

NAHA
AIRFIELD

Marines

USHIJIMA
32nd Army

Itoman

24th Inf.
Div.

Gushichan

Philippine
Sea

Miles

0   2   4   6   8

N NE
NW
W   E
SW   SE
S

Map by Gene Thorp

The United States invasion of Okinawa brought American forces ever closer to the Japanese mainland. It would prove to be one of the bloodiest battles of the war.

2,000 miles. The surrender of Iwo Jima closed the distance to 750 miles. Okinawa is half that. The next obvious assault will be the southernmost islands of Japan itself.

"We were resigned only to the fact that the Japanese would fight to total extinction on Okinawa, as they had elsewhere, and that Japan would have to be invaded with the same gruesome prospects," Marine Corps private Eugene Sledge will later write in a book about his experiences in the Pacific.

The closer to Tokyo the Americans advance, the more brutal the fighting becomes. The invasion of Okinawa is already turning into the bloodiest and most costly battle the US Army, Marines, and Navy will endure in either Europe or the Pacific. One notable casualty is legendary American journalist Ernie Pyle, winner of the Pulitzer Prize for Journalism in 1944, killed by a sniper's bullet through the temple shortly after arriving in the Pacific, after four years covering the European theater.

Unlike the coral and jungle of Peleliu, or the remote black volcanic soil of Iwo Jima, Okinawa is a well-populated island full of farmers. Its citizenry is a mixture of Japanese and Chinese. Many have already committed suicide rather than succumb to the invaders. The verdant fields of okra and eggplant that should be carpeting the countryside have been trampled by soldiers, cratered by shells, and littered with the detritus of war: spent casings, empty food tins, burning vehicles, and, of course, dead bodies.*

The rich clay soil is now mud thanks to monsoon rains. For the first time in many months, the Japanese seem to have an endless supply of ammunition and the big guns with which to fire it. Poncho-wearing American fighting men cower in their flooded foxholes or attack in the slop, their minds and bodies concussed by ceaseless shelling. The stench of rotting corpses carries on the warm subtropical wind. Many a man has slipped in the mud and found himself covered in maggots, face

---

*Okinawa is seventy miles long and averages seven miles wide. The island is part of the Ryukyu archipelago, which Japan annexed in 1879. The island population at the time of the American invasion was approximately 450,000; an estimated 150,000 either committed suicide or were killed in the battle.

to face with a half-buried, decomposing Japanese or American soldier.

"All movements," Private Sledge will add, "were physically exhausting and utterly exasperating because of the mud . . . [and] the ever present danger of shells even far behind the lines."

Sledge will note ruefully, "We tried to wisecrack and joke from time to time, but that always faded away as we grew more weary."

★ ★ ★

Private First Class Desmond Doss would like to pray.

The sun is rising. The men of B Company, First Battalion, 77th Infantry Division are just moments away from assaulting the Maeda Escarpment, a four-hundred-foot-high cliff stretching the five-mile width of Okinawa. While the rest of the island consists of flat or rolling hills, the boulder-covered slopes are steep, and the last sixty feet are completely vertical. Within its limestone rock face the Japanese have concealed a network of tunnels containing machine guns and artillery. From this vantage point, the enemy can monitor American troop movements in three directions, allowing them to lay down pinpoint artillery fire.

It is vital that B Company capture the escarpment. Two full American divisions have failed to reach the cliff top. Now, instead of a full-scale assault, they will try stealth, concealing themselves among the boulders in order to reach the summit before they can be discovered.

Private Doss asks his commanding officer if he can pray. "Sir," he says, "I believe that prayer is the biggest lifesaver there is. I believe that every man should have a word of prayer before he puts his foot on the rope ladder to go up that cliff."

First Lieutenant Cecil Gornto nods. Doss is a devout Seventh-day Adventist who doesn't eat meat, smoke, drink, or work on Saturday. When he was first inducted into the army on April Fools' Day 1942, Doss's behavior was seen as eccentric. Fellow soldiers shunned him. Doss was even offered a discharge on the grounds that he was mentally imbalanced. He refused the ticket out.

Since then, the rail-thin Virginian with the thick twang has distinguished himself at the battles for Guam and Leyte, in the Philippines. His gallantry has earned him two Bronze Stars for heroism under fire. The men of B Company are no longer wary of the twenty-six-year-old's devout ways.

Doss prays aloud just moments before battle. Although some men do not join in the prayer, they respect the private; he is the company medic and the man who might save their lives today. On both Leyte and Guam, Doss amazed his platoon by running through thick enemy fire to drag men to safety.

For the same reasons PFC Desmond Doss has become a hero to the men of B Company, he is also a target. "The Japanese were out to get the medics," Doss will recall of the white armband with a red cross on his left bicep. "They were taught to kill the medics for the reason it broke down the morale of the men. Because if the medics were gone they had no one to take care of them."

Most remarkably, Doss is also a conscientious objector, meaning that he believes quite literally in the words of the Sixth Commandment: Thou shalt not kill. For PFC Doss, war does not excuse him from following this law that he believes was handed down from God. But he is a patriot, and turned down a job in a shipyard back home so that he might march alongside his fellow Americans.

Doss does not carry a firearm. While the other men of B Company attack the Japanese with grenades and carbines, and among the medical corps most carry a pistol, Doss does not.

"Amen," Doss says, completing his prayer. He knows the men are looking at him, hoping to draw comfort from his normally calm demeanor. Doss, however, is terrified, and there is little he can do to hide it.

"Amen," add the men standing around him.

It is dawn, and the temperature on Okinawa is still cool as the men of B Company move out. Within hours, having safely avoided detection, they reach the top of the escarpment, scaling the last fifty feet and then dropping ropes back over the side for other Americans to follow.

Not a single man is killed, and the men of B Company know the reason why: "Doss prayed," marvels one incredulous soldier.

But suddenly, the first cry of "Medic!" echoes across the rocky hilltop.

✫   ✫   ✫

As the rain continues to pour down on Okinawa, the rest of the world waits. Pockets of war still exist in places like Borneo and China, but Okinawa is the linchpin of the final American campaign against Japan. The last great battle of World War II cannot begin until this contest is settled.*

✫   ✫   ✫

In Moscow, Russian leader Joseph Stalin is watching the Okinawa battle carefully. He is also making plans to transport a million men the width of the Soviet Union once the winter snows melt. Now that the war with Nazi Germany has ended, Stalin is free to attack Japanese-held Manchuria, in northern China. As American general George S. Patton has warned US leaders, the Soviet dictator is America's next great enemy. He is proving this by his ruthless stranglehold on the nations of Eastern Europe, now occupied by Soviet forces. The Russian leader actually wants the war between America and Japan to drag on as long as possible, giving him more time to move his troops from Europe to Asia. It is becoming clear that as long as

---

*Five thousand of the American dead in the Battle of Okinawa are sailors killed in kamikaze attacks. An additional thousand more Americans will be pulled off the line with shell shock from enduring the prolonged Japanese artillery bombings. Japan's Okinawa casualties will number more than a hundred thousand dead soldiers.

Soviet aggression remains unchecked, Stalin will expand his empire as he pleases.

✳ ✳ ✳

In Washington, President Harry Truman is keeping a close eye on Joseph Stalin. Unlike his predecessor, FDR, he does not trust the Soviet leader. On May 11, Truman ceases the US Lend-Lease program with the Russians. The Soviet reliance on American trucks and other materials of war, which has been in effect throughout World War II, will soon come to an end. Though the United States and the Soviet Union still consider themselves allies, Harry Truman has given the first indication that America will not tolerate Stalin's brutal global ambition.

✳ ✳ ✳

An early casualty of the Okinawa battle is the USS *Indianapolis*, which now rests in dry dock at Mare Island Naval Shipyard in Vallejo, California. Her crew of 1,196 is enjoying an impromptu break from the war. Some have traveled home to see loved ones, while others spend their days in the nearby barracks playing cards. All of them are lucky to be alive.

Indianapolis, a heavy cruiser, was nearly sunk by a kamikaze pilot off the coast of Okinawa on March 31, during the pre-invasion bombardment. Dropping down in a vertical dive, the suicide bomber loosed his ordnance just twenty-five feet above the ship. The kamikaze dropped only one bomb, but that was enough. The explosive penetrated the deck armor, then passed through the crew's mess and the ship's fuel tanks before exploding deep in the bowels of the vessel. Nine men died instantly.

The blast blew two enormous holes in the hull. *Indianapolis* might have sunk right then and there if not for the damage control crews, who immediately sealed off the flooded compartments. Miraculously, the cruiser then sailed six thousand miles back to San Francisco under her own power for repairs.

Once upon a time, *Indianapolis* was a jewel of the American fleet. President Franklin Roosevelt enjoyed his time aboard her teak quarterdeck so much that he requested it as his personal transport for numerous transatlantic crossings.

Its reputation as a special ship was solidified in December 1941, when *Indianapolis* set sail from her berth at Pearl Harbor across from the ill-fated Battleship Row.* When the Japanese launched their surprise attack two mornings later, *Indianapolis* was safe at sea, seven hundred miles to the southwest of Hawaii. The

---

*Battleship Row was the name given to the dockside location of American battleships in Pearl Harbor. Eight such vessels, all named for states, were in port on December 7, 1941, when Japan attacked: *Nevada*, *Arizona*, *West Virginia*, *Oklahoma*, *Pennsylvania*, *Tennessee*, *Maryland*, and *California*. The USS *Utah* was also in port, but moored in a different portion of the harbor, at the time of the attack. *West Virginia* and *California* were later refloated and returned to service. The wreckage of *Utah* and *Arizona* can still be seen where the ships sank, as memorials to the men who died. The bodies of sailors within the sunken vessels have never been removed.

American battleships *Arizona*, *Utah*, *Oklahoma*, *California*, and *West Virginia* were all sunk, with a loss of almost two thousand lives.

But now *Indianapolis*'s luck has changed. The kamikaze attack has rattled many of the crew, some of whom have requested transfers to other ships before it sails back into battle.

The War Department, however, does not consider *Indianapolis* unlucky. They see her return to America as an act of providence. Even as the damaged vessel is being retrofitted with the latest in communications and radar equipment, the War Department has secretly chosen *Indianapolis* as the ideal vessel to transport the components for two A-bombs all the way across the Pacific, where they will be assembled and prepared for detonation on the island of Tinian. Not a single member of the crew, not even the skipper, Captain Charles McVay III, will be told the truth about the mystery cargo that will soon rest in *Indianapolis*'s hold.

✶　✶　✶

General Douglas MacArthur does not know much about the A-bomb either. In Manila, which he has not left since his wife and son arrived, the general is eagerly planning the invasion of Japan. US Navy chief of staff Admiral Ernest King and US Army Air Forces commander General Hap Arnold oppose the invasion, convinced that control of the sea and skies will eventually strangle the Japanese economically, making the massive loss of American life unnecessary. It is estimated that five million American soldiers, sailors, and marines will be needed, as well as one million British troops. Casualties on both sides are projected to number anywhere from the hundreds of thousands to the millions.*

MacArthur disagrees with his navy and air corps counterparts. He believes that an island blockade will not result in unconditional surrender. He refutes the conventional notion that the Japanese are strong enough to put up anything more than a thin defense of their homeland, despite the fact that they still have four million soldiers in uniform and thousands of planes hidden throughout Japan for the specific task of carrying out kamikaze bombing.

MacArthur believes his command of the largest amphibious landing in history will be successful. He sees glory. Others see death.

A handful of generals from the European theater have been transferred to MacArthur's command, but America's most aggressive and successful general is not among them. General George S. Patton's war is over. The fiery tactician will remain in Germany to oversee postwar rebuilding, entirely unwelcome in a Pacific theater of operations.

As one American officer puts it: "Two prima donnas,

---

*The two-part invasion of Japan was collectively known as Operation Downfall. The first attack would be the invasion of Japan's southernmost island, Kyushu, called Operation Olympic. The second would be the invasion of Honshu, the island on which Tokyo is located. This plan was code-named Operation Coronet.

two colorful personalities in the same theater, were one too many."*

★ ★ ★

Ensconced inside his vast palace in Tokyo, Emperor Hirohito ponders whether or not to move to a secret mountain fortress that has been prepared for his safety.

Japan's cities are in ruins. Hundreds of thousands are homeless. Hirohito's Imperial Japanese Navy has been almost destroyed. The nation is starving. There is growing resentment among famished civilians over the preferential treatment given to the Japanese military, particularly in terms of food distribution. Also, the emperor has known for two months that Russia wants to "secure a voice in the future of Asia"—a diplomat's wording for impending invasion.

But surrender is still not an option for Hirohito.

Instead, he clings to the belief that his military leaders will be able to fight off an invasion of the homeland. New airplanes are being built. Twenty-nine new army divisions are being formed. Tanks and artillery are being stockpiled for the crucial battle.†

---

*There is nearly a six-year age difference between Patton and the older MacArthur. They first met on September 12, 1918, during World War I's Saint-Mihiel offensive. In 1932, MacArthur ordered then major Patton to disperse protesters who had occupied parts of Washington, DC. Historians still debate as to who was the better general.

†The Japanese had been preparing defenses and massing troops on Kyushu since early in 1945. An estimated 750,000 troops were massed around the beachheads in anticipation of the American

"If we hold out long enough in this war," Hirohito believes, "then we may be able to win."

★　★　★

It is Saturday on Okinawa, the Sabbath for PFC Desmond Doss. It is to be a day of rest and prayer, even amid the ongoing battle for the Maeda Escarpment. His leg is bruised and bleeding from falling over the side of the cliff last night, and he can barely stand. As the sun rises, Doss leans back against a rock, thinking of his girlfriend back home and reading his Bible.

A week has passed since Doss's squad launched their attack. The seesaw battle for the escarpment continues; the Japanese are utilizing a "reverse slope" defense, in which the Americans are allowed to occupy the forward portions of the summit but the crest and the reverse side of the mountain remain in Japanese hands. In the process, the Americans have been pushed off the summit many times, only to fight back and regain the high ground. Each day, PFC Doss has climbed the great rope ladders to treat the American wounded. His uniform has turned the color of dried blood from all the men he has treated, frantically performing first aid amid grenades and small-arms fire. Doss refuses to seek cover as he applies tourniquets, stanches blood flow, injects morphine, and drags men from the line of fire. B Company has been reduced from 200 to

---

invasion. Despite heavy aerial bombardment, Japan's factories were still functioning and capable of building new weapons of war, staffed by Japanese laborers and Allied POWs.

155 men, and it is Doss who has tended to each of the fallen. Alive or dead, he has lowered their bodies off the escarpment to safety.

As Doss reclines in the shade, a colonel suddenly stands over him. Senior officers have no place on the front lines, so this man's appearance is highly unusual.

"How are things up there on the hill?" the colonel asks as Doss struggles to rise to his feet. Seeing that Doss's leg is injured, the colonel motions for him to sit back down.

"I haven't been up there this morning, sir."

"I want to see how our artillery is doing," the colonel replies, then walks over and begins climbing the cargo nets to the top.

Doss watches the colonel clamber unsteadily up into the combat zone. It seems like just a matter of seconds before the cry of "Medic!" is shouted down over the side.

Despite the Sabbath, Doss quickly climbs up the rope ladder and comes upon the listless colonel lying on a rock, badly shot up.

The officer is losing blood rapidly. Doss compresses the wound with a surgical dressing, then pulls a liter of plasma from his first-aid bag. Around him, the men of B Company lay down suppressing fire to protect Doss.

The medic pokes a transfusion needle into a vein. In order for the plasma to flow into the colonel's body, the bag must be elevated. The private rises up from his crouched position. Kneeling, exposed to fire, he holds aloft the plasma bag.

A litter arrives. The colonel is eased over the side

of the cliff, alive thanks to Desmond Doss. But not for long—the colonel dies before reaching the rear aid station.

Doss's wounded leg throbs, but he remains on the summit. The company has no other medic. An American attack on a well-fortified pillbox fails, and more men fall. The dead and dying are spread out across the escarpment as the order to fall back is issued.

Every able soldier retreats to safety, scrambling back down the cargo net. Left atop the cliff are Doss, a hundred wounded Americans, and the Imperial Japanese Army.

Doss refuses to leave. "I knew these men; they were my buddies, some had wives and children. If they were hurt, I wanted to be there to take care of them," Doss would later write.

Working tirelessly, exposed to thick gunfire and exploding shells, the private treats every one of the fallen. The wounded who can shoot provide covering fire as they await their turn to be rescued. Ignoring the searing pain in his leg, Doss grabs each of them under the shoulders or by the heels and drags them to the edge of the cliff.

As a child, Desmond Doss once helped rescue victims of a flood. It was then that he was taught a special knot with which he could fashion a sling using a short section of rope. The memory of that knot, something that he had not thought of for twenty years, suddenly comes back to him. Using this impromptu technique, Doss lowers man after man over the side, then rushes back across the escarpment to get another. "Just get one more," he says to himself over and over. "Just one more."

Japanese soldiers take aim at Doss, but they miss. When they advance with bayonets, sometimes coming within just a few feet of the medic, wounded Americans summon the strength to shoot the Japanese soldiers dead.

By nightfall, PFC Desmond Doss has single-handedly saved the lives of seventy-five men.

"I can state without reservation that the actions of this man were the most outstanding display of bravery I have ever seen," First Lieutenant Cecil Gornto will marvel.

"I wasn't trying to be a hero," Doss will tell a newspaper reporter much later in his life. "I was thinking about it from this standpoint—in a house on fire, and a mother has a child in that house, what prompts her to go in and get that child?

"Love," he will respond, answering his own question. "I loved my men and they loved me . . . I just couldn't give them up, just like a mother couldn't give up the child."*

---

* Two weeks later, on May 21, 1945, a grenade exploded against the bottom of PFC Doss's boot. Severely injured, he bandaged his own wounds, then waited several hours while other wounded men were rescued before allowing himself to be placed on a stretcher. On the way back to the aid station, he suffered a compound fracture when hit by Japanese sniper fire. Using a rifle for a splint, Doss ignored the bone protruding from his arm and crawled to safety. Doss spent the remainder of the war in the hospital. While there, he realized that he had lost his Bible in the thick of battle.

★ ★ ★

Thanks to the courage of men like PFC Desmond Doss, the Battle of Okinawa is finally won. The date is June 23, 1945. Due to its proximity to Japan, the island now becomes the staging point for the invasion.

The battle for Okinawa has raged for eighty-two days. More than twenty thousand Americans are dead. Of the half-million Americans who came ashore, one-third have either been killed or wounded.

America did not enter this war by choice, but the days when men fought to avenge the tragedy of Pearl Harbor are long since past. The world will not be safe until Japan is defeated. Yet Japan has not capitulated to another nation in more than two thousand years.

Emperor Hirohito has the power to change all that.

He refuses.

Hirohito's nation is certainly defeated. The emperor's subjects are bleeding and destitute; their land is

---

When word got back to his unit, the soldiers conducted a thorough search of the Maeda Escarpment once the battle was won; they did not stop searching until Doss's Bible was found. Doss received the Medal of Honor from President Harry Truman at a White House ceremony on October 12, 1945, the first noncombatant to receive the nation's highest military award for valor. Doss then spent the next five years in and out of the hospital receiving treatment for his many wounds. Doss had dreams of becoming a florist, but his injuries and the loss of a lung to tuberculosis made regular employment impossible. Desmond Doss died on March 23, 2006, at the age of eighty-seven.

aflame. But Hirohito is not even contemplating surrender to the hated Americans.

However, unbeknownst to the emperor, a force more powerful than any he has ever experienced is about to be unleashed.

The horror of the atomic age will begin in exactly forty-four days.

12

GORA HOTEL
HAKONE, JAPAN
JUNE 24, 1945
7:00 P.M.

A light summer wind brings refreshment to a doomed nation.

In the shadow of the snowcapped volcano Mount Fuji, on an evening when the springtime cherry blossoms have long since fallen from the trees, former Japanese prime minister Koki Hirota is desperate—though trying very hard not to appear that way. Three years from now he will hang by the neck until dead for his part in horrendous Japanese war crimes, but tonight Hirota is attempting to perform the humanitarian act of ending the war, albeit on Japan's terms.

Yet he cannot do this without help from the Russians, which is why the Soviet ambassador to Japan, Yakov Malik, now sits opposite him. The Gora Hotel is fifty miles southwest of Tokyo, in the town of Hakone, making it an unlikely spot for a high-level negotiation, but this is the Russian's choice. He far prefers Hakone to the Japanese capital. Malik enjoys the famous local *onsen*—hot springs—but more important, he appreciates that this wooded resort would be an odd target for American bombers.

The sixty-seven-year-old Hirota is a slender man with a thin mustache, a lifelong diplomat skilled in the deft words and subtle innuendo required of professional statesmen. Malik is broad and gruff, a thirty-nine-year-old foreign affairs officer whose diplomatic talent is of the more brusque Russian variety. His natural arrogance is heightened by his awareness that the Japanese are dealing from a position of great weakness.

The Russians have already declared that they will not renew their 1941 nonaggression pact with Japan on the grounds that the Nippon alliance with Germany makes them an enemy of the Soviet Union. Every day, thirty trainloads of Russian troops and tanks travel to Manchuria in anticipation of a late-summer offensive that the Japanese naively believe will never take place. This misjudgment has led Emperor Hirohito to shift thousands of Japanese troops from Manchuria back to defend the home islands, allowing the Russians to move right in.

As a veteran negotiator, Hirota knows better than to address the obvious. The emperor himself has authorized this discussion; the fall of Okinawa has made Hirohito desperate to find a way to convince Malik to help Japan seek peace. But the former prime minister has been ordered to proceed as if there is no sense of urgency about ending the war, when in fact the Japanese need an answer from the Russians almost immediately. Hirota begins by skirting the issue of peace, making

a halfhearted joke about a new military alliance between the Imperial Japanese Army and the Red Army.

"Our future relations," Malik bluntly replies, in a
subtle reminder that Russo-Japanese history has been
fraught with conflict, "will have to be based on concrete actions."

With that, the meeting abruptly comes to an end.

A desperate Hirota successfully requests a second
session just hours later. He begins by feinting in a new
direction, offering to enter into a trade agreement with
the Soviets: Japanese rubber and lead from its conquered territories in Southeast Asia in exchange for
Soviet oil.

"Russia has no oil to spare," Malik replies, his thick
face impassive.

Having no other choice, Hirota finally gets down to
business.

"Japan," Hirota admits, "seeks an early peace."

This is an astounding statement, overturning more
than a decade of Japanese aggression and effectively
ending its attempts to build an Asian empire. Yet if
Malik is aware that he has just been a party to history,
he shows no sign of it.

"His Excellency, Mr. Hirota, must be well aware
that peace does not depend upon Russia."

The Americans and British have publicly stated
that World War II will only be finished when the Axis
powers "unconditionally surrender." Thus, the war
in Europe did not end until Germany was completely
crushed. "Unconditional surrender will only mean that

our national structure and our people will be destroyed," is how naval admiral Kantaro Suzuki explained the matter to Emperor Hirohito. Tonight's negotiations are not just about the future of Japan but also about the survival of the 2,500-year-old imperial tradition.

However, if the Soviets can intercede on behalf of Japan, convincing the United States and Great Britain that unconditional surrender is unnecessary, that humiliation may be averted.

Instead of giving up, Japan simply wants to stop fighting.

They do not plan on returning the lands they have already conquered in Southeast Asia and China. They also wish to be spared the fate of Nazi Germany, which now endures the indignity of being occupied by American, Russian, French, and British troops, its former leaders soon to be put on trial for war crimes. The punishment for such transgressions, as Koki Hirota well knows, is usually death.

Hirota desperately needs the Russians' help to make this outcome possible.

But that will not happen. Ambassador Malik will not give him the answer he wants. In fact, the Russian refuses to give any answer at all.

The two men talk well into the night, ending their discussion with a round of coffee and liqueurs. The mood is cordial, if strained.

A frustrated Koki Hirota returns to Tokyo, the future of his nation and his emperor still uncertain. He longs to quit these frustrating negotiations, for in his gut Hirota knows that the Russians will never intervene on behalf of Japan.

Japan, the aggressor nation, will not survive. And neither will Koki Hirota.*

---

*Hirota was prime minister of Japan in 1937, shortly before the second Sino-Japanese War began in July of that year. After World War II, he was prosecuted for war crimes based on his knowledge of, and tacit complicity in, the Rape of Nanking. The Tokyo war crimes tribunal convened in April 1946. Hirota was hanged at Tokyo's Sugamo Prison on December 23, 1948.

13

ALAMOGORDO, NEW MEXICO
JULY 16, 1945
1:00 A.M.

Robert Oppenheimer paces, a mug of coffee in one hand and a hand-rolled cigarette in the other. Sunday night has become Monday morning. His face is lined, his every movement betraying extreme tension. A hard rain hammers the tin roof above him. Outside this mess hall, lightning crackles and thirty-mile-per-hour winds lash the former cattle ranch now known simply as base camp.

In less than three hours, the Trinity A-bomb test is due to take place ten miles from where Oppenheimer now fidgets. Five armed guards stand watch at the base of the tower containing Oppenheimer's precious "gadget," making sure that absolutely no one touches or meddles with the explosive. These soldiers will remain there until thirty minutes before the detonation, then get into jeeps and drive away as quickly as possible. Since a weapon like this has never been exploded before, not even a great scientific mind like Oppenheimer knows how big or far-ranging the blast will be.

But there can be no test unless this storm ends. It is anticipated that the bomb will release deadly radioactive particles into the air. Scientists have long known that these waste products of a nuclear reaction are hazardous to human and other forms of life. High winds would carry them across the desert to urban areas, and rain would intensify the damage by saturating the ground with radioactive fallout. Rough weather would also prohibit observation aircraft from taking off. And on a very practical level, rain might ruin the electrical connections necessary to the bomb's detonation.

Throughout the night, Oppenheimer has tried to calm himself. He ignored suggestions that he go to his tent and sleep, instead remaining in the dining hall. At first, he attempted to sit still and read from a book of poetry, but that has proven impossible. Cigarettes and black coffee are his only solace right now.

Robert Oppenheimer has the power to create a literal hell on earth. But he has no authority over the heavens. This annoys him greatly.

General Leslie Groves appears out of the gale. The Manhattan Project's chief executive is adamantly opposed to a postponement, despite the weather. The general's motives are less scientific than political: right now, halfway around the world in a small town outside Berlin known as Potsdam, President Harry Truman is attending a summit meeting with Soviet leader Joseph Stalin and British prime minister Winston Churchill. A successful, on-time detonation of the A-bomb at

4:00 a.m. will immediately be relayed to Truman, who can then share the news about the dawn of the nuclear era over lunch with his fellow world leaders. To the seventy-year-old Churchill, this will come as a triumph, for he has known about the Manhattan Project all along.

For Stalin, however, the news is meant to shock and deter. America's possession of an atomic bomb will be a vivid warning to the Russian leader that he will be the weaker partner in any future US-Russia negotiations.

The 4:00 a.m. detonation time has been chosen because secrecy is still vital to the success of the Manhattan Project. Any potential observers will be sleeping as the white light turns the pitch-black desert night into sudden daytime, if only for an instant.

Groves, who is just as nervous as Oppenheimer, has managed only a few hours of fitful sleep in his own nearby tent. He is now up for the night.

The two men confer. They agree that passing the hours in the base camp dining hall is no way to prepare for the testing of a nuclear bomb. So they step out in the darkness and drive four miles closer to the bomb site. There, at the half-buried command post known as the control dugout, where a small group of technicians and scientists vital to the detonation make last-minute adjustments, Oppenheimer and Groves reluctantly agree to postpone the Trinity explosion.

But only by an hour.

✯ ✯ ✯

More than five thousand miles away in Potsdam, there is also a delay. Harry Truman sits down with Winston Churchill at the same time Oppenheimer and Groves are hunkered together in the control dugout. Truman's lodging in the mansion at Number 2, Kaiserstrasse is plush and ornate, an opulence that does not suit his homespun style. The crucial postwar conference among the world's three most powerful leaders has been postponed indefinitely because Joseph Stalin is nowhere to be found, which gives Truman and Churchill time to get to know each other.

Truman's early days in office were tentative; he merely reacted to the overwhelming events and decisions that had suddenly been thrust upon him. But now, as a noticeably weary Churchill meets with Truman at precisely 11:00 a.m. German time, Truman has found his stride. Rather than be awed by a masterful statesman like Churchill, Truman feels himself to be the man's equal as they spend two hours in conversation.

There is no discussion of the A-bomb testing taking place far away in New Mexico, nor is there talk of a recently intercepted message to the Japanese ambassador to the Soviet Union from his superiors in Tokyo. In the coded communiqué, Ambassador Naotake Sato insists that Japan will never accept unconditional surrender. They do not discuss these topics because it is likely the Russians have planted listening devices at Truman's residence.

As Churchill and his small entourage take their leave, there is a shocking development unfolding in London. Little does either man know it, but they will never have the chance to enjoy a working relationship. The results have not yet been announced in London, but war-weary voters in Great Britain have chosen not to reelect Winston Churchill.* First the death of Franklin Roosevelt and now the ouster of Churchill have cut the list of active Allied wartime leaders down to just two men: Harry S. Truman and Joseph Stalin. These two adversaries who still pretend to be allies will now forge a whole new world.

✳ ✳ ✳

As Winston Churchill departs Number 2, Kaiserstrasse in Potsdam, the Trinity detonation in New Mexico is postponed once again. The blast is rescheduled for 5:30 a.m. With the summer storm now passing, to the immense relief of Robert Oppenheimer and General Leslie Groves, it appears there will be no further delays. Groves leaves Oppenheimer at the control dugout, preferring to drive back to the relative safety of base

---

*Churchill's approval rating stood at 83 percent in May 1945, but he was such an effective war leader that many in Britain feared he might begin a war against the Soviet Union rather than putting an end to the fighting once the Japanese were defeated. With the war in Europe over, the nation turned its focus to rebuilding. British voters were enchanted by the socialist policies of Clement Attlee's Labour Party, whose slogan was "Let us face the future" and who promised to nationalize industries to benefit the working man, causing Churchill's Conservative Party to lose in a landslide. The lifelong politician was later again elected prime minister and served from 1951 to 1955, finally leaving office at the age of eighty due to deteriorating health.

camp. If the blast is as enormous as some fear, there is no telling whether the control dugout will be consumed or not.

At precisely 5:00 a.m., ground zero for Trinity is evacuated. The five soldiers standing guard at the base of the one-hundred-foot tower containing the bomb quickly hustle to their jeeps and race southwest toward base camp. They must drive aggressively over the rough desert roads if they are to arrive before the detonation. In the event of engine trouble, the guards will have a thirty-minute head start on the explosion. "I was sure they would not walk slowly," General Groves will later write with wry understatement.

In the event that the erstwhile guards are still in the open when the A-bomb goes off, they have been told to lie facedown on the ground with their feet toward the explosion. They are not to open their eyes or look at the light in any way, for it has been predicted that the flash will be so brilliant as to blind them.

By 5:05 a.m.—"zero minus twenty-five minutes" until the detonation—the storm's violent winds have died down to a calm breeze. A light drizzle speckles the desert sand. The cloud cover is still too thick to see many stars, and will certainly hamper the observation planes.

Robert Oppenheimer leaves the safety of the control dugout's thick concrete walls. He steps into the fragrant predawn air and stands alone. It has been agreed that base camp is the only place where observers can stand in the open to witness the blast, but Oppenheimer plans to ignore that mandate.

There are two other bunkers just like the control dugout, each situated six miles from the blast site. Both have been covered with dirt to absorb the blast force. Teams of scientists stand ready in these bunkers to analyze the amount of energy released by the explosion and determine whether the bomb detonates in a symmetrical manner.

That is, if the A-bomb explodes at all.

A few days ago, a practice test of the electronic circuitry that would spark the detonation failed miserably. Oppenheimer's engineers have promised him there will be no problem this morning. Nevertheless, Oppenheimer has made a friendly wager of ten dollars with physical chemistry engineer George Kistiakowsky, betting that Trinity will fail to detonate.

The desert air smells of sagebrush. Morning's first rays of sunshine are limning the horizon. Trinity's test site here in the Jornada del Muerto is a flat patch of desert eighteen by twenty-four miles wide. Oppenheimer stares out across that broad expanse, his stomach aching from anxiety and too many cups of coffee. Five miles in the distance, he can clearly see the brightly lit tower containing his gadget. He cannot see the bomb itself, but he knows that it is a round sphere ten feet across, wrapped in a tight coil of wiring. Oppenheimer himself oversaw the moment twelve hours ago when the bomb was hoisted from ground level to the top of the tower.

Inside the control dugout, Oppenheimer's team of scientists is behaving in an almost giddy fashion, some slathering on sunscreen in anticipation of the

Trinity
July 16, 1945

107°W · 106°W · 105°W

36°N

Jemez Mountains

Los Alamos

Santa Fe

Sangre de Cristo Mtns.

44 · 285 · 84 · 85

NEW MEXICO

N NE E SE S SW W NW N (compass)

Albuquerque

285 · 66 · 84 · 54

Rio Grande

Sandia Mountains

35°N

Miles
0 · 10 · 20 · 40

Vaughn

60

60 · 285

Santa Fe

Albuquerque

20 · 10 · 5
30 · 20 · 5 · 3
30 Miles · 40 · 2

Socorro

1 · .5 – Roentgens per hour

34°N

San Antonio

20 MILES

10 MILES

NORTH SHELTER · 380

Ground Zero · Carrizozo

WEST SHELTER · SOUTH SHELTER

BASE CAMP

Jornada del Muerto

105°W

Truth or Consequences

San Andres Mtns.

Sierra Blanca

54 · 70

33°N

Tularosa

Alamogordo

106°W

Map by Gene Thorp

UT. · COLORADO

Santa Fe

Albuquerque

ARIZ. · **NEW MEXICO** · Detail

US · MEXICO · TEXAS

explosion's bright light, others laying down bets as to whether or not the bomb will light the clouds on fire.

Yet no one, not even Robert Oppenheimer, knows exactly what will happen.

An announcement over a nearby loudspeaker breaks the desert silence: "Zero minus twenty minutes."

Robert Oppenheimer gazes at his bomb and waits.

✯　✯　✯

Harry Truman looks out over a most amazing sight: the entire American Second Armored Division standing in formation, awaiting his review. Soldiers, half-tracks, and battle-tested Sherman tanks line the German autobahn just outside Berlin, the olive-drab uniforms of American soldiers stretching as far as the eye can see.

Truman's meeting with Winston Churchill behind him, he now plans to spend the afternoon exploring bombed-out Berlin. But first, the president will enjoy the great privilege of reviewing his conquering army. An old soldier himself, Truman clambers out of his presidential limousine and stands atop a half-track where the crowd can see him.*

As the armored vehicle drives slowly past the troops, Truman is overwhelmed at this display of power. The Second is the largest armored division on earth, a force that has seen action in North Africa, Sicily, and Nor-

---

*Truman was an artillery officer in World War I. His unit provided fire support for Patton's tank brigade in the Meuse-Argonne Offensive. Also in that battle was a soldier from Brooklyn named John O'Reilly, grandfather of Bill O'Reilly.

mandy, and in the battles across Europe that culminated with the German surrender two months ago.

Yet as President Harry Truman looks down into the faces of these brave men—many of them just a year out of high school—he knows that the Second Armored's war may not be over. Already, one million men comprising thirty divisions are making their way around the world to fight the Japanese. It might be only a matter of weeks until the men of the Second board troopships heading for the Pacific.

That is, unless Harry Truman can find another way to convince the Japanese to accept unconditional surrender.

★　★　★

At base camp, General Leslie Groves lies in one of the small trenches bulldozed into the earth for blast protection. The time is "zero minus five minutes"—or 5:25 a.m. All around him, scientists press their faces into the earth. Each clutches a small piece of Lincoln Super Visibility welder's glass, specially designed to protect the eyes from extremely bright light. At the sound of the blast they will be allowed to roll over, sit up, and, through this special glass, witness the world's first atomic bomb explosion. Groves, ever nervous, finds the quiet to be intense. "I thought only of what I would do if, when the countdown got to zero, nothing happened," he later admits.

Four miles closer to the impending blast, Robert Oppenheimer feels time slow down. The sensation is tortuous. So much rides on the events of these next five minutes. "Lord," he says aloud, having temporarily stepped back into the control room, "these affairs are hard on the heart."

Brigadier General Thomas F. Farrell, Groves's executive officer, cannot help but notice Oppenheimer's anguish. "Dr. Oppenheimer, on whom had rested a very heavy burden, grew tense as the last seconds ticked off. He could barely breathe. He held on to a post to steady himself. For the last few seconds he stared straight ahead."

With two minutes to go, a flare is launched to inform one and all that the explosion is near. Oppenheimer once again steps outside the control bunker and lies facedown on the ground next to his brother, Frank.*

At thirty seconds to detonation, the console panel in the control dugout lights up bright red as electrical impulses begin flooding into the bomb. There is still a small chance that the explosion might be scrubbed, but only in the event of electrical difficulties.

At ten seconds, a loud gong echoes through the control dugout as a last reminder for every man to steel himself for what is about to happen.

Chicago physicist Sam Allison, the voice of the control tower, counts down the final seconds. "Three . . . two . . . one . . . NOW!!"

A tremendous light fills the sky, a brightness so in-

---

* Thirty-two-year-old Frank Oppenheimer, a particle physicist, is a scientific director for the Manhattan Project. He has spent the war at various research facilities, and only came to Los Alamos for the final weeks leading up to Trinity.

tense that those who see it will talk about it for the rest of their lives. "The light of the first flash penetrated and came up from the ground through one's lids," Frank Oppenheimer will remember. "When one first looked up, one saw the fireball, and then almost immediately afterwards, the unearthly hovering cloud."

That cloud is purple, radiating heat that can be felt miles away. "It was like opening a hot oven with the sun coming out like a sunrise," in the words of one observer at base camp.

One hundred seconds later, an enormous boom erupts as a shock wave follows the explosion: "About like the crack of a five-inch anti-aircraft gun at a hundred yards," in the eyes of a watching ballistics expert. The explosion is so powerful that more than 180 miles away, in Silver City, New Mexico, two large plate-glass windows shatter.

At the control dugout, the blast bowls over George Kistiakowsky, the man with whom Oppenheimer made a bet that the bomb would not detonate.

"You owe me ten dollars," he screams to Oppenheimer, who is suddenly lighthearted and relaxed.

"I'll never forget his walk," one scientist will remember of Oppenheimer after the blast. "His walk was like *High Noon* . . . this kind of strut.

"He had done it."

★ ★ ★

At the same time Oppenheimer's bomb explodes in New Mexico, twelve hundred miles west in San Francisco, the men of the USS *Indianapolis* are buzzing about the top secret cargo that has been lifted aboard in the dead of night. At 4:00 a.m., two army trucks pulled up to the dock; one contained a fifteen-foot crate and the other a small tube. Boatswain's Mate Louie De-Bernardi directs the work party that now places straps around the crate so that the gantry crane might lift it on board. Meanwhile, two sailors hoist the small cylinder onto their shoulders by running a crowbar through a small eyelet on the tube, then walk the cylinder onto the USS *Indianapolis*.

Curious crew members gossip about what might be coming aboard. Just a few days ago, a shipment of 2,500 life jackets was loaded onto the ship—twice the number needed for the 1,200-man crew. While the men saw that as a routine military screwup, this new cargo is obviously of a much more serious nature.

The crate is secured onto the hangar deck in the middle of the *Indianapolis*. The cylinder is brought into an empty officer's cabin, where it is lowered onto hinged metal straps that have been welded to the floor. The hinges are closed and padlocked.

"I didn't think we were going to use B.W. [bacterial warfare] in this war," remarks Captain Charles McVay III, who has been told nothing about the contents of either package. His orders are to transport the material with all due haste across the Pacific. The *Indianapolis* was specially chosen for her size—as a heavy cruiser, she is large enough to carry such a load, but also much faster than vessels of greater tonnage. Yet "Cherub" McVay, as the forty-six-year-old career officer was known at the US Naval Academy, has been given very specific instructions: no one must go near it except the marine guards who will stand watch day and night. If the ship should sink, these packages should be placed in a lifeboat and saved at all costs. If the *Indianapolis* comes under attack and is in the unlikely danger of being boarded by the enemy, he is to jettison everything overboard to keep it out of Japanese hands.

McVay knows better than to ask questions.

Four hours later, at 8:00 a.m., the *Indianapolis* sails from her berth at the port in San Francisco known as Hunter's Point. By 8:36 a.m., she passes beneath the Golden Gate Bridge and then beside the Marin Headlands, out to sea. Her first stop is Pearl Harbor, where she will deposit the few passengers now catching a lift to the war zone.

After that, *Indianapolis* will return to sea.

Next stop: Tinian Island.

★ ★ ★

Because of the successful Trinity test, scientists now know that the A-bomb material being shipped across the Pacific will produce the explosive force of nineteen thousand tons of dynamite. In addition to the atomic bomb tested in New Mexico, American scientists have built two other A-bombs. One of them is now aboard the *Indianapolis*; the plutonium core of the other is just days away from being flown to the island of Tinian. Neither bomb is yet armed.

Robert Oppenheimer and his crew have discovered that the great fireball will shoot up to a height of over forty thousand feet, sucking up great clouds of dust as it ascends. Even as the giant flames faded, northward winds in New Mexico carried radioactive dust across the desert. Alarmingly, the herds of cattle grazing just beyond the blast zone will soon suffer the loss of their hair, indicating that radiation levels around the site are a threat to human life.

Back at ground zero, the steel tower on which the gadget was perched is gone, completely vaporized. There is not much of a crater; instead, the blast has traveled up and out from the ground. For a quarter mile around the blast site the earth is scorched black. The extreme heat has melted the sand into green glass, a material soon to be known as Trinitite.

Of course, such a horrific explosion and burst of light did not go unnoticed. Answering inquiries, the military responds that an ammunition dump at Alamogordo Army Air Field had caught fire.

However, those who can tell the difference between a simple explosion and an earthshaking bang of epic proportions find this difficult to believe. In New Mexico and Texas, newspapers immediately publish stories speculating about what happened. As far away as California, radio broadcasts wonder about the strange events in the New Mexico desert. News spreads up the coast to the state of Washington, where employees at the Hanford Engineer Works quickly deduce that an A-bomb has been detonated. Like Los Alamos, Hanford is a top secret Manhattan Project facility charged with manufacturing plutonium, a vital ingredient in a nuclear explosion.

At almost 8:00 p.m. in Potsdam, more than seven

hours after the Trinity detonation, Secretary of War Henry Stimson hands Truman a coded telegram announcing its success. "Operated on this morning. Diagnosis not yet complete but results seem satisfactory and already exceeds [*sic*] expectations."

★ ★ ★

Harry Truman's reaction to the news is guarded, pending specifics about the breadth of the blast. In truth, the president is a mere observer of whatever comes next with the A-bomb. He came to the party late, years after FDR foresaw the potential for a nuclear weapon and approved the Manhattan Project. A former World War I artillery officer, Truman sees the bomb as a weapon of war, one with far greater killing capacity than a tank or a missile, but a conventional weapon nonetheless. While he realizes the war's equation has changed in his favor, he does not yet grasp that Trinity is not just a bomb but also a split-second explosion that has changed the future of mankind. From this day forward, any nation, no matter how small, in possession of a nuclear device can unleash the bowels of hell any time it wishes.

As for sharing the news about Trinity with Joseph Stalin, wherever he might be, that can wait.*

★ ★ ★

---

* Stalin was late for two reasons: First, he wanted to show up Truman, letting his tardiness indicate that he was the more powerful of the two men. Second, deeply afraid of flying, the Soviet leader chose to travel a thousand miles by train through territory that

Robert Oppenheimer drinks a brandy at base camp and sends his own special coded message back to his wife, Kitty, who has recently returned to him from Pittsburgh. Oppenheimer chooses words that he had already told her would signal success: "You can change the sheets."

Oppenheimer's euphoria and relief cannot be measured. Unlike President Truman, he is cognizant of the A-bomb's wider implications. He is already haunted by what he saw today, calling it "terrifying," but at the same time recognizes the good in what he has accomplished.

As he later tells a reporter, "Lots of boys not grown up yet will owe their life to it."

★ ★ ★

For General Leslie Groves, the Trinity explosion is not the end of a job, as it is for Robert Oppenheimer. Instead, it is a stepping-stone to his final objective—which is why he immediately boards a plane for Washington, DC.

"They were still upset by what they had seen and could talk of little else," Groves wrote of the handful of scientists who joined him on the flight back east. "I learned later that the effects of the test on all who had witnessed it, particularly the scientists, were quite profound for a number of days.

"As for me, my thoughts were now completely

---

until very recently had been an active combat zone, with all the precautions that entailed.

wrapped up with the preparations for the coming climax with Japan."

It will be a deadly and destructive climax, as an ungodly force will soon be unleashed on the land of the rising sun.

14

Just twelve miles south of the Japanese port of Hiroshima, the Japanese submarine *I-58* slips her berth and glides from the port of Kure, loaded with enough food, torpedoes, and diesel fuel to remain at sea for one month. The rising sun emblem is painted boldly in red and white on her gray conning tower. Above it, perhaps even more patriotically, is painted the *Kikusui* ("floating chrysanthemum") battle standard, in homage to a medieval Japanese warrior who fought to the death against impossible odds for the glory of the emperor.

A muggy, warm day is developing as Lieutenant Commander Mochitsura Hashimoto stands at the helm of his submarine. *I-58* quickly clears the harbor and enters the inland sea that divides Japan's many islands.

The sub leaves behind a city in ruins. Three weeks ago, 162 American B-29 bombers laid siege to Kure, sinking two submarines still under construction and heavily damaging another. Several bombs came close to hitting *I-58*, but she survived unscathed. For the thirty-five-year-old Hashimoto, the fact that his ship has been spared is a source of great relief—second only to the good news that his wife and three sons also lived through the barrage.

American B-29s have begun dropping mines across the entrance to Japan's great ports, closing every harbor on the Pacific and a great number on the Sea of Japan. The mine campaign will effectively isolate the nation from the rest of the world.

Hashimoto is pleased that his vessel is getting away from the homeland before Kure harbor can be mined, for he knows that American planes now dominate the skies over Japan.

It is not just the heavy bombers of the Army Air Forces that are punishing Japan.* Beginning six days ago, on July 10, the United States Navy has taken advantage of newly opened airfields on Okinawa to launch a steady stream of aerial attacks. Naval aviators are now flying hundreds of sorties a day over the Japanese mainland, destroying the nation's shipping, railways, and limited aerial defenses. Instead of the behemoth silver B-29s that drop their payload from thousands of feet in the air, many aviators fly so low

---

*It was not until September 18, 1947, that the US Air Force became a separate entity; army personnel controlled the air force during World War II.

that the Japanese people actually duck as the fighter-bombers thunder overhead. Often they can clearly see the pilots' faces.

American power is slowly crushing Japan's national morale. A cruel blow came just two days ago: eight ferries carrying coal from the island of Hokkaido to Honshu were sunk, with great loss of life. This leaves Japan with no vessels capable of transporting coal from the mines of Hokkaido to the Japanese factories that rely on them for power to run their machinery. Without factories, there can be no bombs, guns, planes, or tanks to fuel the Japanese war effort.

Yet even if the factories could find another energy source, production is all but finished. Industrial leaders are now informing Japan's military leaders that they can produce weaponry "for just a few days more" for lack of raw material.

The psychological toll on the Japanese people is also a liability, yet they represent the nation's last chance for a proper defense of the homeland. Hungry, homeless, and increasingly humiliated, the populace is now being ordered to adopt the suicidal *Ketsu-Go* strategy—that is, that all Japanese men, women, and children will fight to the death. Many households have already been issued sharpened sticks, and family members are expected to use them when the Americans invade.*

Ketsu-Go—Operation Decision—was the official policy of defending Japan to the death. As historian William Manchester points out in *American Caesar*, "Manning the nation's ground

For some Japanese soldiers in the distant battlefields of Asia, it is too late for *Ketsu-Go*. They see for themselves that the tide of war has turned. For the first time ever, many Japanese have begun to surrender—mainly because their weapons have been destroyed.

"From May onwards prisoners in a terrible state came in daily, many of them armed with nothing more dangerous than bamboo spears, and trembling with a mixture of malaria and humiliation," one British soldier in Burma will report.

The Japanese war effort is almost on life support.

But Mochitsura Hashimoto still commands one of the best submarines in the world. Hashimoto has been in charge of *I-58* ever since the state-of-the-art vessel was commissioned in late 1944. She is 356 feet long and 30 feet wide at the beam, making *I-58* larger than most American submarines. She carries nineteen Type 95 torpedoes, which have an accurate range of almost six miles and can travel through the water at more than forty miles per hour. In addition, *I-58*'s deck gun has been removed to make room for six *kaiten* torpedoes—eight-ton, forty-foot-long human-guided suicide

---

defenses were 2,350,000 regular soldiers, 250,000 garrison troops, and 32,000,000 civilian militiamen—a total of 34,600,000, more than the combined armies of the United States, Great Britain, and Nazi Germany. . . . Their weapons included ancient bronze cannon, muzzle loading muskets, bamboo spears and bows and arrows. Even little children had been trained to strap explosives around their waists, roll under tank treads, and blow themselves up. They were called 'Sherman carpets.'"

missiles that are the underwater version of kamikaze aircraft.*

A well-educated man, and a graduate of the Imperial Japanese Naval Academy, Hashimoto knows that Germany's surrender means Japan stands alone against the world. More than two million soldiers and millions of other citizens stand ready to defend the home islands against invasion, but *I-58* and Japan's five other operational submarines represent the nation's last great chance to be the attacker instead of the attacked.

It has been an adventurous, if frustrating, ten months since Hashimoto first took the sub to sea. The *I-58* has seen action off the coast of Guam and during the battles for Iwo Jima and Okinawa. Her job is to harass the American fleet, launching her Type 95s and *kaiten*s at vessels anchored offshore in support of the invasions. But it is US pilots who have often done the stalking, attacking *I-58* whenever she comes close enough to the surface to fire her arsenal. Hashimoto has been forced to dive deep to save his crew on many occasions. On April 25, three American destroyers cornered *I-58*, and there was little Hashimoto and his men could do but wait out the attack from three hundred feet beneath the surface. They survived, and afterward were credited

---

*The *kaiten* torpedo was first developed in summer 1944. Essentially a one-man submarine with an explosive charge that activated upon ramming another vessel, the *kaiten* was launched from a larger host submarine. The program was largely ineffective in comparison with the kamikaze airplane suicide attacks.

with sinking an American tanker and an American aircraft carrier.

But it was all a ruse. The truth is the *I-58* had sunk nothing at all.*

The fact that Hashimoto has not destroyed a single American ship is a matter of shame for him. To become a true man of honor, he needs a kill. He hopes that this voyage will erase the lone blemish on an otherwise spotless service record.

Enemy ships seem to be everywhere in the Pacific now, offering *I-58* a number of targets. Hashimoto's orders are to "harass the enemy's communications," giving him the latitude to attack whenever he wants. And with *I-58*'s range of twenty-one thousand nautical miles, this means Hashimoto can travel almost any place in the Pacific that he wishes, a lone wolf in search of a sheep that has strayed from its flock.

Hashimoto's crew of one hundred officers and men realize that the war may be over by the time they return to port. They are an elite group, hand-selected for service aboard *I-58*. The end of the war will surely mean the dissolution of the Imperial Japanese Navy. This, then, will be their last mission.

Hashimoto, the son of a Shinto priest, has erected

---

*The mistake came about because Japanese submarines relied upon the sound of explosions to confirm a sinking, lacking visual confirmation because they were forced to dive soon after firing their torpedoes. This, plus an Imperial Japanese Navy habit of inflating the number of sinkings of American vessels in order to please superiors, often led to false reports.

a small shrine on board so that he might seek divine intervention. He prays that somewhere out there is an American ship destined to collide with one of *I-58*'s torpedoes.

Soon, his prayer will be answered.

"Dive," orders Hashimoto.

15

President Harry Truman is homesick. On the road for almost two weeks, he has maintained his normal routine of rising early and enjoying a breakfast of oatmeal, orange juice, toast, and milk. Yet he misses his wife, Bess, and the things that make a home a home, like his favorite White House dinner of chicken and dumplings. But right now food is not on Truman's mind. He is immersed in his journal, penning his notes on the Potsdam Conference. The reports of Trinity's power have disturbed him, allowing the president to see at last that America possesses an unparalleled weapon of war.

"We have discovered the most terrible formula in the history of the world," Truman writes with his barely legible handwriting. "It may be the fire destruction prophesied in the Euphrates Valley Era, after Noah and his fabulous Ark."

The words flow quickly onto the page, but each is

chosen with care. For good or bad, Truman knows that history will long judge this journal entry. It was only yesterday that he authorized the dropping of atomic bombs on Japan.

After conferring with his military advisers and with Winston Churchill in Potsdam just before noon on July 24, 1945, Truman has allowed the process to move forward. It was a fairly easy decision, despite the objections of some nuclear scientists at Los Alamos and even General Dwight Eisenhower, Truman's top commander in Europe, who believes that Japan is close to surrendering. In the end, Truman came to the conclusion that an invasion would cost too many American lives.

Though he will later state that "the final decision of where and when to use the atomic bomb was up to me—let there be no mistake about it," the truth is that the decision was made long ago by Franklin Roosevelt, who had no qualms whatsoever about the prospect of using the atomic bomb. FDR was so fed up with the death and destruction in Europe and the Pacific that he had little hesitation in justifying the two-billion-dollar Manhattan Project.

Nonetheless, Truman is the one man in the world with the power to stop the bombing of Japan, and he chooses not to do so. He issues no verbal or written order to announce his decision. Truman does nothing more than get out of the way; what will happen, will happen. It is a rare display of passive behavior by a man so prone to action, but his thinking is clear.

It is late in the night as Truman continues his journal

entry in Potsdam: "This weapon is to be used against Japan between now and August 10th. I have told the Sec. of War, Mr. Stimson, to use it so that military objectives and soldiers and sailors are the target, not women and children. Even if the Japs are savages, ruthless, merciless, and fanatic, we as the leader of the world for the common welfare cannot drop this terrible bomb on the old capital or the new."

The decision to spare the modern capital of Tokyo and the nearby port at Yokohama has made it almost inevitable that Hiroshima will be attacked first. The waterfront city of 350,000 has not once been fire-bombed, making it a prime unscathed target. Many of its residents are Japanese soldiers and marines; the port itself is one of the nation's largest military supply depots. Truman's insistence on military targets makes Hiroshima a natural bull's-eye for the bomb known as Little Boy, which has just reached the island of Tinian and is being unloaded from the USS *Indianapolis* at this very moment.

And with Truman's refusal to destroy the ancient Japanese capital city of Kyoto, the city of Nagasaki is added to the target list in its place.

"The target will be a purely military one and we will issue a warning statement asking the Japs to surrender and save lives," Truman writes. "I'm sure they will not do that, but we will have given them the chance. It is certainly a good thing for the world that Hitler's crowd or Stalin's did not discover this atomic bomb. It seems to be the most terrible thing ever discovered, but it can be made the most useful."

Although it has been more than a week since the successful A-bomb explosion in New Mexico, Truman still had not yet shared the news with Joseph Stalin. Now that the targets have been finalized, the Soviets are to be informed.

The revelation to Stalin comes at the end of another frustrating day of debate about the shape of the postwar world. Russia's bargaining position is to relentlessly demand more control over territories it has seized in Europe. The US position is to refuse Russian expansion.

The Soviets now have more than one million men on the Manchurian border, poised to attack Japanese occupying forces. The presence of such a large Soviet force in China means that the Soviets will soon want a considerable say in the future of Asia. It is a tiresome negotiation, yet Truman has stood up to the Soviets time and again, refusing to allow Stalin to occupy more territory.

The ornate great hall of the Cecilienhof Palace is sweltering. For reasons of decorum, the president will not remove his double-breasted suit coat or even loosen his bow tie. Throughout the afternoon, fifteen leaders and diplomats sit around the ten-foot-wide circular conference table, with Joseph Stalin to Truman's far right and Winston Churchill to his left.

This summit meeting marks the first time Truman and Stalin have met in person. Over the course of the negotiations, the president has been uncowed by the Russian leader, who prefers to wear a military uniform and answers most questions with a simple grunt. This habit amuses Truman, even though he is well aware of Stalin's barbarity.

Shortly before 5:00 p.m., the meeting ends. At the conclusion of a long afternoon around the bargaining table, Truman rises from his seat and walks five chairs to his right, where Stalin stands to stretch his legs. Casually, so as not to alarm the Russian leader, Truman quietly informs Stalin that the United States has "a new weapon of unusual destructive force."

Stalin pauses, then says through his interpreter: "I am glad to hear it."

The truth is, Stalin already knows about the atomic bomb, thanks to his spies inside the Los Alamos research facility. "I hope you will make good use of it against the Japanese," the Russian dictator says—and makes his exit.

Almost immediately, Truman is confronted by Churchill, who is confused, as is Truman's interpreter, Charles Bohlen, a Soviet expert and American diplomat. Secretary of State James F. Byrnes joins them. The men can't believe Stalin is so indifferent.

In fact, Joseph Stalin is panicked. He is a man for whom total power is everything, and the idea that his military might could be diminished is intolerable. Joseph Stalin has murdered millions of his own citizens and has allowed his troops to loot and pillage Germany and Eastern Europe. His goal is to dominate the world. He is terrified that this new weapon will shift the balance of power in favor of the Americans.*

---

*Estimates of the number of people killed by Stalin range from as low as twenty million to as high as sixty-two million "unnatural

After leaving the great hall of Cecilienhof Palace, Stalin quickly dictates a telegram to the scientists at work on Russia's own nuclear program: "Hurry with the job."

---

deaths" during Stalin's time as Soviet leader. The man who is credited with saying that "death solves all problems" and "One death is a tragedy; one million is a statistic" murdered his own citizens through executions, artificial famines, forced-labor camps, incarceration, and torture.

16

The most powerful man in the Pacific has no idea the atomic bomb is operational and that massive destruction is just days away.

At the Potsdam Conference, President Truman's military advisers now know about Trinity, as do Britain and Russia's top generals.

In Germany, American general Dwight Eisenhower, commander of all Allied forces in Europe, was informed of the nuclear weapon's success over dinner one week ago. "They told me they were going to drop it on the Japanese," Eisenhower will later write. "I was against it on two counts. First, the Japanese were ready to surrender and it wasn't necessary to hit them with that awful thing. Second, I hate to see our country being the first to use such a weapon."

But General Douglas MacArthur, the most senior officer on either side of the war, a man who has served under eight presidents, who has been awarded a Medal of Honor and commands a territory five times the size of the United States with more than one million fighting men at his order, has been told nothing.

Even as his staff continues to prepare for the invasion of Japan, an event Douglas MacArthur believes will result in "a million casualties," the general lives a life of leisure. He spends his days regaling with war stories the reporters and delegates from Washington who have come to the Philippines to pay their respects and enjoys long lunches at "Casa Blanca," the mansion he has appropriated for his family amidst the devastation of Manila.

On this sweltering Monday afternoon, another delegation fills his second-floor office. The guests include Assistant Secretary of the Navy H. Struve Hensel and Vice Admiral Ross T. McIntire, who until very recently served as Franklin Roosevelt's personal physician. Their manner is deferential, befitting the respect due a commander of MacArthur's stature. While his guests remain seated, the general paces the room and thinks out loud throughout their visit, as is his custom. MacArthur's top staff, who admire him tremendously, sometimes mimic this behavior to add a little levity to their day.

As the thirty-minute meeting winds to a polite conclusion and the five-man delegation is ushered out the door, MacArthur has a few brief moments to reflect on the shocking news that landed on his desk yesterday:

Japanese troops are pouring onto the island of Kyushu, with "no end in sight."*

Instead of the eighty thousand soldiers MacArthur believed would be defending the invasion beaches, nine Japanese divisions comprising more than five hundred thousand men are now digging in on the coastline, waiting for the Americans to land. Almost all are stationed at Kyushu's southern beaches, site of MacArthur's Operation Olympic invasion zones.

MacArthur is troubled. Allied forces now control most of the Pacific, as MacArthur demonstrated by wading ashore during the invasion of Borneo just a few weeks ago. But the Japanese still own much of Asia's Pacific Rim. Their air force bases in Korea, China, and northern Japan will allow them to launch kamikaze aircraft against an invasion fleet. In addition, the Imperial Japanese Navy's Twelfth Flotilla, based on Kyushu, has nine hundred hidden planes that will be utilized for suicide flights. Vintage wooden biplanes, invisible to American radar, are also being retrofitted for nighttime suicide attacks.

Just as menacing, employees at the Sasebo Naval Station near Nagasaki are working double shifts to build special suicide boats designed to ram landing

---

*American forces captured Japanese codebooks during the battles for Iwo Jima and Okinawa, allowing intelligence units based in Pearl Harbor to read top secret enemy documents. Operation Magic is the code name for the program whose focus is decrypting Japanese messages; the men who decode them call themselves Magicians.

craft laden with US soldiers. The Japanese believe they know precisely where American troops will invade, so vast underground caves are being constructed behind the beaches and stocked with food and ammunition. All civilians are being forcibly removed from the southward-facing coastal regions so that barbed wire, artillery batteries, mines, and antitank defenses can be installed and camouflaged.

As MacArthur continues reading the shocking report, he realizes that the enemy is "changing the tactical and strategic situation sharply." No longer will the Japanese utilize the *fukkaku* strategy employed on Peleliu, Iwo Jima, and Okinawa, lying in wait to repel the American attack from hidden defensive bunkers. Now it is clear to MacArthur that they will defend the beaches with even more fury than the Germans guarded the D-Day landing zones within France. The sands of Kyushu could very well become an American graveyard.

To MacArthur's way of thinking, there are three ways for America to knock out Japan: a naval blockade followed by an invasion; a naval blockade followed by massive aerial bombing; or a straight-up beach invasion. As an army officer and a general committed to commanding the largest military force in history, MacArthur refuses to concede that the navy and the army air corps should determine the outcome of the war. Paranoid by nature, creating conflicts where they might not otherwise exist, MacArthur thinks the other two services are aligned in a conspiracy to prevent his army from getting the glory.

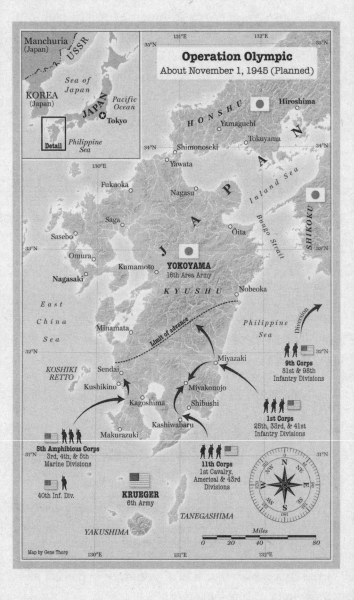

Map by Gene Thorp

Foolishly, MacArthur is openly antagonistic to Admiral Chester Nimitz, his naval equal in rank and power, calling his tactical strategies "just awful." The navy, MacArthur believes, wants to "control all overseas positions after the war, using the army as a sort of home guard."

Nonetheless, he needs the sailors and fly-boys. The cornerstones of Operation Olympic are the ongoing pre-invasion aerial bombardment of Japan's industrial sector and the obliteration of Japan's navy by an American fast-carrier task force. After that, MacArthur's Sixth Army will deliver the decisive blow with its landing on Kyushu.

The general is not a man prone to histrionics, commanding instead with an air of quiet authority. He has confided in friends that he believes the Japanese will surrender by September 1, but the new report indicates that the enemy is spoiling for a fight.

It also puts the timing of Operation Olympic in grave danger. MacArthur cannot attack for four to five months at the earliest, giving the Japanese even more time to prepare.*

The confident tone of other recently intercepted Japanese communiqués makes one thing certain: the

---

* An invasion is more than just the act of sending men ashore; soldiers need to be fed, armed, and cared for in case of injury. MacArthur was awaiting the arrival of troops from Europe, as well as stockpiling weapons, ammunition, landing vessels, food, and hospital supplies.

enemy's determination to slaughter Americans will only increase during this lull.

✯   ✯   ✯

Proof of Japan's determination to kill Americans, even when all seems lost, lies one hundred feet deep in the Pacific, six hundred miles from Manila. Lieutenant Commander Mochitsura Hashimoto eats a fragrant dinner of fresh onions and canned sweet potatoes while plotting his submarine's next maneuver; the Japanese commander is discouraged but far from beaten. The galley, like the rest of the cramped sub, smells of unwashed men, stale breath, and cooked fish. A saunalike humidity fills the hull in these equatorial waters, leading Hashimoto's crew to sleep naked on sacks of rice in an attempt to ward off the heat.

Hashimoto has deliberately positioned his vessel in the middle of the busy shipping lanes between Guam and the Philippines. But despite daily prayers at his makeshift Shinto altar, the gods have not yet blessed Hashimoto. It seemed he might be in luck yesterday, when *I-58* launched two *kaiten* torpedoes after sighting an American cargo ship and its destroyer escort. But the armed freighter, *Wild Hunter*, opened fire with her deck guns, sinking the first torpedo and killing its pilot. The second *kaiten* was rammed by the destroyer, *Lowry*, and blown to bits. There was little damage to the US warship.

More critically, that missed opportunity has turned Hashimoto from the hunter to the hunted. The American destroyer *Albert T. Harris* is currently prowling the

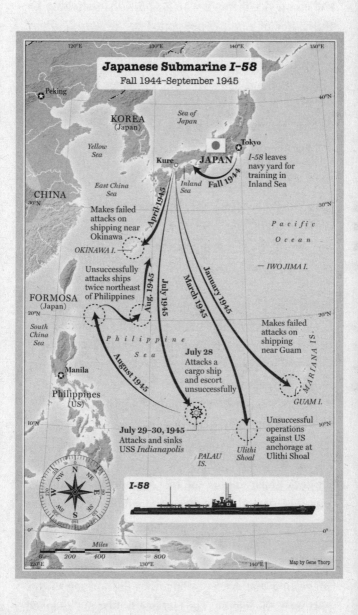

Japanese Submarine *I-58*
Fall 1944–September 1945

I-58 leaves navy yard for training in Inland Sea

Fall 1944

Makes failed attacks on shipping near Okinawa

Unsuccessfully attacks ships twice northeast of Philippines

April 1945

July 1945

March 1945

January 1945

Aug. 1945

Makes failed attacks on shipping near Guam

August 1945

July 28 Attacks a cargo ship and escort unsuccessfully

July 29–30, 1945 Attacks and sinks USS *Indianapolis*

Unsuccessful operations against US anchorage at Ulithi Shoal

I-58

Miles
0   200   400   800

Map by Gene Thorp

same corridor through which *I-58* sails, searching for the source of a periscope spotted by the *Wild Hunter*'s crew.

Midway through *I-58*'s one-month mission, running out of fuel and food, Hashimoto knows he must turn back for Japan very soon. With every passing day of failure, Hashimoto increasingly despairs that he will not get his kill.

★   ★   ★

Thirteen miles from the Japanese submarine, in the dark of night, the USS *Indianapolis* steams toward the Philippines, having dropped her atomic cargo at Tinian Island three days ago. The sea churns; thin clouds drape the moon. Despite the late hour, the heat in the windowless sleeping compartments belowdecks is too intense for many of the crew. Three hundred sailors have made their beds on the hard steel deck, unprotected from the elements and anything else that may come their way tonight.

Weary from the day, Captain Charles McVay takes one last walk around *Indianapolis* before turning in. Three hours ago, content that his ship and men were not in imminent danger, he ordered that the ship's antisubmarine zigzag pattern of motion be ceased to increase sailing speed. He also ordered that hatches and doors remain open, letting in the nighttime air. In the event of an attack, these compartments will flood quickly, but McVay has received no intelligence reports suggesting that enemy submarines are lurking in this portion of the Pacific. The fact that he was not assigned a destroyer escort for this two-day journey further convinces him that his men are safe.

Broad-chested and tall, McVay stoops as he enters his small cabin just off the bridge, strips off his clothes, and lies down for the night. Three days ago, his men off-loaded cargo that they had no idea was in fact the atomic bomb known as Little Boy. Immediately afterward, *Indianapolis* was ordered to sail with all due haste to Leyte, in the Philippines, for two weeks of training.

McVay, himself, would not later be angry that he was denied information about the atomic bomb. In that way, he would never struggle with the moral or ethical dilemma of transporting the most lethal weapon in the history of man six thousand miles across the Pacific, there to be loaded in the bomb bay of the world's most powerful airplane and dropped on a city of 350,000 men, women, and children.

Sweating in the darkness, Captain McVay tries his best to sleep. His ship is due to dock on Leyte at 1100 hours. His mind is focused on the seventeen days of training awaiting *Indianapolis* in the Philippines. After being away from the war for four months, his men will go through a series of refresher courses to get them battle ready. Once that training is completed, *Indianapolis* will sail for Okinawa, there to await the beginning of Operation Olympic.

Midnight.

Sunday night becomes Monday morning.

Far belowdecks, in the ship's galley, dishes are washed and stacked in preparation for breakfast. Incredibly, the sounds of preparation are heard thirteen miles away on board the Japanese submarine *I-58*.

As Captain McVay drifts into a fitful sleep in his Spartan cabin, the rattle of "clinking dishes" alerts a Japanese sonar operator that the USS *Indianapolis* is target ready.

⋆　⋆　⋆

Quickly, Lieutenant Commander Hashimoto gives the order to load six lethal torpedoes. The seas are too rough to launch *kaiten* suicide bombers, so he chooses to fire conventional Type 95 torpedoes. It is better this way: the *kaiten* are unpredictable in rough seas. The Type 95, on the other hand, is the best torpedo in the world, armed with the largest warhead on either side of the conflict, with an effective range of more than six miles.

Hashimoto orders the sub to surface, allowing him to scan the horizon and flood the dank confines of the vessel with fresh air. To the lieutenant commander's shock, his unsuspecting target is running in a straight line and unprotected by an escort vessel. Rather than hurry the attack, Hashimoto patiently levels his vessel at a sixty-foot depth and slows her speed. For twenty heart-pounding minutes, *I-58* edges closer to *Indianapolis*. Hashimoto expects to be discovered at any time, believing the enemy ship has sonar devices that will detect his approach.

But this is not the case. Even though *Indianapolis* was retrofitted with the most up-to-date equipment during her recent repairs in San Francisco, the technology to hear sounds underwater and detect imminent threats was not installed—a situation that proves fatal.*

Hashimoto slows *I-58* to three knots.

Calmly, knowing that he will get just one chance to sink this American ship, Hashimoto brings his sub to within 1,500 yards of his target.

The cold-blooded job of the wartime submariner is to sink enemy ships, but the harsh reality is that the attackers may also be sent to a watery grave. Submarine warfare is the most lethal on earth; in the German navy, for example, 80 percent of all submariners never returned home. The Japanese fatality rate is lower, but not by much. Also, it is not the job of the attacking submarine to rescue survivors in the water. That task is left for other vessels that might be in the vicinity. As soon as torpedoes are launched at an enemy ship, the submarine dives as quickly as possible to escape.

At 12:02 a.m., Hashimoto decides it is time to kill. "Full salvo," he orders. "Two-second intervals—FIRE!"

A look through his periscope shows that *Indianapolis* is still taking no evasive action. Six torpedoes purr silently through the water, on course to slam broadside into the American ship.

Hashimoto maintains his vigil at the periscope, wondering if the attack will be a success or yet another

---

* There are conflicting theories as to why sonar was not installed. The most convincing is that the navy was in a rush to put the *Indianapolis* back to sea.

failure. Minute upon minute passes. He sees nothing but inky blackness.

Then, suddenly, the sky turns bright orange.

"A hit, a hit," Hashimoto shouts to the men crowded around the periscope. Throughout the submarine, the *I-58*'s crew dances with joy. Tonight they will feast on rice and boiled eel as a reward for a job well done.

Lieutenant Commander Mochitsura Hashimoto finally has a kill.

★ ★ ★

Shock envelops the *Indianapolis*.

The lead torpedo blasts a hole in the starboard side of the bow. The engine room powering the ship's mighty propellers—"screws," in navy parlance—is not yet hit, and the vessel keeps pushing forward at a speed of seventeen knots. This causes ocean water to pour into the gaping wound like a torrential river, racing through open compartments and instantly flooding the forward portion of the ship. Radio operators immediately send SOS signals, alerting any vessels in the vicinity that *Indianapolis* needs help. "We are torpedoed and sinking fast," the desperate radio operators add to the standard SOS dots and dashes. "We need immediate assistance."*

The distress calls abruptly end when a second torpedo strikes within an instant of the first, tearing a hole in the right side of the ship and exploding three

---

*In Morse code, this is a system of three dots, three dashes, then three more dots.

thousand pounds of aviation fuel. That cuts the electrical power necessary to send further emergency messages.

Hundreds of men are killed instantly—many of them burned beyond recognition.

In his cabin just off the bridge, Captain Charles Mc-Vay quickly throws on a pair of shorts and walks out to inspect the damage. Thick smoke and the almost total blackness of the dark night prevent him from seeing much. At first the skipper is actually relieved, believing that the blow to his ship is less brutal than the damage *Indianapolis* suffered off Okinawa. So it is that when Lieutenant K. C. Moore, the damage control officer, informs McVay that the forward compartments are flooded and his ship is going down, the captain does not believe him.

Three minutes later, that changes. Second in command, executive officer Joseph Flynn delivers a harsh dose of reality: "I think we are finished," he informs McVay. "I recommend we abandon ship."

The captain is stunned—this a devastating personal blow to the unblemished record of this career naval officer. The *Indianapolis* is a significant command, the vessel so highly thought of that she was once the flagship of the US Navy's Fifth Fleet. Even though McVay was denied the destroyer escort from Guam to Leyte that could have mitigated the attack, he will now have to answer as to why he compounded the mistake by stopping the defensive zigzag sailing pattern and opening all the ship's hatches in hostile waters.

But right now, Captain Charles McVay III must set

aside his own emotions and focus on saving the lives of his men.

Eight minutes after the torpedoes hit, the *Indianapolis* lists 18 degrees to starboard—and leans more to the side with every passing second.

Reluctantly, McVay orders Commander Flynn: "Give the order to abandon ship."

But that order is never delivered to the men. *Indianapolis* is without electricity, and the ship's bugler does not follow the order to sound the command.

By 12:17 a.m., *Indianapolis* is listing 60 degrees, little more than ten minutes after the first strike. The bow of the ship has been sheared off, "just like you had taken a saw and cut if off clean," in the words of one junior officer. Many of the sailors panic, forgetting to don life jackets as they leap into the thick coat of oil now covering the water. They swim frantically, desperate to put distance between themselves and the sinking ship, knowing that *Indianapolis* will suck them into the depths as she goes down if they are too close.

"I started to walk forward to see what I could see, and what I seen was about sixty-foot of the bow chopped off, completely gone," sailor Woody James will recall. "Within a minute and a half, maybe two minutes at the most, the bow is starting to go down. It filled up with water that fast. Everything was open below deck, and the water just flooded in and we were still under way, just scooping water. Complete chaos, total and complete chaos, all over the whole ship. Screams like you couldn't believe and nobody knew what was going on."

Of her crew of 1,196, more than eight hundred men make it into the sea. The military foul-up that saw an extra shipment of life jackets delivered to *Indianapolis* back in San Francisco now seems like an act of providence. But of the ship's thirty-five life rafts, only a dozen are launched because as the ship rolls to its side, the other rafts become inaccessible.

Captain Charles McVay is one of the last to leave *Indianapolis*. He stands on what used to be a vertical section of the port hull, then walks into the water like a man stepping off a curb to cross the street.

McVay looks back and see his ship rise straight up into the air. Her propellers spin slowly, silhouetted by the moon. Then the ten-thousand-ton cruiser knifes straight to the bottom of the Pacific.

The survivors are disoriented. Moments ago they were sleeping, dreaming of the things men dream of when the end of a war is near and the return home is inevitable. Now many are burned and maimed from the blasts. They bob helplessly in the darkness, their bodies rising and lowering on the heavy swell. No longer a crew, they drift off in small packs, borne by the current. Knowing that they are due in the Philippines by morning, most men are confident of rescue when it is clear they are overdue.

But the SOS that should save them has not been heard. No one knows the *Indianapolis* has been sunk, and there is no search under way for the surviving sailors.

The situation seems like it can't get any worse.

Then the sharks appear.

★   ★   ★

Two days after the *Indianapolis* sinks, General Carl "Tooey" Spaatz arrives in Manila to meet secretly with General Douglas MacArthur. The newly appointed commander of United States Army Strategic Air Forces in the Pacific (USASTAF) has been flying for most of the last five days, traveling 8,500 miles from Washington to Manila. Spaatz is here not of his own volition but because he was ordered to brief MacArthur by the acting army chief of staff, General Thomas Handy.*

A man of average height with an Errol Flynn–type mustache, the fifty-four-year-old Spaatz was present in Reims, France, when the Germans surrendered on May 7, 1945, and is now posted to the Pacific to facilitate a similar situation for the Japanese. But his first order of business will be ensuring the deployment of the atomic bomb. Handy gave Spaatz the order verbally, but Spaatz refused to take the assignment unless given instructions in writing. "Listen, Tom," Spaatz told Handy, aware that he could be tried for war crimes if held personally liable for the loss of life that would ensue. "If I'm going to kill 100,000 people, I'm not going to do it on verbal orders. I want a piece of paper."

Handy protested that putting such an order in writing compromised security. Even Harry Truman had

_____

*Handy was serving in that capacity while General George C. Marshall was in Potsdam with President Truman.

refused to affix his signature to any order connecting him with the dropping of the A-bomb. But Spaatz insisted. Finally, Handy caved. "I guess I agree, Tooey," the acting chief of staff admitted. "If a fellow thinks he might blow up the whole end of Japan, he ought to have a piece of paper."

Handy signed the order, but it was actually written by General Leslie Groves of the Manhattan Project.

It is, perhaps, the most important directive in world history.

★ ★ ★

Once satisfied that his posterior was covered, Spaatz endured a grueling journey via military transport from Washington, DC, to Honolulu to Guam, and now to MacArthur's corner office in Manila. There has been nothing comfortable about these flights aboard lumbering military transport planes, whose engines drone so loudly that men cannot speak without shouting; and where sleep is only secured sitting up, numbered in minutes instead of hours.

Yet General Spaatz barely rested after reaching his new headquarters in Guam, even though the luxury of a villa and the comfort of a horizontal bed awaited. The career aviator pressed on, increasing the length of his journey by another two days in order to meet with MacArthur in person. There is a purpose to his haste: he wants MacArthur to know about the atomic bomb before it is dropped. As Groves later comments, "If the weather had been suitable, the bomb would have been dropped before MacArthur had ever been informed by Spaatz, which would have been quite surprising [to MacArthur]."

Spaatz, a man known for his curt speech pattern and matter-of-fact planning, is weary as he greets MacArthur. His body is not used to the tropical heat; he sweats through his uniform. And yet the weight of what he must tell the general compels him so much that he cannot rest until he hands the A-bomb order to a man whose legendary status will soon earn him the nickname "Caesar of the Pacific."

For a moment, the two men speak casually. Then Spaatz hands MacArthur the order. "I didn't try to explain it," Spaatz will later recall. "I just handed it to him and thought that he would ask me lots of questions, but instead he talked about that letter for about five minutes and the rest of the hour proceeded to expound the theories of atomic energy to me."

The order begins specifically: the first "special bomb" will be dropped as soon after about August 3, 1945, as weather will permit visual bombing on one of the targets: Hiroshima, Kokura, Niigata, and Nagasaki.

Secondly: "Additional bombs will be delivered on the above targets as soon as made ready by the project staff. Further instructions will be issued concerning targets other than those listed above."

The third clause is a warning: "Discussion of any and all information concerning the use of the weapon against Japan is reserved to the Secretary of War and the President of the United States. No communiqués on the subject or releases of information will be issued by Commanders in the field without specific prior authority. Any news stories will be sent to the War Department for specific clearance."

The fourth and final directive of the order includes one caveat targeted specifically at Spaatz: "It is desired that you personally deliver one copy of this directive to General MacArthur and one copy to Admiral Nimitz for their information."

Nimitz, whose Pacific Fleet is headquartered in Guam, has already read the order.

So it is that General Douglas MacArthur is the last to know about Japan's doom. He scribbles his initials—"MACA"—in the right margin to verify that he has received the one-page document.

The general is not alone among US military leaders in initially opposing the bomb. Generals Hap Arnold and Dwight Eisenhower have gone on record in top secret circles as objecting, as have Admiral William D. Leahy, Rear Admiral Lewis L. Strauss, Assistant Secretary of War John J. McLoy, and Assistant Secretary of the Navy Ralph A. Bard. The consensus of these men is that the atomic bomb is too destructive and too many civilians will be killed.

Those in favor of the A-bomb attack, such as Secretary of War Henry Stimson and Army Chief of Staff George C. Marshall, are more closely tied to the White House than actual combat operations in the field.

But MacArthur's displeasure runs much deeper than that of the other dissenters.

The general is a brilliant tactician. He also has a deep understanding of Japanese culture, believing that the nation will never completely cooperate with surrender and an ensuing national occupation unless Emperor Hirohito is allowed to remain in power after the war ends.

But there is a harsher truth.

MacArthur is so determined to command Operation Olympic that he has lied about projected casualties to Marshall. In a June 17 cable to the general, meant for the eyes of President Harry Truman, he assured them that losses would be less than a hundred thousand men.

"Your message arrived with thirty minutes to spare," Marshall cabled back to MacArthur, having received the erroneous estimate just before a big meeting with Truman, "and had determining influence in obtaining formal presidential approval for Olympic."

But now, Operation Olympic will never happen. Douglas MacArthur understands that his dream of conquering the nation of Japan by leading a ground invasion is over.

This is a cruel blow for MacArthur. Convinced of his own military genius, MacArthur has openly disparaged fellow army generals Dwight Eisenhower and George Patton, stating that they "made every mistake that supposedly intelligent men could make." In an interview with the *New York Herald Tribune* in November 1944, MacArthur went on to say, "The European strategy was to hammer stupidly against the enemy's strongest points." With "just a portion of the force" given to Patton in North Africa, MacArthur bragged that he "could have retaken the Philippines in three months."

General Douglas MacArthur does not want to bomb the Japanese—he wants to crush them up close and personal.

To his mind, that kind of victory would make him immortal.

★ ★ ★

As Douglas MacArthur digests the news about the atomic bomb, sailors of the USS *Indianapolis* are dying. It is day four in the sea for them. The men are blinded by the daytime sun, desperate for food and water. Many are burned, and others are coated in oil from the massive slick that now spreads across more than twenty square miles of the Pacific. Almost all have swallowed oil and seawater, thanks to the rolling swells. Dehydration is making men hallucinate, causing them to see ships, planes, islands, and even hotels that do not exist. In their thirst, some of the crew seal their own fates by drinking seawater. The salt makes them delirious before eventually causing them to slip into comas.

American planes have flown over the *Indianapolis* victims several times. But despite the crew's best efforts to wave their arms and make themselves visible, they have not been seen.

Captain Charles McVay is fortunate, having secured a spot in a raft rather than floating in a life jacket. He once commanded a warship with a crew of twelve hundred, but now his authority is limited to a rectangular raft and a handful of men who still revere him as their skipper.

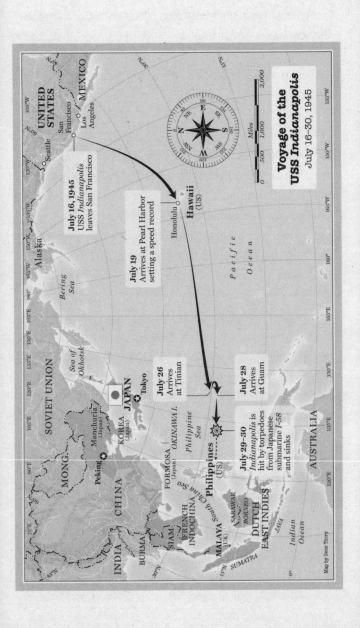

Voyage of the USS *Indianapolis*
July 16–30, 1945

July 16, 1945
USS *Indianapolis* leaves San Francisco

July 19
Arrives at Pearl Harbor setting a speed record

July 26
Arrives at Tinian

July 28
Arrives at Guam

July 29–30
Indianapolis is hit by torpedoes from Japanese submarine *I-58* and sinks

UNITED STATES

MEXICO

Seattle

San Francisco

Los Angeles

Alaska

Hawaii (US)

Honolulu

Bering Sea

SOVIET UNION

Sea of Okhotsk

MONG.

CHINA

Peking

Manchuria (Japan)

KOREA (Japan)

JAPAN

Tokyo

FORMOSA (Japan)

OKINAWAI.

Philippine Sea

Philippines (US)

Pacific Ocean

INDIA

BURMA

SIAM

FRENCH INDOCHINA

South China Sea

MALAYA (UK)

SUMATRA

SARAWAK

BORNEO

JAVA

DUTCH EAST INDIES

AUSTRALIA

Indian Ocean

Miles
0   500   1,000   2,000

Map by Gene Thorp

Within hours of the sinking, hungry sharks added to the horror.

"The day wore on and the sharks were around, hundreds of them," sailor Woody James later remembered. "You'd hear guys scream, especially late in the afternoon. Seemed like the sharks were the worst late in the afternoon than they were during the day. Then they fed at night too. Everything would be quiet and then you'd hear somebody scream and you knew a shark had got him."

A massive shark with a white dorsal fin has made Captain Charles McVay's raft his focus, swimming underneath it and circling. Rather than focus on the danger, McVay maintains hope by using a small hook and length of line from the emergency kit to fish, firing a flare gun to alert passing airplanes, and doing his best to calm the men aboard his life raft.

As for the sailors in the water, McVay can do nothing. They are a collection of floating groups and individuals spread out over miles of open ocean. On the first night, light winds blow men in rafts northeast, away from the Philippines, even as ocean currents push those in life jackets in the opposite direction. Now, on the fourth day since their ship sank, two-thirds of these floating men are already dead.

Those who remain alive are enduring torture. At first, some sailors killed each other while fighting over buoyancy vests. But now so many men are dead that there are life jackets to spare.

The current has carried the men far from the *Indianapolis*'s resting place. Some sailors have drifted more than fifty miles. All across the sea, dead men bob on the surface. Many corpses are just torsos, the legs and lower bodies already eaten away by sharks. Other men are still alive, but some have given up hope that help will arrive. A few commit suicide by slipping out of their life vests and descending into the ocean.

One sailor counts twenty-five shark attacks on his group. Another counts eighty-eight. So far from land, the ocean is a clear blue. In daytime, the sailors can look beneath them and see the predators circling below. There is no logic to the shark attacks, with one exception: sailors who eat the Spam rations in the emergency kit are hit first, the sharks attracted to the smell of the salty meat product. But the reality is that no one is safe. The tactic of holding absolutely still when a shark is spotted seems no more or less effective than splashing the water and making a commotion to drive it away—the sharks are relentless, no matter what the terrified sailors do.

On the fourth day in the ocean, time is running out. Only providence can save the remaining men.

It does.

★   ★   ★

Four days after the *Indianapolis* disappears beneath the waves, Brigadier General Bill Ritchie lingers in Douglas MacArthur's office as yet another delegation from America finishes paying its respects. MacArthur's schedulers have cryptically informed their boss that Ritchie will remain behind for a short chat.

Ritchie is a forty-three-year-old Arkansas native and West Point graduate who has just flown six thousand miles to the Philippines from the Potsdam Conference in Germany. Like General Spaatz two days ago, he is weary from the long hours of travel that have taken him a fourth of the way around the world in the hold of a cargo plane.

Soon it is just Ritchie and MacArthur in the general's office. The two men know each other well, having worked together in the past. The door is closed. A tropical breeze wafts in from the balcony.

In calm, lucid tones, the easygoing Ritchie confirms that Douglas MacArthur knows about the atomic bomb.

He also confirms that the bombing may take place as soon as tomorrow.

✳　✳　✳

The *Indianapolis* rescue operation begins by accident. PV-1 bomber pilot Wilbur G. Gwinn left his base on Peleliu on the morning of August 2 in search of enemy submarines. Instead, a surprised Lieutenant Gwinn radios back to his base that he has found "many men in the water." A PBY-5A Catalina is immediately dispatched to investigate the findings. The pilot is twenty-eight-year-old Lieutenant R. Adrian Marks, a man who has been part of the war in the Pacific since its very first day, when he survived the Japanese sneak attack on Pearl Harbor.

As Marks flies to the scene, he alerts the destroyer USS *Cecil J. Doyle* about his emergency mission. Immediately, the *Cecil J. Doyle* changes its course and races toward the survivors.

Marks and his eight-man crew soon spot survivors in the water. He is stunned to see sharks openly attacking some of the men. Three life rafts are dropped down to the sailors, but Marks accurately assesses that this will do little good. He can clearly see the wounded men, their arms and faces covered in oil to protect them from the sun, rising and falling on the twelve-foot swells. The sharks seem to be ignoring those sailors clustered in groups, instead targeting men who have drifted off alone.

Lieutenant Marks knows he must act.

Navy regulations prohibit him from landing the "Dumbo," as his seaplane is nicknamed, on anything but calm waters. But Marks wants to land anyway. He polls his crew, knowing that if he crashes their lives will be on his hands. To a man, they agree to land, despite the fierce seas.

On his first pass, the Dumbo bounces off a swell, soaring fifteen feet in the air before landing hard in the trough. Immediately, Marks directs his plane across the ocean surface, focusing first on rescuing lone survivors. Each time his plane draws near a man in the water, his crew tosses a life ring attached to ropes, then pulls the man in.

Marks and his crew work feverishly. The interior of the plane is soon filled. Word reaches the cockpit that these men are from the *Indianapolis*, a fact especially poignant to Lieutenant Marks, for he grew up in a small Indiana town close to that city.

By nightfall, the courageous work of Marks and his

crew has resulted in fifty-six men being saved. However, the Dumbo will never fly again because of the damage it received on landing in the sea. Instead, it is now a refuge from the sharks and the oil, allowing the men of the *Indianapolis* to finally get a fitful night of sleep—some of them lashed to the wings with parachute cord.

The sea once again turns stormy, and Marks becomes worried that his overloaded aircraft might sink.

"Scores of badly injured men were softly crying with thirst and with pain," Marks will later recall. "And then, far out on the horizon, there was a light."

The USS *Cecil J. Doyle* has arrived.

✷ ✷ ✷

Captain Charles McVay and the men in his raft are not among those rescued by Lieutenant Marks or the *Cecil J. Doyle*. As the sun rises on their fifth day in the water, McVay's group can see the rescue operations in the distance, but they despair that they are too far away to be found.

On Friday, August 3, at 11:30 a.m., McVay spots another plane.

This time, it sees him.

An empty metal ammunition can on board his raft has miraculously been picked up by a search ship's radar, and rescue planes are quickly dispatched.

After five days in the ocean, without a drop of water to drink, Captain Charles McVay and the men in his life raft are rescued. More than eight hundred of his men leapt into the water on the night the USS *Indianapolis* sank. The tally of survivors is listed as 317 officers and sailors.

In actuality, it is one less.

Twenty-three years from now, unable to blot out these memories and considering himself to blame for the deaths of nearly nine hundred men, Captain Charles McVay will place his navy service revolver to his head and pull the trigger.*

---

* Just one week after his rescue, Captain McVay was asked to stand before a board of inquiry into the sinking of the *Indianapolis*. It was found that McVay was at fault because he had stopped the anti-submarine zigzag evasion pattern shortly after nightfall. Admiral Chester Nimitz, commander of all naval forces in the Pacific, opposed a court-martial; however, he was overruled by navy leaders in Washington. McVay was found guilty in 1945, though many of the *Indianapolis*'s surviving crew believed he was made a scapegoat. McVay's conviction was later set aside at the request of Admiral Nimitz and McVay retired in 1949 with the rank of rear admiral.

17

---◆---

T he angry drone of B-29 bomber engines is not an unusual sound for the people of this densely populated port city. On a heavily overcast morning, air-raid sirens once again announce the arrival of the silver behemoths, thundering overhead unopposed at an elevation of twenty thousand feet. Since Hiroshima has not been bombed during the war, most citizens think the sirens are just another false alarm. There is no stampede to take refuge in the bomb shelters.

But this raid is different. It is rush hour in Hiroshima, and as commuters on their way to work by streetcar, bicycle, and bus can clearly see, bombs are tumbling out of the warplanes, soon to inflict the same horrific damage on Hiroshima that has been visited on almost every other major city in Japan.

Until today, this city located at the mouth of the Ota River delta has been spared, even as B-29 raids have systematically destroyed most of Japan. Major cities like Tokyo were bombed first. Now General Curtis LeMay is directing his bombers toward secondary targets, such as Toyama, a hub for ball-bearing and aluminum production. Four days ago, 182 B-29s literally leveled Toyama by dropping 1,466 tons of conventional and incendiary bombs on the city. No home or industry was left unpunished, with one estimate showing 99.5 percent of Toyama wiped off the map.

On August 1, during attacks focusing on Japan's ability to transport men and matériel, the rail hub of Hachioji was obliterated by the Army Air Corps's 58th Bomb Wing. In addition, the 313th Bomb Wing decimated the rail hub of Nagaoka, and the 314th vaporized the tiny rail center of Mito.

Since the Tokyo firebombings in March, the full scope of LeMay's aerial attacks has emerged: one million Japanese have died in sixty-six targeted cities. Ten million more have been made homeless.

But as the B-29s open their bomb bay doors over Hiroshima this morning, it is not fire that falls from the sky. Instead, unarmed five-hundred-pound canisters hurtle toward the ground. At four thousand feet, an altitude charge automatically opens them. Hundreds of thousands of four-by-eight-inch slips of paper known as "LeMay bombing leaflets" are released into the sky and flutter to the ground.

"Civilians!" they read in Japanese. "Evacuate at once!

"These leaflets are being dropped to notify you that your city has been listed for destruction by our powerful air force.

"This advance notice will give your military authorities ample time to take necessary defensive measures to protect you from our inevitable attack. Watch and see how powerless they are to protect you. Systematic destruction of city after city will continue as long as you blindly follow your military leaders whose blunders have placed you on the very brink of oblivion. It is your responsibility to overthrow the military government now and save what is left of your beautiful country.

"In the meanwhile, we encourage all civilians to evacuate at once."

One week ago at the Potsdam Conference, President Harry Truman issued a simple warning that if Japan did not surrender immediately it would face "prompt and utter destruction," which soon became known as the Potsdam Declaration. Many citizens throughout Japan know of this ultimatum because of American radio broadcasts delivered in Japanese.*

As the leaflets reach the ground, the people of Hiroshima open them to see aerial photographs of five B-29s unleashing scores of bombs on Japan. A series of small circles form the border, each representing a city that has been targeted. B-29s have been dropping

---

*Empowered by possession of the atomic bomb and determined to minimize the Soviet Union's role in the postwar Pacific, Harry Truman issued the Potsdam Declaration before showing it to the Russians. Thus, in a diplomatic slap in the face, the Soviets were not allowed to sign the definitive mandate about the ending of the war. They retaliated by accelerating their timetable for the invasion of Manchuria, in an attempt to get a toehold in Japanese-held territory before the end of the war.

these leaflets on cities all over Japan for more than a week.

By any estimate, Hiroshima is a perfect target. Japanese authorities are so convinced of this that they have already evacuated almost a hundred thousand citizens to safer locations.

Hiroshima is entirely flat and just a few feet above sea level, meaning that an explosion will expand outward with maximum effect. The city is also the headquarters of Japan's Second Army, whose twenty-five thousand soldiers will be vital to thwarting the American invasion. In addition, Hiroshima possesses a massive armament storage depot. It is a thriving port and communications hub, and—as American intelligence was relieved to report on July 30—not a single Allied prisoner of war is being held within the city's twenty-six square miles.*

As American B-29s pass over the city, then out over the Sea of Japan and back to their bases in the Mariana Islands six hours from now, the people of Hiroshima are left to wonder what these leaflets really mean.

★   ★   ★

On the island of Tinian, 1,500 miles southeast of Hiroshima, final preparations for the dropping of the atomic bomb are in place. Today, August 3, might have seen the B-29 crews release the bomb known as Little Boy

---

*Later reports would find that eight American POWs were being held in the Hiroshima Castle.

instead of warning leaflets. But a typhoon approaching Japan made flying conditions less than ideal.

Little Boy has been ready to go for three days. The five-ton explosive device rests on a special trailer, covered in canvas to conceal its appearance. All Little Boy lacks to be activated are the four cordite charges that will initiate the explosion. These will not be secured in the bomb until the B-29 carrying it to Hiroshima has taken off, just in case the plane crashes on the runway.

The pilot flying the bombing mission is Colonel Paul W. Tibbets, a thirty-year-old career officer from Quincy, Illinois. During the early part of the war, he served as the personal pilot for General George S. Patton in Europe. As part of his assignment, Tibbets also went on to fly more than forty combat missions over the Third Reich. He has been flying the B-29 since its debut in 1943. At this moment, the aircraft he will fly has no catchy name, no artwork emblazoned across its nose. Right now, it is only known by the number painted on its fuselage: 82.

Tibbets was personally selected by General Leslie Groves to lead the elite detachment of pilots who will drop atomic weapons on Japan. He has been practicing the bombing for weeks, flying out over the Pacific with a dummy version of Little Boy and dropping it in the ocean. Now Tibbets is waiting on the weather. The skies have to be clear enough over Hiroshima for him to visually see his target and deploy the bomb.

The final word will come from General Curtis LeMay, who will then inform Washington that he has given the order for Tibbets to take off. "Firm decision is expected from LeMay at 4 August 0400," reads a top-secret classified telegram to the War Department.

Colonel Tibbets knows it is almost time. "The actual and forecast weather were almost identical," he will later remember.

"So we got busy."

☆   ☆   ☆

In Tokyo, Emperor Hirohito is not concerned. The words "prompt and utter destruction" delivered by President Harry Truman have not resonated with the emperor. Like his prime minister, Kantaro Suzuki, he believes those words to be recycled rhetoric from previous meetings among Allied leaders. So he ignores Truman's ultimatum, still believing that the Soviet Union will help broker a peace to his liking with the West—completely oblivious to the fact that Russian leader Joseph Stalin is just five days away from invading Japanese-held Manchuria.

At a point when Hirohito's nation desperately needs him to show wisdom and discretion, the emperor is behaving like a deluded fool.

Meanwhile, a joint session of Hirohito's cabinet and the Supreme Council for the Direction of the War is in session. Their topic of debate is whether or not any surrender is permissible. They have argued the matter for more than a week, with no conclusion in sight.

Like their divine emperor, this assemblage of politicians and military leaders believes that President Harry Truman will not follow through on his demand of unconditional surrender. Time, they believe, is on *their* side. In a statement to the world's media on July 28, the Japanese formally reject any notion that they will accede to Truman's demands. Later that day, Japanese prime minister Kantaro Suzuki holds a press conference to reiterate those sentiments, stating that "the only alternative for us is to be determined to continue our fight to the end."

Joining their emperor in delusion, the Japanese leadership believes they still control their destiny.

As Navy Minister Mitsumasa Yonai states about Truman's promise of total annihilation: "America is beginning to be isolated. The government therefore will ignore it.

"There is no need to rush."

18

Colonel Paul Warfield Tibbets Jr. is always on time. Cradling a Kaywoodie briar pipe in his left hand, the commander of America's nuclear strike force strides past a cordon of armed guards, hurrying into the Quonset hut that will serve as today's briefing room. Tibbets is obsessively punctual, and today is no exception. The meeting is due to start at precisely 3:00 p.m. As he pushes into the crowded room, he is not a second late.

At thirty years of age, Tibbets—raised in Illinois, Iowa, and Florida—is short, compact, and very young for the advanced rank of full colonel. His hair is cut short, per military regulations, but everything else about his appearance suggests a man with a strong streak of individuality: that thick, dark hair is uncombed; a tuft of chest hair fluffs out of the unbuttoned collar of his wrinkled khaki uniform shirt; and, somewhat incongruously for such a vital mission, Tibbets wears shorts

Colonel Paul Tibbets and Captain Deak Parsons briefing B-29 crews in advance of the Hiroshima bombing

on this hot Saturday afternoon, making the moment appear almost casual.

Tibbets surveils a packed room as he takes his place on the briefing platform. A photographer captures the moment on film. Each B-29 requires a crew of eleven men.* Seven aircraft are now being readied for flight. The crews, all in lightweight khaki uniforms, sit on hard wooden chairs. Tibbets handpicked these men.

_____

* A crew consists of the aircraft commander, copilot, navigator, bombardier, electronics countermeasures officer, tail gunner, flight engineer, assistant flight engineer, ordnance expert, and two radar operators. Tibbets will also carry a twelfth crew member on the Hiroshima mission as weaponeer, in charge of arming the bomb.

All are in their twenties and thirties. They are the best of the best, soon to fly a world-changing mission over what they refer to as "the Empire."

Tibbets does not mince words. "The moment has arrived. This is what we have all been working toward. Very recently the weapon we are about to deliver was successfully tested in the States. We have received orders to drop it on the enemy."

Behind Tibbets are two blackboards covered by thick cloth. Two intelligence officers step forward and remove the drapes, revealing maps of Hiroshima, Kokura, and Nagasaki. Tibbets states that these are the intended targets.* He then breaks down each crew's responsibilities: Captain Charles McKnight, in the B-29 named *Top Secret*, will fly to Iwo Jima and remain there as a backup in case of emergency; Major Ralph Taylor Jr.'s *Full House*, Captain Claude Eatherly's *Straight Flush*, and Major John Wilson's *Jabit III* will fly over Japan the day prior to the bombing to check the weather; *Necessary Evil*, piloted by Captain George Marquardt, will photograph the explosion; and Major Charles Sweeney's *The Great Artiste* will measure the blast by dropping scientific instruments that will float to the ground by parachute and then radio details back to Guam and Tinian.

---

*Niigata was ultimately removed from the list of bombing sites. Its location in northwest Honshu was too far from Tinian, allowing little room for error in terms of fuel for the B-29s.

Tibbets will pilot the lead plane containing the A-bomb. As of now, the aircraft has no nickname.

Since the "509th Composite Group" was activated in December 1944, these crews have trained in utter secrecy. They are not popular here in Tinian, where other bomber squadrons mock their many privileges and top secret compound. But they ignore the taunts, knowing that they have been training for a high-level mission that could end the war. Tibbets was given fifteen B-29s, and a top secret training location in the Utah desert. Once the crews Tibbets handpicked flew to Tinian a month ago, they began simulating a most unique sort of bombing mission: instead of dozens of bombs, they practiced dropping just one rotund "pumpkin bomb." At five tons, twelve feet in length, and five feet in diameter, the pumpkin bomb approximated the size of the atomic bomb known as Fat Man. This allowed pilots to get a feel for how the actual bomb will fall as it is deployed from their forward bomb bay.

Little Boy is a different shape from Fat Man, measuring ten feet long and just a bit more than two feet in diameter. The men of the 509th successfully drop-tested a nonatomic replica of Little Boy on July 23.

Tibbets calls forty-three-year-old navy officer William S. "Deak" Parsons to the platform. An ordnance expert by training, Captain Parsons has served in a most unique capacity during the war, spending much of his time at Los Alamos, where he worked not only with Robert Oppenheimer on the design and development of Little Boy but also with General Groves on the Target Committee. He even observed the Trinity explosion less than a month ago.

Since then, Parsons has been Little Boy's constant companion, overseeing its delivery to Tinian. It was Parsons who personally met with Captain Charles McVay of the USS *Indianapolis* in San Francisco to convey the order that his ship "will sail at high speed to Tinian" with the bomb components.

Throughout his two years in Los Alamos, Captain Parsons's primary motivation for designing the bomb has been to end the war. This ambition became personal shortly after the *Indianapolis* set sail from San Francisco, when Parsons made a rapid detour to see his young half brother in a San Diego naval hospital.

Bob Parsons was among the twenty thousand American casualties during the fierce fighting on Iwo Jima. Once handsome, the Marine Corps private's face is now permanently disfigured: the right side caved in, his jaw gone, a pink prosthesis in the orb where his right eye once rested.

Deak Parsons knows he can do little to help his younger brother but believes dropping the A-bomb will prevent the same thing from happening to other young American men.

At the podium, Captain Parsons looks at the faces of the aviators gathered in this stuffy Quonset hut and tells them all about the weapon that will win the war.

"The bomb you are about to drop is something new in the history of warfare," Parsons begins. "It is the most destructive weapon ever produced."

Parsons then tells the men about the Trinity blast, an explosion "ten times more brilliant than the sun." Following orders to keep the source of the detonation a secret, he does not use the words "atomic" or "nuclear."* Instead, he draws a picture of the enormous mushroom cloud in chalk on a blackboard, describing how the cloud vacuumed sand up off the desert floor and carried it thousands of feet into the air.

"We think it will knock out everything within a three-mile area," Parsons tells the men, adding that Little Boy might be even more powerful than the Trinity explosion: "No one knows what will happen when the bomb is dropped from the air."

The B-29 crewmen are stunned. Such a weapon is beyond their comprehension.

Tibbets once again takes his place on the briefing platform.

"Whatever any of us, including myself, has done until now is small potatoes compared to what we are going to do," he tells his men. "I'm proud to be associated with you. Your morale has been high, even though it was difficult not knowing what you were doing, thinking that maybe you were wasting your time, and that the 'gimmick' was just somebody's wild dream.

"I am personally honored—and I'm sure all of you are, too—to take part in this raid which will shorten the war by at least six months."

---

*Only Tibbets, Parsons, and bombardier Major Thomas W. Ferebee are allowed to know that the bomb to be dropped on Hiroshima is atomic.

Tibbets gazes out over the room one last time.

"Depending on the weather, this mission will go off on August sixth."*

---

*Tibbets's speech is paraphrased, taken from an illegal diary of the meeting kept by radio operator Sergeant Abe Spitzer.

19

———— ◆ ————

It is bedtime on this Sunday night. Throughout Hiroshima, citizens rest up for the coming workweek. In the city's Ujina district, thirty-two-year-old firefighter Yosaku Mikami is well past the halfway point of his twenty-four-hour shift. If all goes well, he will sleep through the night before getting off work at 8:00 a.m. Then Mikami will ride by streetcar to his house on the edge of town, in the Sakaemachi district, heading in the opposite direction of commuters traveling to their places of work in the city.

Most mornings, Mikami returns home to the smell of breakfast being cooked over burning coals in a hibachi. His wife greets him warmly as his two young children prepare for school.

But the morning of August 6, 1945, will be different.

Many in Hiroshima use the word *bukimi*—strange or otherworldly—to describe the uneasy awareness in recent days that the Americans have not leveled their city. Some predict with grisly humor that it is only a matter of time before their luck runs out. As a firefighter, Mikami approves of the firebreaks being cleared throughout Hiroshima—wide-open areas in the middle of the city where wooden homes and buildings have been knocked down and the rubble removed to prevent fire racing from house to house, as it did during the Tokyo firebombings of March 1944.

Mikami is saddened and relieved at the same time by precautions that civil authorities are taking to spare women and young children. Thousands are being evacuated to the countryside; among them are Mikami's wife and children, who departed just this morning. Their final destination is uncertain right now. If relatives will not take them in, they will be forced to sleep in temples or public halls along with the thousands of other Japanese citizens being sent away for their own safety.

Tomorrow morning will be lonely for Yosaku Mikami, for he will walk into his empty home and begin to think about this missing family.

⋆　⋆　⋆

Air-raid sirens suddenly awake sixteen-year-old Akira Onogi inside his family's home, adjacent to a small warehouse. The sound has become a regular part of many nights, often the result of American bombers flying overhead en route to other targets. Thus, Akira feels no rush to go to an air-raid shelter. Japan's 1937 Air Defense Law was created for a night like this, but the long war and the reluctance of America to bomb Hiroshima have desensitized its residents. A second siren signaling a false alarm means that all is clear; on the other hand, the unmistakable thunder of an approaching B-29 bomb squadron means young and old alike must immediately get to an air-raid shelter. Despite the risk, Akira and the other four members of his family prefer to remain comfortably in bed.

Tonight, 588 B-29s are attacking five target cities throughout Japan, though Hiroshima will not be one of them. Not a single plane will be shot down. The Americans, it seems, can bomb wherever they want, whenever they want, and whatever they want.

Soon enough comes the all clear. Akira rolls over and goes back to sleep. Though in his second year of junior high school and an avid student, Akira is no longer allowed to attend classes. Instead, like his fellow students, he has been mobilized to aid the war effort by laboring in the factories. He is due to rise early for work at the Mitsubishi shipbuilding plant. It is his patriotic obligation but not a job that he enjoys.

The August night is pitch-black but warm. The only sound Akira hears is that of light snoring from his parents. But the boy is not worried that his rest is being disturbed, for he has made other plans for the morning of Monday, August 6. In a minor act of protest, he plans to stay home from work and read a book.

Little does Akira know that he will soon play a role in a real-life story beyond anything the written word can accurately describe.

★ ★ ★

Akiko Takakura needs to be up early on Monday. Someday she hopes to be a preschool teacher, but for now the twenty-year-old is a bank employee. In the morning she will eat her breakfast of breakfast corn, soybean draff, and rice before taking the streetcar to the Hatchobori Station and then walking to her job at the Geibi Bank. It will be the height of rush hour, the streets teeming with commuters. But it will also be a lovely stroll, enhanced by views of the Ota River, the parade ground where Japanese soldiers perform their morning calisthenics, and Hiroshima Castle, a revered local landmark dating back to the sixteenth century. If all goes well, Akiko will climb the nine stone steps to the double doors leading into the three-story Geibi Bank building by 8:15 a.m.

The bank is built of stone and features protective armored shutters on the first and second floors to deter robbers. Female employees must arrive at work thirty minutes before the men in order to clean the office space, so once inside, Akiko will stamp the bank's attendance log and then step behind the teller windows to begin the dusting of desks and other minor organizational tasks that form the start of her workday routine.

She is a model employee. Her superiors appreciate that she likes to arrive early for work.

It is a trait that will soon save her life.

★ ★ ★

After the Trinity A-bomb test took place in the New Mexico desert three weeks ago, British physicist William

Penney of the Manhattan Project measured the blast and reported that another such explosion "would reduce a city of three or four hundred thousand people to nothing but a sink for disaster relief, bandages and hospitals."

The force of the test explosion was equivalent to ten thousand tons of dynamite. A brilliant fireball was followed by a purple cloud glowing with radioactivity that soared into the stratosphere. Everything within the blast zone was vaporized.

If a man had been standing within that zone, he would have died in a fraction of a second, but not before his bone marrow boiled and his flesh literally exploded from his skeleton. In the next millisecond, nothing of that person would remain except compressed gas, which would be instantly sucked up into that great purple cloud racing high into the sky.

The Trinity A-bomb test killed no one. But now a new chapter of warfare is about to begin.

20

—◆—

The bringer of death sits in the front seat of a six-by-six army truck. Approaching the B-29 he personally selected for this mission, Colonel Paul Tibbets wears a one-piece tan flight suit and a billed cap. In preparation for the coming twelve-hour mission, he carries cigars, cigarettes, loose tobacco, and a pipe. Should his plane be shot down, Tibbets also has a handgun. And, if capture becomes a possibility, he also carries twelve cyanide pills, one for each member of his crew. Better to end their lives than be tortured into giving away A-bomb secrets.

Tibbets knew there would be commotion about tonight's mission. But he never expected the sight before him: floodlights turn the black tropical night into day. Flashbulbs pop as Tibbets and his crew arrive at the flight line. Scientists and technicians flit around the bomber, fussing over last-minute details. Inside the forward bomb bay, safely concealed from view, is the bulbous, 8,900-pound shape of Little Boy, soon to be dropped from a height of five miles onto Hiroshima. The target point is the concrete-and-steel Aioi Bridge, whose T shape is easily visible from the air.

Just hours ago, the B-29 with the number 82 painted on the rear of the fuselage finally got a nickname. Tibbets wrote the words on a scrap of paper and handed it to a sign painter in midafternoon. In the past, he has favored aggressive names such as *Butcher Shop* and *Red Gremlin* for his aircraft. But the plane he will fly

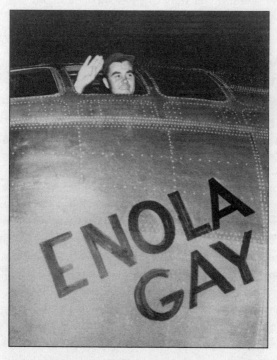

Colonel Paul Tibbets just moments before taking off to drop the atomic bomb on Hiroshima

tonight will hold a special place in history, so he indulges in a rare display of sentiment.

By 4:00 p.m. the aircraft was formally christened *Enola Gay*, in honor of Tibbets's fifty-four-year-old mother. Years ago, when the colonel angered his father by quitting his job as a physician's assistant at a venereal disease clinic to pursue a flying career, it was Enola Gay who calmed the waters. "If you want to go kill yourself," his father had said angrily, "I don't give a damn."

To which the former Enola Gay Haggard added quietly, "Paul, if you want to go fly airplanes, you're going to be all right."

Now, with the black block-letter painting of Enola Gay's name on the silver fuselage, she and her son will forever be linked in history.*

"There stood the *Enola Gay*," Tibbets will later write, "bathed in floodlights like the star of a Hollywood movie. Motion picture cameras were set up

---

*The seldom-used name "Enola" is the word "alone" spelled in reverse. It is believed that Enola Gay Tibbets's parents were inspired to give her the name by the 1867 Laura Preston novel *In Bonds*, in which Enola is the name of a special place to a main character. When Enola Gay Tibbets later learned that her name was painted on the aircraft that dropped the Hiroshima bomb, her face displayed no visible emotion. However, her stomach would often jiggle when something made her happy. "You should have seen the old gal's belly jiggle on that one," Tibbets's father told his son of the moment it was announced on the radio.

and still photographers were standing by with their equipment. Any Japanese lurking in the surrounding hills—and there were still some who had escaped capture—had to know that something very special was going on."

Soon, the thrum of the 2,200 horsepower B-29 Wright Cyclone engines fills the air as the advance weather planes *Jabit III*, *Full House*, and *Straight Flush* lumber down the 8,500-foot east-west Runway Able, which has been nicknamed the "Hirohito Highway." One by one, the planes take off and ascend into the night for the twelve-hour round-trip flight to the Empire.

The time is 1:37 a.m.

Colonel Paul Tibbets and *Enola Gay* are set to take off in one hour.

★ ★ ★

Preparation has been intense. At 2:00 p.m., Little Boy was pulled by tractor to a special loading pit. Due to its size, it cannot fit beneath the B-29's fuselage for loading like normal bombs. Instead, a concrete-lined pit has been dug into the earth. At 2:15, *Enola Gay* was backed over the pit before the atomic weapon was loaded into the bomb bay with a hydraulic lift. Captain Deak Parsons entered the bay at 3:30 to practice the eleven steps necessary to arm the bomb midflight, which he has never done before. Just this morning, four B-29s rolling out for standard bombing missions crashed on takeoff, detonating all their explosives.

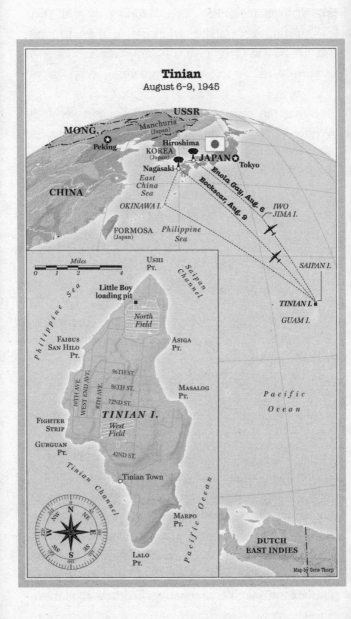

Tinian
August 6–9, 1945

USSR

MONG.

Manchuria
(Japan)

Peking

KOREA
(Japan)

CHINA

Hiroshima

JAPAN

Tokyo

Nagasaki

East
China
Sea

Enola Gay, Aug. 6

Bockscar, Aug. 9

OKINAWA I.

IWO
JIMA I.

FORMOSA
(Japan)

Philippine
Sea

SAIPAN I.

TINIAN I.

GUAM I.

USHI
Pt.

Saipan
Channel

Little Boy
loading pit

North
Field

Philippine Sea

FAIBUS
SAN HILO
Pt.

ASIGA
Pt.

96TH ST.
86TH ST.
72ND ST.

10TH AVE.
WEST END AVE.
8TH AVE.

MASALOG
Pt.

*Pacific
Ocean*

FIGHTER
STRIP

TINIAN I.

West
Field

GURGUAN
Pt.

42ND ST.

Tinian Channel

Tinian Town

Pacific Ocean

MARPO
Pt.

N
NW NE
W E
SW SE
S

LALO
Pt.

DUTCH
EAST INDIES

Miles
0   1   2   3   4

Map by Gene Thorp

Little Boy being loaded into the bomb bay of Enola Gay

Parsons is openly fearful that a similar crash of *Enola Gay* will wipe Tinian off the map.

By 5:30, with the words "Enola Gay" painted in block letters just beneath the cockpit, the B-29 was ready for preflight testing, which went off without incident.

At 8:00 p.m., Colonel Tibbets conducted a final briefing. In addition to flight routes, altitudes, and departure times, he pinpointed the location of rescue ships and submarines that would be in the area in case a plane had to ditch in the ocean. This information was particularly vital because the US Navy had just issued a warning for all ships to stay at least fifty miles away from Hiroshima. This reduced the potential number of rescue vessels, meaning that only a pinpoint water landing would save Tibbets and his crew in an emergency.

Catholic Mass was prayed at 10:00 p.m. A Protestant service followed immediately at 10:30. Almost every man attended one or the other. Tibbets, a man whose only faith is in the physics of aviation, attended neither. The men are loose but pensive—trained professionals who have flown scores of combat missions. However, during the final preflight midnight meal of sausage, blueberry pancakes, and real eggs in the mess hall—affectionately nicknamed the "Dogpatch Inn"—Tibbets was nervous, though trying not to show it. He ate little, preferring to drink black coffee and smoke his pipe. His time had almost come.

★ ★ ★

Three hundred miles southwest of Tinian, the USS *Oneida*, a fast attack transport, has just arrived in the bustling anchorage at Ulithi, an island atoll four hundred miles northeast of Palau. She dropped anchor at 1500 hours on August 5, the same time Little Boy was being loaded into *Enola Gay*'s bomb bay. *Oneida* is carrying a cargo of fresh army soldiers traveling from Pearl Harbor to Okinawa, where they will train for the invasion of Japan.

The *Oneida* is a new ship, commissioned just last December. She is 455 feet long and 62 feet wide at the beam, with a top speed of 17.7 knots. In her short time afloat, she has taken a nearly full tour of the Pacific, maintaining almost nonstop motion carrying men and cargo in and out of combat zones. Since leaving San

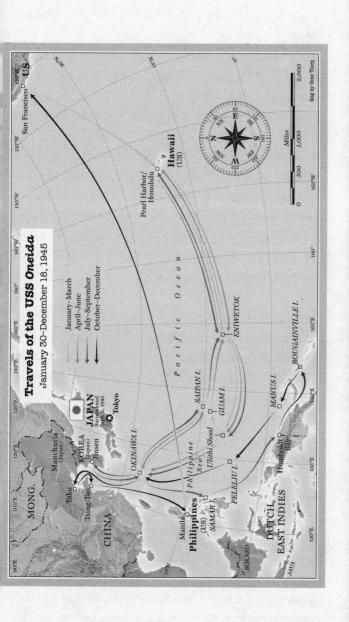

Travels of the USS Oneida
January 30–December 18, 1945

January–March
April–June
July–September
October–December

San Francisco   US

Hawaii
(US)

Pearl Harbor/
Honolulu

Pacific Ocean

ENIWETOK

SAIPAN I.

GUAM I.

Ulithi Shoal

Philippine
Sea

OKINAWA I.

JAPAN
Surrendered
Sept. 2, 1945
Tokyo

Manchuria
(Japan)

KOREA
(Japan)
Jinsen

Taku
Tsing-Tao

CHINA

MONG.

PELELIU I.

MANUS I.

BOUGAINVILLE I.

Humboldt
Bay

DUTCH
EAST INDIES

BORNEO

JAVA

Manila
Philippines
(US)

SAMAR I.

N
NE
E
SE
S
SW
W
NW

Miles
0   500   1,000   2,000

Map by Gene Thorp

90°E   105°E   120°E   135°E   150°E   165°E   180°   165°W   150°W   135°W   120°W
90°N
15°N
0°
15°S

Francisco on January 30, *Oneida* has visited nineteen ports or anchorages.*

A young ensign from Brooklyn, New York, is among the ship's fifty-six-man officer corps. He is twenty-one and quick-witted, the son of a New York City policeman. In his nine-month stint aboard *Oneida*, the recent graduate of the navy's V-12 Navy College Training Program at the College of the Holy Cross has seen action off the coast of Okinawa, witnessed defeated Japanese soldiers up close when the *Oneida* ferried 1,050 prisoners of war to Pearl Harbor last month, and experienced all manner of weather—most of all rain, heat, and tropical humidity. In one month's time, the ensign will even endure a typhoon aboard *Oneida*.

As with so many soldiers and sailors, the young officer does not know what lies ahead for him. There are, of course, rumors of a massive American invasion of the Japanese mainland. All American military personnel know that would lead to catastrophic casualties on both sides.

The ensign will do his duty, whatever happens, but

---

*The Oneida are an Iroquois tribe living in upstate New York who gave their name to counties in New York, Wisconsin, and Idaho as well as to the ship. The USS *Oneida* from World War II was actually the third ship bearing that moniker, the first being a brig of war in the War of 1812. The second was a storied sloop of war that served gallantly in the American Civil War from 1862 to 1865 and sank off the coast of Yokohama, Japan, in 1870 when she collided with a British steamer. Seven crew members of the ship's second incarnation were awarded the Medal of Honor for their courageous actions.

he would like to make it home alive. There is a young woman waiting for him.

★ ★ ★

A methodical man, Colonel Tibbets makes one last walk around *Enola Gay*, scrutinizing her for signs of trouble. With seven thousand gallons of fuel and a four-ton bomb, she is almost seven tons overweight, so even the slightest malfunction could be deadly.

"I made sure there were no open pieces of cowling, no pitot covers left hanging, and that the tires were inflated and in good condition. I also checked the pavement for telltale evidence of hydraulic leaks and looked into the bottom of the engine cowlings with a flashlight to be sure there was no excessive oil drip."

Tibbets enters the cockpit through a ladder at the aft end of the nose gear. The other eleven members of the crew also get on the plane, find their seats, and arrange themselves for the long flight.

Tibbets sits in the seat on the left reserved for the aircraft commander. Copilot Bob Lewis takes the right seat. There is tension between the two men, for *Enola Gay* was Lewis's aircraft before Tibbets chose to change the name and fly it on this mission.

Outside, spectators wait patiently on the tarmac for *Enola Gay* to take flight. Tibbets is in no hurry, unworried about his audience or the bruised feelings of Captain Lewis as he runs through yet another preflight check of instruments and systems.

Once all four engines are running, Tibbets does a final check of the oil-pressure, fuel-pressure, and RPM gauges. The thrum of the propellers causes *Enola Gay* to shake; only when she takes flight will the vibration cease. "The entire checkout and starting procedure required about thirty-five minutes and it was now 2:30," Tibbets will remember.

"Waving to the crowd of almost one hundred who were standing by, I gunned the engines and began our taxi.

"Destination: Hiroshima."

21

The humid air is filled with warning. Air-raid sirens again awaken the citizens of Hiroshima. The morning has dawned warm and clear, with just a few wispy clouds in the sky. A single American B-29 has been seen flying toward the city, causing the alert to sound and disrupting the start of the business day—a time for cooking the morning meal and boarding the streetcar to work. Air-raid warnings are now a constant nuisance, but at this late point in the war it seems unlikely the Americans will finally bomb the city. So while some residents dutifully flee into bomb shelters, others go about their day.

In the huge harbor, shrimp fishermen tend to their nets, as their ancestors have done for centuries. They ignore the air-raid warnings, as they have nowhere to flee. In the southern section of town near the port, the Ujina fire station is relatively calm, and fireman Yosaku Mikami looks at the clock. He is less than sixty minutes away from the end of his twenty-four-hour shift, but any bombing will cause fires, meaning Yosaku's services will be needed immediately.

Despite the evacuation of his family yesterday and the empty house that awaits him, Yosaku is eager to get home. He patiently waits for the sound of the all-clear siren, and at 7:32 he hears it. The danger has passed—or so it seems.

★   ★   ★

On the other side of town, sixteen-year-old Akira Onogi is executing his plan to take the day off from work at the Mitsubishi shipbuilding plant. A studious boy, Akira is angry that he can no longer attend school due to the war. But he now lies content on the floor of his parents' home, reading a book. Akira is looking forward to a day of leisure—he has no plans at all.

★   ★   ★

The all-clear siren alerts the people who took shelter at the Hatchobori streetcar station that they can now emerge. Twenty-year-old Akiko Takakura is a cautious young woman, but she now resumes her journey to the Geibi Bank, where she does secretarial work. The bank, with its stone walls and armored window coverings that let in almost no light, is less than a half mile from the T-shaped Aioi Bridge spanning the Ota River—what will soon be ground zero.

Three days ago, the clock tower at Hiroshima University stopped working at precisely 8:15. The city lacks the spare parts and material to fix it, so the great clock looking down on all of Hiroshima remains frozen in time.

As Akiko enters the lobby of her workplace, she notices that the bank clock in the lobby is just a few moments away from striking 8:15.

It is an omen Akiko will never forget.

★ ★ ★

Enola Gay flies over Japan at an altitude of 30,700 feet. The overloaded bomber can climb no higher. Weather plane *Straight Flush*, which caused the air-raid sirens to sound in Hiroshima this morning, has reported that the weather is fine for visual bombing. With that message, the fate of the city is sealed.

"It's Hiroshima," Colonel Paul Tibbets barks into *Enola Gay*'s intercom.

Six hours ago, shortly after taking off from Tinian, Captain Deak Parsons and his assistant, Lieutenant Morris Jeppson, wriggled through the small pressurized opening separating the bomb bay from the rest of the aircraft. Little Boy almost entirely fills the cavernous space. The ugly bomb is bulbous, with four square tail fins to guide its descent, a design predicated upon performance instead of appearance.

A single shackle holds Little Boy in place. Braces keep the bomb from swaying side to side. Standing on a small catwalk, Parsons positions himself at the rear of the device. He needs light to see what he is doing, so Jeppson, a physicist educated at Harvard, Yale, and MIT, provides it.

The captain works quickly, running through an

eleven-step checklist that arms Little Boy. Opening a small panel, he inserts four silk packages of cordite powder. This smokeless propellant will detonate the uranium "bullet" at one end of the bomb's inner cannon barrel. The small chunk of enriched U-235 will race down the barrel and collide with a separate sphere of uranium known as the nucleus at the opposite end. Within one-trillionth of a second of the bullet striking the nucleus—a "picosecond," in technical terms—the splitting of one atom into two smaller atoms will begin the process of nuclear fission. The explosion will follow immediately, releasing deadly heat and radioactive gamma rays.

As Parsons arms Little Boy, the sharp, machined edges of the rear panel cut his fingertips. Undaunted, he finishes the job in twenty-five minutes. His final act is to insert three green dummy plugs between Little Boy's battery and its firing mechanism.

Little Boy is armed but fragile. Anything that ignites the cordite charges will cause it to explode, killing all the men on *Enola Gay*; thus, the green plugs placed between the electrical connections. As long as those plugs are secure, Little Boy will not detonate.

★ ★ ★

Just before they enter Japanese airspace, Deak Parsons sends Morris Jeppson back into the bomb bay one last time. The blond lieutenant replaces the green plugs with three red arming plugs, thus establishing an electrical circuit between the battery and the bomb.

Little Boy is now alive.

⭐ ⭐ ⭐

One hour later, *Enola Gay* bombardier Thomas Fere-bee announces, pointing straight out the front bubble window of the aircraft, "I've got the bridge."

The Aioi Bridge was chosen as Little Boy's aim-ing point because of its location in the center of Hi-roshima and its unique T-shaped appearance, visible from the air.

Looking down, Colonel Tibbets can see the white buildings of downtown Hiroshima; he can actually see a mass of movement that looks like people walking to work. "My eyes were fixed on the center of the city, which shimmered in the early morning light," he will later remember.

Enola Gay flies the last miles to Hiroshima un-contested. No enemy planes or antiaircraft fire greet the Americans. Japanese air defense officials, having already sounded three air-raid warnings during the night, choose to ignore the B-29's approach, thinking it to be on a simple reconnaissance mission.

With ninety seconds to go, bombardier Thomas Ferebee positions his left eye over the Norden bomb-sight's viewfinder. If he does his job properly, allowing for *Enola Gay*'s airspeed of 330 miles per hour and the slight amount of wind that will cause the bomb to drift, Little Boy should fall to the ground with pinpoint accuracy.

"One minute out," Tibbets announces, breaking radio silence.

Ferebee flicks a switch that sends a sharp tone into

the headphones of the *Enola Gay* crew and those of the men in the two scientific planes following behind, reminding them of what is to come. They are to put specially darkened goggles over their eyes to protect their vision. All three planes have been ordered to flee the vicinity as soon as possible to avoid the aftershock of the atomic explosion.

"Thirty seconds," says Tibbets.

"Twenty."

The bomb bay doors open at precisely 8:15 a.m.— the exact moment at which the Hiroshima University clock froze three days ago.

"Ten . . . nine . . . eight . . . seven . . . six . . . five . . .

"Four . . . three . . . two . . . one . . ."

At 8:15:17 a.m., Little Boy is set loose from its shackle.

☆   ☆   ☆

Instantly, *Enola Gay* lurches upward, finally rid of the four extra tons beneath her nose. Tibbets wrestles her sharply to the right, almost standing her on a wing as he turns away from Hiroshima. He has less than fifty seconds to distance himself from the blast. If he fails to cover enough ground, *Enola Gay* will be destroyed by shock waves.

Despite the 60-degree bank, a move more suited to a lithe fighter aircraft than a massive bomber, bombardier Ferebee keeps his left eye affixed to his Norden bombsight, allowing him to watch Little Boy plummet to earth. The bomb wobbles after first being dropped, but the four stabilizing fins soon force the nose down, propelling it toward the heart of Hiroshima.

Ferebee is transfixed, knowing that he is witnessing history. Ten seconds pass. Twenty. Thirty. Almost too late, he remembers that the explosion's brightness will blind anyone who stares at it. Just in time, Ferebee unglues his eye from the bombsight and turns away from Little Boy's descent.

Forty-three seconds after its release, at an altitude of 1,890 feet over the Aioi Bridge in downtown Hiroshima, Little Boy's radar proximity fuse detonates. Within the bomb's inner cannon, the four cordite charges explode, sending the uranium bullet hurtling the length of the barrel, where it collides with the second mass of U-235. The chain reaction is instantaneous. In the blast that follows, a fireball spreads out over the target zone. It travels at one hundred times the speed of sound, rendering it silent. One-millionth of a second later, the people of Hiroshima begin to incinerate.

Almost twelve miles away, the shock wave slams into the escaping *Enola Gay* so hard that Tibbets shouts "Flak," thinking the plane has been hit by ground fire. He feels a strange "tingling sensation" in his mouth, the result of his fillings interacting with the radioactive elements now billowing thousands of feet into the air.

But *Enola Gay* is safe. All twelve men on board are alive. In six hours they will celebrate with whiskey and lemonade and spend the night far from the hell they have just created.

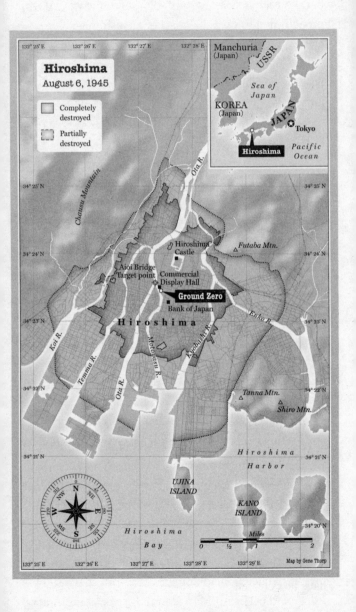

Hiroshima
August 6, 1945

Completely
destroyed

Partially
destroyed

Manchuria
(Japan)

USSR

Sea of
Japan

KOREA
(Japan)

JAPAN

Tokyo

Hiroshima

Pacific
Ocean

132° 25' E   132° 26' E   132° 27' E   132° 28' E

34° 25' N   34° 25' N

34° 24' N   34° 24' N

34° 23' N   34° 23' N

34° 22' N   34° 22' N

34° 21' N   34° 21' N

34° 20' N

Chausu Mountain

Ota R.

Futaba Mtn.

Hiroshima
Castle

Aioi Bridge
target point

Commercial
Display Hall

Ground Zero

Bank of Japan

Enko R.

Koi R.

Temma R.

Ota R.

Motoyasu R.

Kyobashi R.

Hiroshima

Tanna Mtn.

Shiro Mtn.

Hiroshima
Harbor

UJINA
ISLAND

KANO
ISLAND

Hiroshima
Bay

N
NE
E
SE
S
SW
W
NW

Miles

0   ½   1   2

Map by Gene Thorp

132° 25' E   132° 26' E   132° 27' E   132° 28' E   132° 29' E

★ ★ ★

Little Boy explodes three hundred yards from its primary target. The temperature inside the bomb at the moment of nuclear fission is more than a million degrees Fahrenheit, which sends out a white flash of light ten times the brightness of the sun. Millionths of a second later, the heat on the ground directly below the bomb spikes to 6,000 degrees, bringing with it deadly radioactive gamma rays.

A thirty-five-year-old widow, Mrs. Aoyama, has sent her young son off to his mandatory work detail early. Per her daily routine, she is outdoors, working in the vegetable garden she shares with monks from a nearby Buddhist temple. The vegetable garden is located directly beneath the exploding Little Boy, the precise spot on the earth that will be known as the hypocenter.

Mrs. Aoyama is vaporized.

Death comes so quickly that her nerve endings do not have time to react to pain, nor even acknowledge the presence of the light and heat liquefying her bones and boiling her brain at a temperature five times greater than that of boiling water.

Thousands of men, women, and children within a half-mile radius of Mrs. Aoyama are simultaneously reduced to lumps of charcoal, their internal organs evaporating inside their charred corpses. Downtown Hiroshima is instantly covered in smoking black piles that were once human bodies. One woman standing in front of the Hiroshima Central Broadcasting Station tries to flee, only to be carbonized in a running position, her baby pressed tightly to her body.

But that is just the beginning.

Three milliseconds later, the sky erupts into a fireball three hundred yards wide as the surrounding air ignites, liquefying everyone in its proximity.

Then comes the blast as the explosion rockets outward with the force of twenty thousand tons of TNT, followed immediately by a billowing mushroom cloud that rises more than fifty thousand feet into the air, sucking up dust, dirt, and bodily gases from the vaporized remains of those killed at the hypocenter.

Within seconds, seventy thousand people are dead.

Almost every person and building within a one-mile radius of the hypocenter has vanished.

Pets, birds, rats, ants, cockroaches—gone.

Homes, fishing boats, telephone poles, the centuries-old Hiroshima Castle—all disappeared.

Day turns into night as the mushroom cloud blots out the sun. Beyond the one-mile radius of the hypocenter, some have survived, though at a horrible cost. Flash burns blind all those unfortunate to be caught looking in the direction of the blast, while the intense heat maims and disfigures thousands, many of whom live miles away. One group of Japanese soldiers is burned so badly that their faces literally melt away; it is impossible to distinguish the back of their heads from the front.

No one is spared the suffering. A group of students from the Hiroshima Girls Business School are "covered with blisters the size of balls, on their backs, their faces, their shoulders and their arms. The blisters were

A Hiroshima streetcar amid the ruins of what was once downtown Hiroshima

starting to burst open and their skin hung down like rugs," Japanese photojournalist Yoshito Matsushige will remember.

The heat incinerates the clothes of many victims, such as the fifteen passengers on a streetcar on the outskirts of the city. They all now lie dead in a naked pile. Because dark colors absorb heat while light colors reflect it, some of the unclothed women have burns in the shape of flowers on their bodies as a result of the designs on the kimonos they were wearing at the time of their death.

★ ★ ★

If the designers of Little Boy imagined a single bomb blast would inflict instant death on thousands, they were correct. The truth is that it does not take much imagination to foresee puncture wounds caused by shards of exploded glass and wood hurtling through the air. The atomic blast wave travels at two miles per second, knocking flat anything in its path. Then there is the horror of radiation—radioactive particles of dust that will slowly kill residents of Hiroshima for months and years to come. But there is even more.

Thousands of Japanese die from fire and water. The flames come first, individual blazes that begin at the instant Little Boy explodes. Within five minutes, almost every structure within a two-mile radius of the blast is ablaze, a raging firestorm that propels a powerful flaming wind. Soon, that wind reaches hurricane strength, reducing much of Hiroshima to cinders.

Many residents are now buried in the rubble of their collapsed homes. Trapped beneath thick wooden beams and tons of ceramic roof tiling, they frantically plead for rescue as the fires burn closer. Their screams echo throughout the streets of Hiroshima.

To escape the firestorm, or to cool the burns covering their bodies, many Japanese leap into the city's firefighting cisterns. But what happens next is yet another cruel twist of fate: the explosion has superheated the water, and everyone immersing himself or herself in it immediately boils to death.

Others try to escape the flames by diving into one of the seven rivers that flow through Hiroshima, only to find the water clogged with dead bodies. Many are actually pushed into the water by the enormous crowds trying to flee the firestorm. Once they are caught in the current, the number of corpses makes it impossible to swim. "I saw a few live people still in the water, knocking against the dead as they floated down the river," one eyewitness will later recall. "There must have been hundreds and thousands who fled to the river to escape the fire and then drowned."

Hiroshima is chaos. Some confused citizens maintain almost total silence as they endure the horrors of Little Boy. Many wander the streets in a daze, arms held away from their bodies to prevent them rubbing against their burns, staring at the carbon lumps on the street, picking their way through the debris, and absorbing the surreal nature of what has happened. Others, their homes destroyed, join the long line of Hiroshima's citizens frantically retreating to the safety of the countryside.

$\star$ $\star$ $\star$

Just seconds after Little Boy's detonation, the Japan Broadcasting Corporation in Tokyo notices that their Hiroshima station is off the air. The control operator gets on the phone to see if he can help fix the problem but gets no response.

Soon it becomes clear that Hiroshima's train station, telegraph operators, and military garrison have also severed communications. Fearing an American bombing, the headquarters of the Japanese military, the general staff office, dispatches a young officer from Tokyo to investigate. His orders are to fly to Hiroshima immediately and ascertain whether or not the city has been the target of an American attack.

The next day, the chilling results of what the young officer saw from the air are reported on Japanese radio: "Practically all living things, human and animal, were literally seared to death."

☆　☆　☆

Those who survive the bombing of Hiroshima will forever be known in Japan as the *hibakusha*—the "explosion-affected people."

The difference between survival and death is often luck: standing inside a concrete building that blocks the shock waves, or having the good fortune of not being pinned beneath a large beam when a house collapses.

"The atomic bomb does not discriminate," Hiroshima weatherman Isao Kita will remember. "The atomic bomb kills everyone from little babies to old people. And it's not an easy death. It's a very cruel and very painful way to die."

☆　☆　☆

Among the *hibakusha* is fireman Yosaku Mikami, who is spared death on his way home because his streetcar is shielded from the blast by a tunnel.

"The car passed through Miyuki Bashi and was approaching the train office, when I saw the blue flash from the window. At the same time, smoke filled the car, which prevented me even from seeing the person standing directly in front of me."

Yosaku returns to the fire station, where he joins his colleague on the fire truck. They are confronted by utter chaos and unimaginable horror as they come upon scores of victims "swearing, screaming, shouting, asking for help." Yosaku and his fellow firefighters immediately go to work, hoping to find a hospital where they might take the worst of the victims. "We tried to open the eyes of the injured and we found out they were still alive. We tried to carry them by their arms and legs and to place them onto the fire truck. But this was difficult because their skin was peeled off as we tried to move them. . . . But they never complained they felt pain, even when their skin was peeling off."

Yosaku and the other firemen travel through the city, tending to the wounded and visiting other fire stations to determine the fate of their brother firefighters. They find many still alive, combating the blazes. But they also come upon scenes of horrifying death.

At one station Yosaku finds a fireman scorched to death inside his truck: "He looked as if he was about to start the fire engine to fight the fire."

★   ★   ★

Stunned by the shock waves, sixteen-year-old Akira Onogi is thrown through the air and knocked unconscious. When Akira comes to, he walks outside to find his neighbor standing naked in the rubble of his ruined home, too consumed with searching for lost family members to care about the flaps of burned flesh hanging off his own body.

"I talked to him but he was too exhausted to give me a reply. He was looking for his family desperately," Akira will long remember.

"We found this small girl crying and she asked us to help her mother . . . trapped by a fallen beam on top of the lower half of her body." Akira and a group of onlookers work together to lift the crushing section of wood, but their efforts are in vain.

"Finally a fire broke out, endangering us. So we had no choice but to leave her. She was conscious and we deeply bowed to her with clasped hands to apologize to her and then we left."

For the next ten years, sparks given off by electric streetcars will startle Akira, reminding him of the A-bomb's instantaneous flash—the *pikadon*, or "spark and bang," as it is so often called by survivors. And he will never sit by a window, having seen far too many corpses pierced by exploding panes of glass.

But the most vivid moment, the one that will stay with Akira the rest of his life, is the memory of the daughter and her doomed mother. Thirty years after the atomic bomb blast, Akira will immortalize his sorrow on canvas, painting the scene with unbridled emotion. He places himself in the painting's bottom right-hand corner, hands pressed together in remorse as the sobbing little girl begs him to save her mother's life.*

---

*Akira's painting will become one of the iconic images of the Hiroshima bombing, frequently to be seen on display at the Hiroshima Peace Memorial Museum.

Akira Onogi's vivid memories of the aftermath of the Hiroshima atomic bomb would haunt him for years to come.

★ ★ ★

Geibi Bank employee Akiko Takakura is also among those spared. She stepped into work just moments before her workplace exploded at 8:15, stopping the bank's clock at that precise time. "When I was doing my morning routine, dusting the desks and things like that, the A-bomb was dropped. All I remember was that I saw something flash suddenly."

Though the bank is just three hundred yards from the center of the bomb blast, its stone walls and armored window coverings provide perfect protection. Just on the other side of those walls, on the steps leading into the bank, Akiko would have been instantly burned into a carbon lump.

Momentarily knocked unconscious from the blast, Akiko wakes up a short time later and staggers out into the street to a scene of profound horror: "Many people on the street were killed almost instantly. The fingertips of those dead bodies caught fire and the fire gradually spread over their entire bodies from their fingers. A light gray liquid dripped down their hands, scorching their fingers. I was so shocked to know that fingers and bodies could be burned and deformed like that."

Akiko wanders through the city in a daze, her progress slowed by the countless dead bodies she carefully steps over. She makes her way to the former military garrison, where bare-chested soldiers were performing their morning calisthenics just an hour ago.

"At the drill ground, the burnt field was strewn with what must have been dead soldiers."

She lies down on the ground to rest. "I don't know how much time passed, but at dusk I suddenly vomited what must have been the remnants of my breakfast. . . . I vomited bloody phlegm twice. I knew then that I, too, would die in that place."

Despite 102 cuts on her back from flying glass and debris, along with two serious burns and many bruises, Akiko finds the will to go on. "I'm going to live. I've got to live," she tells herself. A half century from now, determined that a new generation of Japanese must never forget the horror she is experiencing today, Akiko will write the poem "To Children Who Don't Know the Atomic Bomb," describing that morning in graphic detail and ending with the following unforgettable image.*

> One woman walking on the road
> died and then
> her fingers burned,
> a blue flame shortening them like candles.

★   ★   ★

The time in Tokyo is 7:50 p.m. It has been eleven hours and thirty-five minutes since Little Boy was dropped on Hiroshima. Many in the Japanese high command believe that the bomb was atomic, but the generals have withheld this news from their emperor all afternoon.

It is dusk, and Hirohito takes advantage of the warm August night to stroll the gardens of the Imperial Palace, completely unaware of what has happened in Hiroshima.

Suddenly, an aide from the Imperial Japanese Army approaches, which can only mean bad news. Such an

---

Eyewitness Testimonies: Appeals from the A-bomb Survivors, Hiroshima Peace Culture Foundation. Decades after the blast, at the age of forty-five, Akiko was diagnosed with a tumor on her spine, which was successfully removed. In 2012, at the age of eighty-six, she was diagnosed with myelodysplastic syndrome (MDS), a blood anomaly that is often a precursor to leukemia. Both of these conditions are common in survivors of the atomic bomb. At the age of eighty-nine, Akiko currently carries out the duties of the head priest's wife at the Hoonji Temple in the Asa Kita ward of Hiroshima.

intrusion on the emperor's solitude is unheard of except in a time of tragedy. In somber tones, the aide informs Hirohito that Hiroshima has been "attacked with a special bomb from a US bomber." The aide goes on to state that the Navy Ministry, which has been investigating the attacks, believes that "most parts of the city" have ceased to exist.

The aide leaves, allowing Emperor Hirohito to ruminate on what he has just heard. Since the fall of Okinawa six weeks ago, he has known that Japan cannot win this war. For a reminder of the Americans' dominance, Hirohito need only look around the Imperial Palace: despite standing orders by the US military that the emperor's palace should not be bombed, fires started by B-29 raids on Tokyo have leaped the great stone walls and moats surrounding his fortress and burned Hirohito's wooden residence to the ground. Hirohito and his family now live in the imperial library, adjacent to the enormous gardens in which the emperor now walks. All of the emperor's official business is conducted in a bunker sixty feet underground. In that way, he is similar to his deceased ally, the German leader Adolf Hitler.

Like Hitler, Hirohito has refused to surrender. He has persisted in the belief that the Russians will help him negotiate peace with America. The emperor still believes that now. However, he is staggered by the news from Hiroshima.

If the reports from the city are true, Hirohito knows that only unconditional surrender will save Japan from complete destruction. This will mean the end of the

2,500-year-old imperial dynasty—and perhaps the end of Hirohito's own life, should he be tried and found guilty of war crimes.

But five hours later, when American president Harry Truman once again demands unconditional surrender from Japan, Hirohito's response is utter silence.

While his devastated people suffer and die, the god-man continues his stroll.

22

Harry Truman is feeling powerful. Holding court just before lunch in the USS *Augusta*'s enlisted men's mess hall, he banters with the six sailors at his table, asking about their hometowns and life in the navy. Truman could have flown home after his three-week stay at the Potsdam Conference in Germany, but his security agents recommended making the five-day transatlantic journey by sea because they feared an attack in the sky.

The voyage has been blustery, the windblown Atlantic covered in whitecaps and rolling swells. Yet Truman has risen early each morning for a walk on deck in the open air. The crew has been surprised to see the president wearing a broad smile during these morning constitutionals, despite the ongoing conflict in the Pacific. They cannot possibly know the tremendous feeling of success he feels after holding his own on the world stage at Potsdam, and even more important, they do not know that Truman is awaiting confirmation that an atomic bomb has been dropped on Japan.

The president has had a hard time keeping this top secret news to himself. There are a handful of journalists on board the ship, and on the day *Augusta* set sail from Plymouth, England, Truman met with them to explain that America possessed the atomic bomb. He shares this staggering news safe in the knowledge that the media are forbidden from using the ship's radios and have no way of communicating the information. In this particular isolation, the talkative Truman gets to explain the A-bomb on his terms, and yet the weapon maintains its confidential status.

As Truman now chats with the young sailors prior to eating lunch, Captain Frank H. Graham approaches the table holding a map of Japan and a teletype message. Hiroshima is circled in red pencil on the map. The message reads: "Hiroshima bombed visually . . . Results clear cut successful in all respects. Visible effects greater than in any test. Conditions normal in airplane following delivery."

Truman's face lights up. "This is the greatest thing in history," he proclaims to Graham, enthusiastically shaking his hand. "It's time for us to get home."

The president then orders Graham to share the secret message with Secretary of State James F. Byrnes, sitting just a few tables away. A second teletype arrives moments later from Secretary of War Henry Stimson confirming the previous report. "Big bomb dropped on Hiroshima August 5 at 7:15 p.m. Washington time. First reports indicate complete success."

Truman can't help himself: leaping to his feet, he taps his water glass with a fork. At first, there is confusion. These military men immediately rise to attention, realizing the impropriety of the president standing as they sit. But Truman waves them back down: "Please keep your seats and listen for a moment. I have an announcement to make. We have just dropped a new bomb on Japan which has more power than twenty thousand tons of TNT. It has been an overwhelming success!"

Bedlam sweeps through the mess hall. Cheers echo down the ship's passageways. A grinning Truman holds the teletype message aloft as he races from the mess hall and runs down the corridor to share the news with *Augusta*'s officers. "We won the gamble," he shouts above the jubilant celebration.

Everyone believes that the end of the war has arrived.

They are wrong.

⭐　⭐　⭐

Within moments, dressed in a tan double-breasted suit and dark tie, President Truman films a message to the American people from his stateroom aboard the *Augusta*. He sits at a desk, a porthole visible over his right shoulder. The text of his speech was prepared long ago but only just released to the national media by the White House. But Truman's words, which are also being broadcast live on the radio, have a far more powerful effect than a print dispatch. For while this message may seem to be aimed at the American people, it is in fact a warning to the Japanese leadership.

"Sixteen hours ago an American plane dropped one bomb on Hiroshima and destroyed its usefulness to the enemy," he begins. Truman's tone is somber, but there is no doubt he feels justified in his decision. Even as he speaks, more leaflets are being dropped on Japan, encouraging the people to rise up and demand that their leaders surrender.

"The Japanese began the war from the air at Pearl Harbor. They have been repaid many fold. And the end is not yet. With this bomb we have now added a new and revolutionary increase in destruction to supplement the growing power of our armed forces. In their present form these bombs are now in production and even more powerful forms are in development.

"It is an atomic bomb. It is a harnessing of the basic power of the universe. The force from which the sun draws its power has been loosed against those who brought war to the Far East."

Truman then tells the history of the bomb's development, concluding with an unmistakable reminder that the job is not yet done. Only Japan's acceptance of the Potsdam Declaration and its terms of unconditional surrender will stop the bombings.

"We are now prepared to destroy more rapidly and completely every productive enterprise the Japanese have in any city. We shall destroy their docks, their factories, and their communications. Let there be no mistake: We shall completely destroy Japan's power to make war. . . . If they do not now accept our terms they may expect a rain of ruin from the air, the like of which has never been seen on earth."

Finally, Truman signs off. He does not need to order a second bomb to be dropped on Japan, for that command was given two weeks ago, on the same date he approved the Hiroshima attack. In fact, the order allows for bombings to continue as long there is a supply of atomic bombs.

The *Augusta* is just north of Bermuda as Truman completes his speech. The temperature is finally warming. Knowing that a media whirlwind awaits him upon his arrival home tomorrow, the president settles in to enjoy a day of sunshine, hoping for news of a Japanese surrender.

★   ★   ★

In Manila, General Douglas MacArthur is appalled. It is just after midnight on Tuesday when an aide awakens him with news of the Hiroshima bombing. The general is hypersensitive to slights both perceived and real, and when it comes to the atomic bomb there have been many. For the past three years, MacArthur has waged war on *his* terms, attacking when and where he wants. He knows the Japanese culture from his decades living in the Pacific and is confident that they are on the verge of surrender.

Even though MacArthur wears the five-star rank of general of the army, President Truman has rarely consulted him about the state of the Pacific conflict, unlike George Marshall and Dwight Eisenhower, who routinely advise the president on matters of war. While Marshall has long known about the bomb and Eisenhower was made aware of it shortly after the Trinity explosion, MacArthur learned of its existence only one week ago.

MacArthur was never once asked about the A-bomb's tactical use in his theater of war. It is a situation, he believes, no different than if the A-bomb had been dropped on Europe without Eisenhower being informed.

MacArthur knows that would never happen.

Now, on top of those insults, comes the stunning realization that Harry Truman does not *trust* Douglas MacArthur.

On Sunday, August 5, the general received verbal confirmation that the bomb would be dropped the following day. However, this courtesy also contained a key element of misdirection: instead of Hiroshima, the courier from Washington informed the general that ground zero would be a lightly populated industrial district south of Tokyo,

Someone, somewhere, believes Douglas MacArthur cannot keep a secret.

Unfortunately, MacArthur's behavior lends credence to the view that he can't keep his mouth shut. On the morning of the Hiroshima explosion, still not knowing its true location or whether the mission has been a success, MacArthur calls reporters to his office at Manila City Hall and, in off-the-record comments, coyly predicts, "The war may end sooner than we think."

The truth is that MacArthur approved of the Tokyo strike. Showcasing the power of the explosion in an area almost completely devoid of civilians made military sense to him. The tragic slaughter of Manila's residents by the retreating Japanese just a few months ago is still fresh in MacArthur's memory; even before those senseless killings, the general has been openly opposed to targeting civilians. When Japanese commanders accused his troops of firing artillery at a hospital in Rabaul, on the island of New Britain, MacArthur immediately denied the charge and used a neutral embassy in Tokyo to send a message to the Japanese general, telling him that an artillery battery next to the hospital was the real target. But there is inconsistency in his stance: MacArthur does support the bombing of civilians when it suits his purposes, such as the aerial attacks designed to soften up the island of Kyushu for Operation Olympic.

At this point in his career, MacArthur's military training precludes him from publicly criticizing his commander in chief, but for the rest of his life he will privately share his views about August 6, 1945. "MacArthur once spoke eloquently to me about it," Richard Nixon will one day recount to reporters. (The future president served a year in the Pacific during World War II as a naval officer.) "He thought it a tragedy that the bomb was ever exploded. . . . MacArthur, you see, was a soldier. He believed in using force only against military targets, and that is why the nuclear thing turned him off."

Others will reveal that MacArthur saw "no earthly justification for dropping the bomb."*

MacArthur's personal pilot, Lieutenant Colonel Weldon "Dusty" Rhoades, will remember MacArthur's opinion of the bomb even more vividly, writing in his journal, "General MacArthur definitely is appalled and depressed by this Frankenstein monster."

Accurately, MacArthur believes that bombing Hiroshima will *not* lead to a Japanese surrender. The shame would be overwhelming.

According to MacArthur, a Japanese surrender will happen only if President Truman allows the emperor to remain in power after the war. "The retention of the institution of the emperor . . . will allow the Japanese nation to seek peace with dignity, knowing that their divine emperor will continue to guide them."

✶　✶　✶

But most Americans see the situation far differently.

"Thank God for the atomic bomb" is a common refrain among American soldiers and sailors, who have been dreading the bloodbath sure to come if American troops invade the beaches of Japan. To many of them, the bombing of civilians is not an issue—it's payback for the Japanese attack on Pearl Harbor. And if the destruction could lead to peace, US enlisted men almost unanimously believe it is worth it. For the first time

---

*Quoted from a postwar interview with journalist Norman Cousins later published in the book *The Pathology of Power*.

since they put on that uniform, these soldiers and sailors can start planning for the distant future. "For all the fake manliness of our facades," a twenty-one-year-old infantry lieutenant will write, "we cried with relief and joy. We were going to live. We were going to grow up to adulthood."

★　★　★

In Los Alamos, New Mexico, Robert Oppenheimer stands before an auditorium filled with the scientists who designed and produced the atomic bomb. Clasping his hands over his head like a boxer entering the ring, he tells the cheering audience that it is "too early to determine what the results of the bombing might have been, but I'm pretty sure the Japanese didn't like it."

Oppenheimer soon leaves the stage, but not before bringing down the house with his final comment: "My only regret is that we didn't develop the bomb in time to use it against the Germans."

★　★　★

A Gallup poll reports that 85 percent of Americans believe that the use of the atomic bomb is justified. Most of the media also support the decision. Across the country, newspapers trumpet the A-bomb blast in banner headlines. The *New York Times* reports the event with six front-page stories.

The *Times*, however, sounds a rare cautionary note on its editorial page, predicting that the use of the A-bomb will now be justified by other nations in the future.

"Yesterday man unleashed the atom to destroy man, and another chapter in human history opened, a chapter in which the weird, the strange, the horrible becomes the trite and the obvious. We clinched victory in the Pacific, but sowed the whirlwind.

"Americans have become a synonym for destruction. And now we have been the first to introduce a new weapon of unknowable effects which may bring us victory more quickly, but will sow the seeds of hate more widely than ever."*

There are others who display trepidation. Manhattan Project physicist Luis Alvarez, after observing the explosion aboard *The Great Artiste*, begins questioning the bomb's morality. In a letter to his son written on the return flight to Tinian, he ponders what he has just seen: "What regrets I have about being a party to killing and maiming thousands of Japanese civilians this morning are tempered with the hope that this terrible weapon we have created may bring the countries of the world together and prevent future wars."

David Lawrence, the conservative founder of the *United States News*, will pen one of the most damning criticisms of Truman's decision: "We shall not soon purge ourselves of the feeling of guilt which prevails among us. Military necessity will be our constant cry in answer to criticism, but it will never erase from our minds the simple truth that we, of all civilized nations, though hesitating to use poison gas, did not hesitate to

---

*The editorial was written by journalist Hanson Baldwin, military editor of the *New York Times*.

employ the most destructive weapon of all times indiscriminately against men, women and children. What a precedent for the future we have furnished to other nations even less concerned than we with scruples or ideals!"*

⋆ ⋆ ⋆

In Japan, there is simply shock, but no talk of accepting the Potsdam Declaration and surrendering. Instead, as a wave of 385 B-29 bombers attacks four targets in Tokyo with conventional bombs, the military broadcasts a series of defiant radio messages from the capital. The people of Japan are directed to remain calm in the face of American bombings and to renew their pledge to continue the fight.

An August 8 broadcast in English, aimed at North America, accuses the United States of an "atrocity campaign" that will "create the impression that all Japanese are cruel people." And while Japan has ignored the terms of the Geneva Conventions and Hague Conventions throughout the war, it is the United States that the Japanese now accuse of war crimes. "This is made clear by Article 22 of The Hague Convention. Consequently, any attack by such means against open towns and defenseless citizens are unforgivable actions."†

---

*The *United States News* would later become the *U.S. News & World Report*.

† Article 22 of the Hague Convention reads, "The right of belligerents to adopt means of injuring the enemy is not unlimited."

The broadcast asks: "How will the United States war leaders justify their degradation, not only in the eyes of the other peoples but also in the eyes of the American people? How will these righteous-thinking American people feel about the way their war leaders are perpetuating this crime against man and God?

"Will they condone the whole thing on the ground that everything is fair in love and war or will they rise in anger and denounce this blot on the honor and tradition and prestige of the American people?"

In an unusual attempt to win the sympathy of Europeans, a third broadcast is transmitted in French. "As a consequence of the use of the new bomb against the town of Hiroshima on August sixth, most of the town has been completely destroyed and there are numerous dead and wounded among the population.

"The destructive power of these bombs is indescribable, and the cruel sight resulting from the attack is so impressive that one cannot distinguish between men and women killed by the fire. The corpses are too numerous to be counted.

"The destructive power of this new bomb spreads over a large area. People who were outdoors at the time of the explosion were burned alive by high temperatures while those who were indoors were crushed by falling buildings."*

---

*It is difficult to get exact statistics regarding Hiroshima casualties. The transient nature of the military population and the number of civilians evacuated to the country in the days leading up to the bombing skew precise population numbers, but it is esti-

⋆ ⋆ ⋆

The Tokyo broadcasts can be heard quite clearly 1,500 miles away on the island of Tinian, where a B-29 bomber is now loaded with the second atomic weapon, an even more lethal plutonium bomb code-named Fat Man.

American aircrews are gearing up to unleash more hell on what is now a defenseless Japan. In addition, the dictator Joseph Stalin is set to attack Japanese-held territory in Manchuria. The plan for that sneak attack has been kept from Harry Truman and America, as Stalin has rightly assessed Japan's weakness. In just three short days, the world has changed—and it will now be altered even further.

The next A-bomb destination is about to be revealed.

---

mated that Hiroshima's population was 255,000 at the time of the bombing. More than 50,000 people are thought to have died instantly, and another 70,000 were injured. One Japanese study later showed that burns accounted for approximately 60 percent of all deaths, falling buildings and flying debris made up 30 percent, and gamma radiation accounted for 10 percent. By November 1945, three months after the blast, the estimated death toll had climbed to 130,000 due to lingering infection from burns and radiation poisoning. Seven decades later, the residual effects of the atomic bomb—such as cataracts and leukemia and several other forms of cancer—still plague the people of Hiroshima. Statistics at the Hiroshima Peace Memorial Museum put the death toll at 200,000.

23

TOKYO, JAPAN
AUGUST 9, 1945
10:30 A.M.

Emperor Hirohito is morose. He again walks through the elms and pine trees of his extensive garden, knowing the war is lost. He is brooding about the destruction of Hiroshima—he knows it has crushed the spirit of the Japanese people, and now there is even more horrible news: the Soviet Union has invaded Manchuria.*

---

*The Soviet Union's invasion of Manchuria was the last epic battle of the Second World War. While often overlooked, the clash occurred on a scale comparable to the Allied invasion of Normandy on June 6, 1944; 1.5 million Russian soldiers faced off against 713,724 Japanese troops. The Soviets routed the Japanese within a matter of weeks, losing an estimated 12,000 men killed and 24,000 men wounded. Japanese casualties were 22,000 killed and another 20,000 wounded, but just as debilitating was a historical rarity: mass desertion in the ranks. As in so many Russian conquests throughout Europe, rape and looting in Manchuria quickly followed. The joy many Chinese felt upon being liberated from

Although he is protected in a bunker, Hirohito understands that his people are not. The United States has been bombing Japan for months, destroying so many cities that they are running out of targets. Tokyo itself has been hit more than a dozen times. Just last night, the emperor once again heard air-raid sirens throughout his capital city as sixty B-29s bombed a nearby aircraft factory. The Japanese people are weary of war, but they continue to endure it, hoping to save their god-king from shame.

The invasion of Manchuria makes surrender inevitable. Russia and Japan signed a nonaggression pact four years ago, which Stalin has now violated. Hirohito knows the Russians to be an aggressive people, as evidenced by their continued occupation of Eastern Europe three months after the European war. The Soviet entry into the Pacific war makes it possible that the Russians may also attempt to invade Japan. Hirohito's nation has neither the men nor the arms to hold off a two-pronged American and Soviet invasion.

Ignoring the heat, Hirohito continues to ponder the possibility of surrender. But this path is fraught with peril: the Japanese military might not cooperate. Some military and civilian leaders actually welcome the coming invasion for the chance to make a historic last stand against people they consider to be barbarians. "If it came to a final battle on Japanese soil," War Minister Korechika Anami believes, "we could at least for a

_____

their Japanese captors was soon replaced by fear and loathing for the Soviets.

time repulse the enemy, and might thereafter somehow find life out of death."

Even as the emperor absorbs the terrible news about the Soviet attack in Manchuria, the top military and civilian cabinet known as the Supreme Council for the Direction of the War is meeting in the concrete bunker beneath the residence of Prime Minister Kantaro Suzuki to discuss whether or not to accept the Potsdam Declaration and take the first steps toward surrender.

Hirohito knows that surrender to the Americans will require the complete backing of his military. Despite Hirohito's deity and his imperial reign, it is the military that truly holds power in Japan. It has been almost ten years, but Hirohito well remembers the terrible events of 1936, when a military mutiny saw the assassination of several top government officials and the takeover of downtown Tokyo.

A faction loyal to Hirohito was successful in crushing the revolt, but there is no certainty the results will be the same should such a coup happen again.

✶ ✶ ✶

In his Spartan Manila office, General Douglas MacArthur greets the news of the Manchurian invasion with great joy: "I am delighted at the Russian declaration of war against Japan. This will make possible a great pincers movement which cannot fail to end in the destruction of the enemy. In Europe, Russia was on the eastern front, the Allies on the west. Now the allies are on the east and the Russians on the west, but the results will be the same."

Like many other top American military leaders, MacArthur still sees Joseph Stalin as an ally, not an enemy. He has previously told other officers that "we must not invade Japan proper unless the Russian army is previously committed to action in Manchuria," believing that such an invasion would pin down Japanese divisions that might otherwise be shifted to fight against American forces. The general also thinks that Russian occupation of large segments of China and Korea is "inevitable"—not realizing he will one day be called upon to fight the Communist advance in those areas.

It has now been three days since the atomic bomb was dropped. The Japanese have chosen not to surrender, and MacArthur is still hoping to lead the greatest amphibious invasion in the history of the world. To the general's way of thinking, another A-bomb is not needed.

America has *him*.

★   ★   ★

In Hiroshima, the stench of burned flesh and rotting corpses still hangs over the city as citizens search for missing family members. In scenes played over and over again, the living wander into first-aid stations, calling out the names of lost loved ones. They are rarely answered.

The surviving soldiers of the Akatsuki Corps lead relief efforts, distributing rice, using wood to burn dead bodies, and arranging transportation out of the shattered city for the living.

"A light southerly wind blowing across the city wafted to us as an odor suggestive of burning sardines. I wondered what could cause such a smell until somebody, noticing it too, informed me that sanitation teams were cremating the remains of people who had been killed . . . the dead were being burned by the hundreds," one survivor will later remember.

The mayor of Hiroshima at the time of the blast was a teetotaling Christian named Senkichi Awaya. His official residence was in the city's Kakomachi district, well within the blast-zone radius. At the time of the detonation, he was eating breakfast with his son and three-year-old granddaughter; all three were killed instantly. Awaya's wife, the mother of his seven children, survived the bombing, only to die one month later from radiation poisoning.*

The head of Hiroshima's rationing department is a

---

* The radioactivity caused by the fission of uranium most severely affected those within two miles of the blast center, causing vomiting, diarrhea, hair loss, damage to the bone marrow (which affects the body's ability to produce blood), and large bumps on the skin known as keloids. The lack of white blood cells in victims led to sepsis and infection. Delayed effects included the abnormally high mortality rate among fetuses subjected to high levels of radiation and high levels of mental impairment for those in utero who survived birth. The radiation poisoning was caused not just by the initial blast but also by the highly radioactive black rain that began falling twenty minutes later. Even those who visited Hiroshima's hypocenter in the weeks after the explosion were subjected to extremely high levels of radiation and began displaying symptoms. Most victims (90 percent) of radiation poisoning die within the first sixty days after exposure; those who live more than

man named Shinso Hamai, who will one day become mayor himself. Before the bombing, concerned that the people of Hiroshima would not have food in the event of a major disaster, Hamai arranged that rice balls should be delivered to the city. So it is that villagers in the surrounding countryside make rice balls and deliver them to the hungry survivors in Hiroshima.

Within days, the exodus from Hiroshima is complete. More than 150,000 residents travel by military truck or train to temporary shelters. The island of Ninoshima, five miles offshore in Hiroshima Bay and untouched by the A-bomb blast, is a storehouse for medical supplies and becomes the region's biggest relief center, providing comfort to more than ten thousand burn victims. The number of wounded quickly overwhelms the available hospital beds, leading many of the burned and maimed to sleep in stables and other enclosures.

Bacterial infection stemming from the extreme smoke and debris of the blast runs rampant. Teams of doctors perform surgery around the clock, seeing so many patients that there is no time to clean the operating theater between victims; the most common procedure is amputation. The island facility is not actually a hospital but a quarantine center that once housed military men and horses returning from duty in foreign lands. There is no provision for the removal of medical waste, so surgeons dispose of severed limbs by throwing

___

five months are still subject to a higher rate of cancer mortality than the general population.

them out hospital windows. Piles of arms and legs soon rise higher than the level of the window itself.

Yet the amputees are the lucky ones. At least they are alive and can begin planning for a new future; many victims of the blast who come to Ninoshima seeking medical help die within days from their infections and burns. At first, their corpses are stacked one on top of the other for burning. But soon the number of dead bodies is so great that mass cremation becomes impossible. Instead, the dead are carried to air-raid shelters and caves, where they are left to rot. These impromptu burial sites will be excavated decades later, uncovering not just bone fragments and ashes but artifacts like rings and shoes that will help reveal the identities of the dead.

This is the new reality in Hiroshima as Emperor Hirohito walks his gardens. Despite the unprecedented carnage, the god-man continues to dither.

24

Colonel Paul Tibbets still has not seen the awful destruction that he and his men delivered to Hiroshima. Right now that is not his primary concern. Radio contact with *Bockscar*, the aircraft flying the second A-bomb mission over Japan, has ceased; there has been a report that the aircraft and crew are lost at sea. Whether this means they've crash-landed in the Pacific or the new plutonium bomb exploded en route to the target, Tibbets does not know. Fearing the worst, he can only hope that the ominous radio message stating that "*Bockscar* is down" was garbled in transmission.

Even though General Curtis LeMay wanted Tibbets to lead the second atomic bombing mission, Tibbets chose to hand over the job to Major Chuck Sweeney, his close friend. Tibbets wanted Sweeney to have a chance to go down in history. The twenty-five-year-old Bostonian

The nose of Bockscar, *whose dramatic bombing run over Japan would be long overlooked by history*

flew *The Great Artiste* in the Hiroshima mission, witnessing the giant mushroom cloud that rose over the city as the plane's scientific instruments measured radioactivity and blast force. Sweeney seemed an ideal choice to lead the second atomic bombing run over Japan, having served as a squadron commander for four months and flown five simulated A-bomb attack missions. Tibbets also knows him to be a rule follower, a man who will execute his orders precisely as they have been written.

The one flaw in Sweeney's résumé is that he has never before flown in combat.

★   ★   ★

Major Chuck Sweeney and his plane, *Bockscar*, did not crash. Now, Sweeney sees nothing but storm clouds and antiaircraft fire as he flies over Japan, searching for his target.

Three days after dropping the first atomic bomb, America is now just moments away from dropping a second. Ground zero is Kokura, a historic tree-lined city just 130 miles southwest of Hiroshima. It is one of Japan's most heavily defended targets, a hub of steelworks and munitions factories. Many Hiroshima residents who survived the first A-bomb blast have come here seeking refuge.

Sweeney's bomb bay doors are already open. The plutonium weapon known as Fat Man is ready for release. Yet Sweeney's orders forbid him from dropping Fat Man without a clear aerial view of the target, and the thick clouds are making it impossible to see Kokura from the air. The nearby industrial city of Yawata—an area so thick with industrial facilities that it has been called "the Pittsburgh of Japan"—was bombed last night with conventional weapons. Smoke from those still-smoldering fires now drifts over Kokura, mingling with low, gray summer-storm clouds.

Frustrated bombardier Captain Kermit Beahan presses his left eye to the Norden bombsight's viewfinder, straining to see the target. Today is his twenty-seventh birthday. Through the crosshairs, Beahan glimpses a few random buildings but cannot see the large arms factory that is the aiming point for Fat Man.

An increasingly angry Charles Sweeney turns *Bockscar* in a steep bank. Determined to follow orders, he is taking a great risk by flying a second bombing run over the city because there is now determined opposition. Japanese antiaircraft fire explodes all around him as Sweeney flies straight over Kokura, proving to the surprised American crew that the enemy still possesses hidden defenses. Commander Frederick Ashworth, a naval officer who outranks Sweeney and serves as the mission's chief weaponeer, climbs into the cockpit to speak with him. Ultimately, Ashworth has the power to order Sweeney to stop the bombing mission and fly home to Tinian.

Bockscar has a fully armed A-bomb in her belly. She is behind schedule and running out of gas. Everything that can possibly go wrong on this mission has gone wrong.

"Major," tail gunner Sergeant Albert "Pappy" Dehart says over the radio as he watches the antiaircraft explosions coming their way, "flak is closer."

"Roger," Sweeney answers, his voice flat and grim.

Dehart's voice comes over the radio once again, this time high and tight: "Flak right on our tail and coming closer."

"Skipper," barks Staff Sergeant Edward K. Buckley, "Jap Zeros coming up at us. Looks like about ten."

And still Captain Beahan cannot see a thing.

"Let's try it from another angle," Sweeney barks over the intercom, ignoring the approaching fighter planes as he lines up for a third run.

But when Beahan still cannot find the target,

Commander Ashworth effectively takes control of the aircraft, steering it away from Kokura.

"It's Nagasaki," he tells Sweeney, calling out the name of the secondary target. "Radar or visually, but drop we will."

Bockscar's bomb bay doors are immediately closed. The tone warning of the impending bomb drop abruptly ceases. The Japanese Zeros have not yet arrived, and Sweeney pushes *Bockscar* to the limit in order to escape.

The crew, which has grown fearful, cheers: "Nagasaki, here we come."

✭ ✭ ✭

The complications began the day before takeoff, when nuclear engineers assembling Fat Man's firing unit almost detonated the device by inserting a cable into the assembly backward. The problem was fixed, but not before the two engineers spent several nervous hours in the middle of the night sweating fearfully as they switched and resoldered the connectors, terrified all the while that Fat Man would blow them up.

The next problem was fuel. Monsoon conditions over Japan required *Bockscar* to fly at higher altitudes than on a normal bombing run, thus burning more fuel. This problem was compounded just prior to takeoff, during the preflight systems check: the electrical switch designed to shuttle 640 gallons of gasoline from the reserve tank into the main tank was found to be ineffective. If this had been the *Enola Gay*, the mission would have been scrubbed. But severe weather was now forecast for Japan, meaning that the window for dropping the second A-bomb was closing fast. It was either go now or wait a week. The mission had to proceed.

✭ ✭ ✭

And so *Bockscar* took off shortly before two o'clock on the morning of August 9, 1945. Like *Enola Gay*, she used the entire length of Tinian's runway before Sweeney could coax her up into the thick tropical air. This was also the moment when, two thousand miles west, the Soviet Army launched its invasion of Manchuria.

Already exhausted and wanting to be sharp later in the flight, Major Sweeney immediately handed the controls off to his copilot, First Lieutenant Charles Donald Albury, so he could catch a few hours' sleep. The weather was volatile, a mixture of lightning, rain, and winds from the distant monsoon. *Bockscar* fought through the chop as she climbed to nine thousand feet, burning more and more fuel. In the bomb bay, Commander Ashworth and his assistant weaponeer, Lieutenant Philip M. Barnes, removed the bomb's green safety plugs.

Fat Man was armed.

Three hours later, shortly after sunrise, red lights on the weaponeer's control panel began flashing in rapid sequence, indicating that detonation could take place at any second. Terrified, Lieutenant Barnes hurried to alert Ashworth, whom he found asleep in the bomb bay, using Fat Man as a pillow.

"Hey," Barnes said, shaking Ashworth awake, "we got something wrong here. We got a red light going off like the bomb is going to explode right now. Armed. It's armed. Fully armed."

"Oh, my God," exclaimed Ashworth.

The two men told no one. For ten anxious minutes, they analyzed the bomb's blueprints, searching for a clue to the problem. Finally, after removing the outer casing so they could peer into Fat Man's inner workings, the two men realized they had made a mistake while arming the bomb. The solution was simple: they flipped two small switches.

The red light stopped flashing.

Ashworth rested his head on the bomb and went back to sleep.

But that was not the end of *Bockscar*'s problems. The rendezvous with the instrument plane and the photographic plane was supposed to take place at thirty thousand feet at 0900 hours. Sweeney had specific orders from Colonel Tibbets to remain at the rendezvous point for no more than fifteen minutes. *The Great Artiste*, still outfitted with scientific instruments, showed up on time, but the photographic plane was nowhere to be seen.

"Where's Hoppy?" Sweeney demanded, referring to the pilot of the missing B-29. "Where the hell is Hoppy?"

Defying Tibbets's order, Sweeney circled for fifty

long minutes, burning more and more fuel. He wanted this mission to be perfect, just like that of *Enola Gay*. He waited at the rendezvous until he could wait no more.

Finally, just before 10:00 a.m., Sweeney broke off and flew toward Kokura.

Major James I. "Hoppy" Hopkins and the B-29 that will be nicknamed "Big Stink" shortly after the mission were in fact in the area the entire time. But Hopkins was at an incorrect altitude, nine thousand feet above *Bockscar* and *The Great Artiste*.

Growing more concerned by the minute, Hopkins finally disobeyed orders and broke radio silence. "Is *Bockscar* down?" he asked the personnel back on Tinian.

The control tower heard only the words "*Bockscar* down"—leading to Colonel Tibbets's current angst and causing one general to step outside the mess hall and vomit up his breakfast. All ships and planes standing by for rescue operations are now told to stand down, as *Bockscar* is considered lost.

But nobody has told that to *Bockscar*'s crew. They are now on their own.

✦   ✦   ✦

Grasping the steering wheel tightly, Sweeney banks southwest toward Nagasaki, 95 miles away. He turns so severely that *Bockscar* almost collides midair with *The Great Artiste*, which has been following them to record the power of the blast. Sweeney's jitters are compounded by the knowledge that his aircraft only has enough fuel for one bombing run if he hopes to land 450 miles away at Okinawa on his return. Even that is a stretch—he may have to crash-land *Bockscar* in the Pacific after dropping the bomb. The thought is weighing heavily on his mind.

★ ★ ★

Nagasaki is a town of some romance, first visited by Portuguese sailors in the sixteenth century and so beloved by European tourists that it became the setting for Italian composer Giacomo Puccini's opera *Madama Butterfly*. It is also a major port city for the Japanese war effort and home to both the Mitsubishi Steel and Arms Works and the torpedo-producing Mitsubishi-Urakami Ordnance Works.

Sweeney levels off at twenty-eight thousand feet for the bombing run, but Nagasaki is just as covered by clouds as Kokura. Captain Kermit Beahan, *Bockscar*'s bombardier, is prepared to violate orders and use radar to locate the target as Sweeney begins the five-minute bombing run over the city.

"I got it," an excited Beahan suddenly yells, seeing the unmistakable shape of a Nagasaki racetrack through a hole in the clouds. He immediately switches from radar to visual bombardment. *Bockscar*'s airspeed is just two hundred miles per hour.

Within forty-five seconds, Beahan spots the target and drops Fat Man.

"Bombs away," he announces. The black five-ton bomb tumbles out of the bay, destined to explode in forty-three seconds.

Immediately, Sweeney dives *Bockscar* down and banks to the right, racing away from the coming mushroom cloud. *The Great Artiste* follows. The blast force far exceeds that of Little Boy. Five shock waves pound the two planes as they make their escape, a sensation that feels like "being beaten by a telegraph pole" to Sweeney. Within moments, both planes are out over the sea.

"Mayday, Mayday," Sweeney says, breaking radio silence. He is desperately trying to signal any American military craft in the area that the *Bockscar* is in trouble—almost out of fuel. His radio call is heard back in Tinian, reassuring them that the mission has not been aborted and that the men of *Bockscar* are still alive. Yet there is little anyone but Sweeney can do to get *Bockscar* safely to Okinawa; all rescue operations were suspended when it was feared that *Bockscar* had crashed. The flight engineer, Master Sergeant John D. Kuharek, estimates that their three hundred remaining gallons of fuel will leave them fifty miles short.

For more than an hour, Sweeney and the men of *Bockscar* pray. They fly over open ocean, estimating their remaining fuel and knowing all too well that there is no margin for error. Each man dons his "Mae West," the flotation device that will keep the men from drowning in case of a water landing.* Sweeney slows

---

*The Mae West was a personal flotation device worn on the outside of the aircrew uniform. In the event of a forced water landing, the vest could be inflated by blowing into a small tube to provide

the propellers to increase fuel range and lowers his elevation incrementally, allowing gravity to provide airspeed. Many of the men believe they will not make it. *Bockscar*'s navigator, Second Lieutenant Fred Olivi, wonders if the water will be cold.

Okinawa finally comes into view. In the short few weeks since America conquered the island, its runways have become congested and busy; rows of bombers preparing for takeoff line the runway apron. Unable to raise the control tower on the radio, Sweeney orders that emergency flares be fired out of the plane's upper porthole, hoping the runways will be cleared.

They are.

Bockscar lands at 1:51 p.m., traveling so fast that upon initial impact she bounces twenty-five feet into the air. One by one, her engines shut down for lack of fuel. Struggling to control his floundering aircraft, Sweeney just misses a row of B-24 bombers laden with incendiary bombs, which would have killed him and his crew in a massive fiery explosion.

Finally, *Bockscar* comes to a halt. Emergency fire trucks and ambulances race to her assistance. The bomber does not even have enough fuel to taxi off the runway. Incredibly, no one has informed the airfield that *Bockscar* is en route.

"Who the hell are you?" demands base commander

---

buoyancy. Made of highly visible rubber-coated yellow fabric, the Mae West was nicknamed for the buxom film actress because the wearer appeared to assume her physical endowment.

Lieutenant General Jimmy Doolittle, the man whose daring raid on Tokyo in 1942 marked the first American attack on Japanese soil. It is a fitting moment: the first man to bomb Japan in the Second World War is standing toe-to-toe with the man who hopes to be the last.

"We are the 509, *Bockscar*," Sweeney replies. "We dropped an atomic bomb on Nagasaki."

Not having lingered to assess the aftereffects of Fat Man, Sweeney tells Doolittle, "I think we were a little off target."

✳   ✳   ✳

Fat Man is indeed off target, missing the Mitsubishi torpedo plant by almost two miles.

It doesn't matter.

"The pillar of fire became a living thing," *New York Times* journalist William Laurence will write, watching the explosion on board *The Great Artiste*. "A species of being born right before incredulous eyes. It seethed and boiled in white fury like a thousand geysers."*

---

*Laurence was born in 1888 in Lithuania, then emigrated to America in 1905. He graduated from Harvard Law School but chose to pursue a career as a journalist. In September 1940, he wrote an article about the potential of atomic explosion as a means of waging war. Laurence was so prescient in his observations that General Leslie Groves later insisted that anyone who checked the article out of a library be investigated. Thanks to this expertise, the *Times* and the Manhattan Project formed an alliance that would allow Laurence to witness the Trinity explosion and the launch of

*Nagasaki as the mushroom cloud from Fat Man rises up and
out over the city*

On the ground in Nagasaki, an estimated forty-five
thousand men, women, and children die instantly; another sixty thousand are badly injured. There is no
firestorm, as in Hiroshima, because Fat Man detonates in the foothills of the steep, wooded folds of the
Urakami Valley, thus preventing the blast from ex-
panding outward. However, the traumatic flash burns
and the carbonization of the dead and dying are no
less intense.

Once again, thousands are crushed in the rubble of
their own homes and businesses. The unique construc-

---

the *Enola Gay* from Tinian, and ultimately to fly over Nagasaki as
an observer on the second atomic bombing run.

tion of Nagasaki's bomb shelters, which are mostly caves dug into the hillsides, turns the stone passageways into ovens that burn hundreds alive in an instant. Throughout the city, many of the burned walk for miles before collapsing and dying. Still others suffer not just from burns but also from vomiting and bloody diarrhea, which kill them within a week of Fat Man's detonation. Thousands of victims watch their skin grow yellow; they are doomed to die weeks and months later from radiation poisoning. The city of Nagasaki, having no place to bury all the bodies, establishes open-air crematoriums to burn the dead.

In one haunting incident, a young boy no more than ten years old approaches the operators of a crematorium. He carries his infant brother in a small pack on his back. Head lolling peacefully to one side, the infant appears to be sleeping.

He carefully removes his backpack and hands his brother to the men working the flames, who see that the baby is dead. As the infant is placed on coals to be cremated, his older brother stands at rigid attention like a soldier and watches, fighting off tears by biting his lip so hard that a trickle of blood soon runs off the corner of his mouth.

Only when he is certain that his baby brother has received a proper cremation does the young boy turn and leave.

"The general impression, which transcends those derived from our physical senses, is one of deadness, the absolute essence of death in the sense of finality without hope for resurrection," one eyewitness to the destruction will write.

"It's everywhere, and nothing has escaped its touch."*

---

* Nagasaki's population at the time of the attack was estimated to be more than 200,000. Eight weeks after the blast, the total number of dead stood at 140,000. One hundred sixty-five individuals were "double survivors"—*nijyuu hibakusha*, or "twice bombed person"—having been present in both Hiroshima and Nagasaki at the time of their bombing. In addition to Japanese citizens, some 20,000 Korean slave laborers were killed in Hiroshima and an estimated 2,000 more in Nagasaki. The *hibakusha* (those men and women who survived the atomic bombs) and their relatives are still discriminated against in Japan, as many believe that radiation sickness is hereditary and possibly contagious.

25

———— • ————

THE WHITE HOUSE
WASHINGTON, DC
AUGUST 9, 1945
10:46 A.M.

A vicious wave of heat and humidity envelops the nation's capital as President Harry Truman meets for ninety minutes in the Oval Office with his select team of atomic weapons advisers.* News of the successful Nagasaki mission reached the White House overnight, and as foul summer storms lash Japan, delaying further bombing for the near future, Truman must decide whether, once the weather clears, the United States should drop a third atomic bomb. Target: Tokyo.

Truman does not wish to obliterate the Japanese; he wants them to surrender. Early reports show heavy

---

*Those present at the meeting were Secretary of War Henry L. Stimson, scientists Vannevar Bush and James B. Conant, Special Assistant to Secretary of War George L. Harrison, and Manhattan Project supervisor Major General Leslie Groves.

civilian casualties in Nagasaki, just as in Hiroshima. Yet the Japanese military seems willing to endure such horrific losses.

"For myself, I certainly regret the necessity of wiping out whole populations because of the 'pigheadedness' of the leaders of a nation," Truman will write to his friend, Georgia's Democratic senator Richard Russell. "My object is to save as many American lives as possible but I also have a humane feeling for the women and children in Japan."

Truman is expressing his sympathy, not reversing his position. He is as adamant as ever that he will do what it takes to defeat the Japanese.

The president makes this abundantly clear to Samuel McCrea Cavert of the Federal Council of Churches of Christ in America, who has demanded that the president justify the dropping of atomic bombs.

A telegram from Cavert to the president reads, "Their use sets extremely dangerous precedent for future of mankind." The cable goes on to urge that "ample opportunity be given Japan to reconsider her ultimatum before any further devastation by atomic bomb is visited upon her people." Cavert's message angers Truman; the clergyman actually threatens the president by saying his group will soon make a public statement condemning the bomb.

But Truman will not be cowed. He would not normally respond to such a threat, particularly at a time when he is immersed in the high-stakes decisions of warcraft. But the president is a man who loves a good game of poker.* This is not a time for bluffing. Truman dictates a direct response.

"Nobody is more disturbed over the use of Atomic bombs than I am but I was greatly disturbed over the unwarranted attack by the Japanese on Pearl Harbor and the murder of our prisoners of war," Truman writes.

"The only language they seem to understand is the one we have been using to bombard them. When you have to deal with a beast you have to treat him as a beast. It is most regrettable but nevertheless true."

✳   ✳   ✳

In Tokyo, the leader of the beast, Emperor Hirohito, rises to speak in his underground bunker. It is 2:00 a.m., and Hirohito wears a full-dress military uniform. The weariness of yet another day and night of ruination is etched upon his face. Witnesses to this moment will remember the emperor being disheveled, his face flushed, his hair unkempt.

The emperor has entertained the Supreme Council

---

*The sign bearing Truman's famous motto, "The Buck Stops Here," was not given to the president until October 2, 1945, and so would not have been on his desk during World War II. The reverse side of that sign, seen only by Truman, featured the words "I'm from Missouri." The phrase "the buck stops here" derives from poker as played on the American frontier: a buckhorn knife was passed around the table from player to player depending upon whose turn it was to deal. If a player chose not to take his turn as dealer, he could "pass the buck."

for the Direction of the War and their assorted secretaries and assistants in the underground conference room for almost three hours. The thick wooden door is closed and the air-conditioning is not working, causing every man to sweat from the extreme humidity in the chamber that is no bigger than a large bedroom. Even the lacquered wall panels bead with perspiration.

The subject of this midnight meeting is unconditional surrender. It is the continuation of a long day of high-level war discussions, following close on the heels of the Soviet invasion and the Nagasaki bombing. Every man is exhausted. Each individual in this room has a personal stake in the discussion, for not only would surrender mean the end of the Japanese empire but, just yesterday, the United States and England formalized a treaty stipulating the proper punishment of war criminals. The first men to be tried will be the Nazis; their trials will convene in the German city of Nuremberg starting this November.

If they surrender, the men in this overheated room will be next—and they know it.

-All associated with the war realize they will most likely be tried and found guilty, even the emperor. Prime Minister Kantaro Suzuki, War Minister Korechika Anami, Navy Minister Mitsumasa Yonai, Foreign Minister Shigenori Togo, Navy Chief of Staff Teijiro Toyoda, and Chief of the Army General Staff Yoshijiro Umezu recognize that whether they committed atrocities or not doesn't matter—they directed the soldiers and sailors who did.

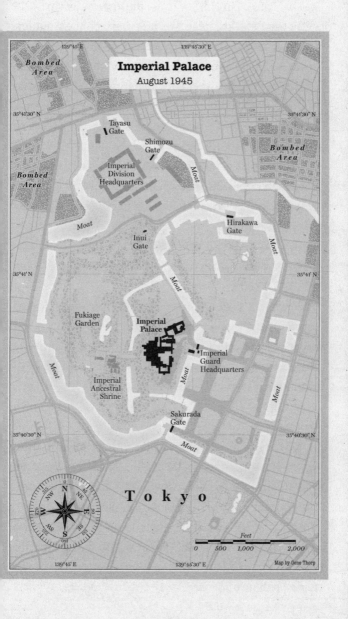

Imperial Palace
August 1945

Bombed Area

139°45' E

139°45'30" E

35°41'30" N

Tayasu Gate

Shimozu Gate

Imperial Division Headquarters

Bombed Area

Bombed Area

Moat

Moat

Inui Gate

Hirakawa Gate

Moat

35°41' N

Moat

Fukiage Garden

Imperial Palace

Imperial Guard Headquarters

Moat

Imperial Ancestral Shrine

Moat

Sakurada Gate

35°40'30" N

Moat

T o k y o

139°45' E

139°45'30" E

Feet

0   500   1,000   2,000

Map by Gene Thorp

Of course, Hirohito was the ultimate authority.

Throughout the war, the members of the Supreme Council chortled with delight as a dozen English-speaking Japanese women—among them American citizen Iva Ikuko Toguri, a twenty-nine-year-old Los Angeles native stranded in Japan when the war began—broadcast taunting propaganda attacks to American soldiers and sailors. These women, collectively known as "Tokyo Rose," told lonely Americans throughout the Pacific that their girlfriends back home were sleeping with other men, among hundreds of other lies designed to sap morale.

But radio broadcasts that many Americans dismissed as laughable are the least of the Supreme Council's indiscretions.

The men in this bunker handed over power to the ruthless Hideki Tojo, the psychopathic architect of the Japanese war effort who had served as prime minister from October 1941 until July 1944. It was the unassuming but manipulative Tojo who convinced Hirohito that war was necessary "to establish a new, stable order in East Asia."

Tojo, viewed worldwide as the Hitler of Japan, oversaw the surprise attacks throughout the Pacific that began this brutal war—a conflict that has now claimed twenty-four million lives in the Pacific and Asia alone. And it was Tojo who not only started the war but also authorized the inhumane policies that will define the Japanese war effort far longer than any moment of strategic brilliance.

But the men in this bunker allowed it all to happen.*

* * *

Soon the rest of the world will discover that the Japanese leadership not only brutalizes captured soldiers but has also sanctioned the use of women in conquered territories as prostitutes for the gratification of Japanese troops. These innocent civilians are forced into sexual slavery and have become known as comfort women. Some two hundred thousand of these victims have been abducted or sold to brothels favored by Japanese troops. The penalty for becoming pregnant is often death or disembowelment, for fear of diluting the purity of the Japanese race with the blood of a mixed-race child.

---

*Planning for the Pearl Harbor attack was already under way when General Hideki Tojo became Japan's prime minister in 1940, but it was Tojo who ultimately led the country into war. In addition to advocating the abuse and even death of prisoners of war, Tojo instituted new pro-military curricula for Japanese schools, ordered the sterilization of individuals deemed to be mentally incompetent, and aggressively pursued the war effort on several fronts at the same time—fighting the Chinese in China, the British and Australians in Burma and on the Malay Peninsula, and the Americans throughout the western Pacific. He was extraordinarily popular in the early days of the war, but as the tide turned and US forces began creeping ever closer to Japan, it was Tojo who bore the brunt of the criticism. The fall of Saipan in June 1944 put American bombers in range of Tokyo for the first time, forcing Tojo to resign.

The Japanese military carefully regulates the "comfort stations" in which these women are forced to work, controlling security to make sure the victims do not escape and regularly checking them for sexually transmitted diseases. The practice began after the invasion of China and continued to other nations as Japan took control of the Pacific. Women from Taiwan, the Philippines, Korea, Indonesia, Burma, and Holland have been taken captive and repeatedly raped by Japanese soldiers.

"Sometimes twelve soldiers would force me to have sex with them and then they would allow me to rest for a while, then about twelve soldiers would have sex with me again," a Filipino woman will recount almost fifty years later. "You cannot say no as they will definitely kill you. During the mornings, you have a guard. You are free to roam around the garrison, but you cannot get out."

The ratio of soldiers to comfort women could range as high as 150 to 1, depending upon the region. The Japanese war leadership actually incorporated forced prostitution into its war plan, believing that it elevated troop morale.

"When the soldiers came back from the battlefields, as many as twenty men would come to my room from early morning," another comfort woman will one day recount. "They rounded up little girls still in school. Their genitals were still underdeveloped, so they became torn and infected. There was no medicine except something to prevent sexually transmitted diseases and Mercurochrome. They got sick, their sores became septic, but there was no treatment."

Not all the "comfort stations" are buildings.

"The soldiers made Chinese laborers lay straw in the trenches and the girls were put in there," one woman will remember. "There was no bedding . . . underneath was earth. There was no electricity at that time, only oil lamps, but they weren't even given a lamp. They cried in the dark, 'Mummy, it hurts!'"

★   ★   ★

The leaders of Japan also know they have honored soldiers who beheaded, set ablaze, enslaved, and even cannibalized prisoners of war. The majority of the estimated 150,000 American, British, and Dutch citizens held as slave labor in Japanese POW camps are denied food, medical treatment, and clothing and are subjected to squalid living conditions. Escape is all but impossible.

In the jungle, the POWs sleep in hundred-man bamboo barracks with mud floors that are often covered with excrement as a result of the high dysentery rate. Officers and enlisted men alike quickly learn that the Japanese do not honor the Geneva Conventions. POWs are slaves; they work in coal mines, factories, and shipyards and on tropical plantations. More than 12,000 American, British, and Dutch prisoners and 150,000 civilian slaves have died of exhaustion and disease while constructing the Burma-Siam Railway alone.*

---

*This stretch of train tracks was also known as the "Death Railway" for the many POWs and civilian laborers who died during its

Prime Minister Tojo went so far as to issue a mandate that all POWs were expendable and even instituted a "Kill All the Prisoners" policy.

One document obtained by the US government puts this mandate in specific terms: "Whether they are destroyed individually or in groups, or however it is done, with mass bombing, poisonous smoke, poisons, drowning, decapitation, or what, dispose of the prisoners as the situation dictates. In any case it is the aim not to allow the escape of a single one, to annihilate them all, and not to leave any traces."

In one infamous massacre, the Japanese attempt to slaughter 150 Americans in a prisoner-of-war camp on the island of Palawan rather than let them be rescued by advancing Allied troops. While the Americans take refuge in an air-raid shelter, their captors fill the shelter with gasoline and set it on fire. Prisoners attempting to escape from the bunker are mowed down by machine-gun fire. Nevertheless, though 139 men die, 11 lucky men live to tell the tale.

Of the estimated 27,465 Americans held in POW camps, more than 11,000 will die. By stark comparison,

---

construction, which began in October 1942 and lasted a year. The 250-mile length of track ran from Ban Pong, Thailand, to Thanbyuzayat, Burma. Allied forces successfully bombed the railway's pivotal bridge, destroying three sections; this span became legendary in 1957 with the release of the movie *The Bridge on the River Kwai*, starring Alec Guinness and William Holden. Loosely based on actual events, it has long been considered one of the great motion pictures of all time. *The Bridge on the River Kwai* went on to win seven Academy Awards, including Best Picture.

of the 93,941 Americans taken captive by the Germans, 92,820 survived the war.*

✫   ✫   ✫

Hirohito himself approved one of the war's most heinous depredations, Unit 731. This medical group performed tests on human subjects in the name of pathological research, amputating arms and legs without anesthetic, replacing blood with antifreeze, splitting a man's body down the middle from top to bottom and then pickling him in a six-foot-tall glass jar of formaldehyde, and injecting diseases such as bubonic plague and cholera into healthy human beings.

It was through Unit 731 that many Japanese battlefield doctors prepared for war—alive and conscious victims were shot with a rifle or machine gun, then surgeons operated on their wounds without anesthetic to rehearse emergency battlefield procedures. Thousands

---

* There are various figures pertaining to the number of American prisoners of war in Japanese hands. This reputable statistic is provided by the National WWII Museum in New Orleans. It should be noted that the Japanese maintained roughly five hundred POW camps in Asia, stretching from Burma all the way across the Pacific to the Philippines. The first prisoner captured by the Japanese was a British pilot, Flight Lieutenant William Bowden, captured on December 8, 1941, after crashing in the Gulf of Siam. He survived the war. The last POW to be captured was another Royal Air Force pilot, Sublieutenant Fred Hockley, shot down over Japan nine hours after Japan surrendered. He was executed. The officers responsible were tried for war crimes in 1947, found guilty, and hanged.

of non-Japanese Asian citizens and Allied prisoners of war were murdered as a result of Unit 731 procedures.

Even as the war has turned against Japan, the atrocities have continued. On May 5, 1945, an American B-29 crashed on the island of Kyushu. The pilot was taken away for interrogation while ten members of the crew were bundled off to a secret laboratory in the city of Fukuoka and subjected to the amputations and vivisections endured by Unit 731's other human guinea pigs.

Each man died a grisly death.

All approved by the divine emperor.*

☆   ☆   ☆

Hirohito is at last ready to offer his opinion to the Supreme Council. Every man in the room rises and bows to his ruler. As they take their seats, the emperor is momentarily overcome by what he is about to say. But he gathers himself and proceeds. "Thinking about the world situation and the internal Japanese situation . . .

---

* Many of Unit 731's barbaric medical procedures were committed against the Chinese, but a medical research facility was also maintained in Tokyo. Excavation of the remains of those buried outside the facility did not begin until 2011, thanks to the Japanese government's ongoing denial that the war crimes of Unit 731 ever took place. The United States is complicit in this silence, having granted Unit 731 commander General Shiro Ishii and many of his subordinates immunity from prosecution in exchange for the data harvested from their experiments on human subjects. This agreement was personally approved by General Douglas MacArthur.

to continue the war now means that cruelty and bloodshed will still continue in the world and that the Japanese nation will suffer severe damage."

The emperor's voice is high. He speaks in staccato sentences with rounded vowels. His quiet words come from a man not known for graceful speech. As Hirohito's emotions get the best of him, he begins to cry. Many in the room are also overcome; they hurl themselves forward onto their communal tables and begin to sob.

Hirohito continues: "When I think about my obedient soldiers abroad, and of those who died or were wounded in battle, about those who have lost their property or lives by bombing in the homeland—when I think of all those sacrifices I cannot help but feel sad.

"I cannot stand the disarming of loyal and gallant troops and punishment of those responsible for war . . .

"It is now necessary to bear the unbearable."*

★　★　★

It is 6:30 a.m. on August 10 when President Truman receives the Japanese surrender letter in his private quarters at the White House. In the absence of a Japanese embassy in Washington, which has not existed since the attack on Pearl Harbor, Hirohito has sent the

---

*Hirohito's speech was transcribed by Prime Minister Suzuki's chief cabinet secretary, Sakomizu Hisatsune, who knew in advance that the emperor would speak.

communiqué to the embassy of neutral Switzerland, which then passed it on to the War Department.

"In obedience to the gracious command of His Majesty the Emperor," the document begins, "the Japanese Government are [*sic*] ready to accept the terms enumerated in the joint declaration which was issued at Potsdam on July 26th, 1945, by the heads of the Governments of the United States, Great Britain, and China, and later subscribed to by the Soviet Government."

Thus far, there is nothing in the language to deflate Truman's hopes for an unconditional surrender. This unlikely man who was nominated for the vice presidency just one year ago and who assumed the mantle of president of the United States at a most pivotal moment in world history is just a few sentences away from ending the Second World War. The German surrender in May was inevitable; the Japanese situation has been much more tricky and has required Truman to show diplomatic steel to match America's military might. He has made many difficult decisions, doing so with poise and focus. The slip of paper he now holds in his hand is the culmination of four agonizing months in office. Yet he reads on with trepidation, making sure that the entire document is in accord with the surrender terms put forth by the United States.

It is not. The Japanese are attaching one vital condition to their surrender: "the understanding that the said declaration does not comprise any demand which prejudices the prerogatives of His Majesty as a Sovereign Ruler."

Truman has been expecting this, and a small part of him may be willing to let Hirohito stay on the throne. Secretary of War Stimson has long argued that this is necessary to restore order in a postwar Japan. Certainly, General Douglas MacArthur has also made his conviction on this subject known.

But Truman is unsure: "Could we even consider a message with so large a 'but' as the kind of unconditional surrender we had fought for?" he will later write. It is a question that weighs heavily upon him.

The president is due to meet with his cabinet at 2:00 p.m. on this Friday, but he hastily convenes a more discreet meeting to discuss the Japanese terms. In attendance are Stimson, Secretary of State Byrnes, Secretary of the Navy James Forrestal, and Admiral

President Truman informs reporters of Japan's surrender from his desk in the Oval Office.

William Leahy, chief of staff to the commander in chief of the army and navy.

The room splits. Byrnes favors pushing for unconditional surrender; Stimson still maintains that the emperor is vital to Japan's postwar rehabilitation. Truman, who has already decided that no further atomic bombs will be dropped without his specific orders, listens patiently to both sides. It is Forrestal who suggests there might be a loophole in the Potsdam terms that would allow the acceptance of Japan's surrender offer.

So it is that Truman orders that Japan be sent a counteroffer: Hirohito can remain, but he will not have immunity from war crimes prosecution.

"Ate lunch at my desk and discussed the Jap offer to surrender," Truman writes in his journal that night. "They wanted to make a condition precedent to the surrender. Our terms are 'unconditional.' They wanted to keep the Emperor. We told 'em we'd tell 'em how to keep him, but we'd make the terms."

The message is cabled to Switzerland, then on to Tokyo.

It reads: "With regard to the Japanese Government's message accepting the terms of the Potsdam proclamation but containing the statement, 'with the understanding that the said declaration does not comprise any demand which prejudices the prerogatives of His Majesty as a sovereign ruler,' our position is as follows:

"From the moment of surrender the authority of the Emperor and the Japanese Government to rule the state shall be subject to the Supreme Commander of the Allied powers who will take such steps as he deems proper to effectuate the surrender terms."

One day passes without word from the Japanese. Then another.

And still another.

Truman seethes.

26

The Imperial Japanese Army is cornered. Six hundred miles from Tokyo, in the low, forested hills above this provincial Chinese crossroads, the Fifth Army has assumed a defensive position for a last stand against the invading Soviet army. Odds are overwhelmingly in favor of the Russians: 290,000 soldiers to 60,000 for the Japanese. The Soviets possess four thousand artillery pieces and rocket launchers, the IJA just slightly more than one hundred. A thousand Soviet Tiger tanks and Sherman tanks "on loan" from the Americans face absolutely no armor on the Japanese side.*

Making matters worse for the Japanese, their troops

---

* Despite President Truman's discontinuation of the Lend-Lease assistance to the Soviet Union, the Soviets asked for, and received, five hundred Sherman tanks, almost a million tons of dry goods, and more than two hundred thousand tons of fuel. All this for the

are on the verge of starvation; many are armed only with bayonets (often fashioned from pieces of scrap metal) because ammunition is scarce. The situation is so dire that the Japanese cannot even escape because of an absence of mechanized vehicles.

Fifteen hundred miles to the west, Soviet forces are also racing across the searing heat of Mongolia's desert even as the center of the Russian advance travels through the rugged mile-high Greater Khingan mountain range. It is here, in eastern Manchuria, where victory will allow the Soviets unchallenged access to the Sea of Japan for their proposed invasion of the island nation.

Thus far, the Russian troops have been unstoppable. They are a combination of callow young recruits and hardened veterans of the war against Germany—robust men who looted Berlin just three months ago. The new soldiers, most of whom endured garrison duty in eastern Russia, are bone thin because nutritious food is scarce. Many of these "easterners" lack proper clothing and boots, instead wrapping their feet in fabric.

It doesn't matter. The Russian army has opened a twenty-mile-wide front, pushing the Japanese forces ten miles back. The Soviets have used a relentless ground attack and unchallenged aerial bombardment to destroy the enemy; Russian paratroop forces are dropped far behind Japanese lines, successfully securing vital bridges and train tunnels. These attacks are

---

Manchurian invasion about which the United States was largely kept uninformed.

accomplished with all possible stealth—some Japanese sentries have their throats slit without even realizing what is happening.

As usual, Russian troops leave behind scenes of gross violence.

The nauseating stench of war envelops the Chinese countryside. Craters pock the earth where Russian pilots have bombed and strafed the outmatched Imperial Japanese Army. The bloated corpses of the dead litter the forests and swamps of eastern Manchuria, their personal photographs and letters floating away on the wind, the smell of their rotting bodies mingling with that of their dead horses.

The Soviet goal is to advance into China from three different directions, meeting up in Manchuria's capital city of Changchun—or Hsinking, meaning "new capital," as the Japanese have renamed it. This is the home of China's last living emperor, a foppish thirty-nine-year-old with a bizarre fascination for England's King Henry VIII. When the Japanese conquered parts of China, they installed Emperor Pu Yi as a puppet ruler. It is Joseph Stalin's intention to install a puppet of his own.*

---

*Pu Yi ascended to the Chinese throne at the age of two, only to endure a tumultuous time of change that saw him gain and lose his title several times over the course of his life. This man who knew a life of luxury in his youth, with concubines and forty-course dinners, eventually lost power altogether and died in Beijing at the age of sixty-one while working as a gardener. His life story was the subject of the 1987 Bernardo Bertolucci film *The Last Emperor*, which won nine Academy Awards.

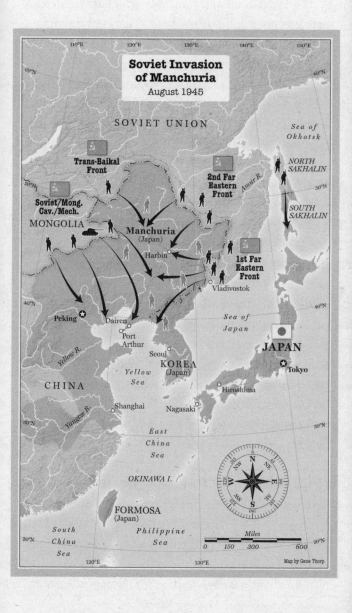

Soviet Invasion of Manchuria
August 1945

SOVIET UNION

Sea of Okhotsk

Trans-Baikal Front

2nd Far Eastern Front

Amur R.

NORTH SAKHALIN

SOUTH SAKHALIN

Soviet/Mong. Cav./Mech.

MONGOLIA

Manchuria (Japan)

Harbin

1st Far Eastern Front

Vladivostok

Peking

Dairen

Port Arthur

Seoul

Yellow R.

KOREA (Japan)

Sea of Japan

JAPAN

Tokyo

CHINA

Yellow Sea

Hiroshima

Shanghai

Nagasaki

Yangtze R.

East China Sea

OKINAWA I.

FORMOSA (Japan)

South China Sea

Philippine Sea

Miles

0   150   300   600

Map by Gene Thorp

The Soviet commander, Marshal Kirill Merets-kov, is enjoying his finest hour. The Russian victory in Manchuria will earn Meretskov the Soviet Union's highest World War II military honor, the Order of Victory. The burly, fish-eyed general led the defeat of the German army at Leningrad, a years-long siege that ended on January 27, 1944. This was an incredible turn of events, because just a little more than two years earlier Meretskov had been imprisoned and tortured by Joseph Stalin, who thought him disloyal.

Now all is forgiven.

The all-important transportation hub of Mutanchiang is now within Soviet reach. Pre-invasion planning projected the Russians might reach the city in seventeen days; Meretskov has done it in four. Heavy rains now drench eastern Manchuria, but even the strongest of downpours will not stop the Russian army.

As an indication of what is to come, Soviet tanks obliterated a thirty-car Japanese relief troop train just this morning. Nine hundred reinforcement soldiers now lie dead in the dirt.

The last great battle of World War II is under way.

★   ★   ★

Half a world away in Washington, DC, President Harry Truman is tired of waiting. His surrender counteroffer was cabled to the Japanese the evening of Friday, August 10, but the weekend has come and gone without a Japanese response.

"We are all on edge waiting for the Japs to answer,"

Truman writes in his journal on Saturday, August 11. "Have had a hell of a day."

Sunday, August 12, is no better. Starting early on his typical day of rest, the president dons a suit and prepares to conduct official business. "9 a.m.," Truman's scheduler will write in the official calendar. "Came to Executive Office to await word on Japanese surrender."

Yet nothing happens.

On Monday, August 13, the president starts work in the Oval Office again at 9:00 a.m. Sensing that the Japanese will not accept his counteroffer, he authorizes the resumption of B-29 bombing raids utilizing conventional and incendiary bombs. Truman also spends the afternoon with Lieutenant General Richard Sutherland, chief of staff for General Douglas MacArthur. The topic of discussion is the upcoming invasion of Japan. But there is another item Truman wishes to discuss with the fifty-one-year-old Sutherland, having to do with a secret plan the president has concocted to have Douglas MacArthur oversee the postwar rebuilding of Japan.

Meanwhile, as they have for almost a week, exhausted reporters and photographers crowd into the White House press briefing room, awaiting surrender news. If and when Truman makes an announcement, the journalistic horde will race to the Oval Office to shout questions, per custom.

Outside, on the streets of Washington, rumors of an impending surrender are the talk of the day. In Lafayette Square, just across the street from the White House, citizens hold a vigil, longing to be at the epicenter of events when news of the Japanese capitulation is finally announced.

And still, there is nothing but silence from Japan.

Tuesday, August 14, is more of the same.

August is normally a time when the government goes on holiday to avoid the heat of Washington, but Truman obviously cannot leave. Were he not waiting for World War II to end, Harry S. Truman might be enjoying this summer day in a much cooler location.*

Truman's outward behavior is calm. Reporters comment on his "cool stride" and "matter-of-factness."

Outside the White House, the crowd in Lafayette Square has now swelled to ten thousand. The press is still on round-the-clock standby, afraid of leaving the White House for even an instant.

★   ★   ★

Seven thousand miles away in Manchuria, the Imperial Japanese Army and the Soviets are in the midst of a fierce firefight for a place known as Ssutaoling Hill. Strong Japanese resistance has stopped Russian tanks from reaching the summit, so they have regrouped

---

* After a devastating electrical fire on Christmas Eve, 1929, which severely damaged the West Wing, President Herbert Hoover ordered that air-conditioning be installed in the West Wing and in the White House living quarters. Two years earlier, the Carrier Corporation had installed air-conditioning in the House of Representatives. These simple technological additions changed the way business was done in the nation's capital, which had previously emptied out in August due to extreme heat and humidity.

on the slopes and begun a four-hour "concentration of fire" to obliterate the enemy stronghold. The Japanese respond with direct fire and one-man suicide attacks, destroying twenty-one Russian tanks. The battle, however, is soon lost. In the morning, Japanese forces will retreat after five ferocious days of combat, leaving behind only those fanatics who wish to fight to the death.*

⭐　⭐　⭐

In Tokyo, hundreds of thousands of leaflets fall into the streets, dropped by American B-29 bombers. They tell the Japanese people that resistance is no longer realistic.

Hours later, prompted by the ongoing silence of the Japanese leadership, another massive flight of 821 B-29s thunders unopposed over Tokyo—only this time, their payload is not paper. In an act of redundancy, the Twentieth Air Force bombs what has already been bombed and obliterates what has already

---

* The Soviet Union remained in Manchuria after the war to bolster the spread of global communism, using the region as a base of operations for Chinese revolutionary Mao Tse-tung. The Soviets began to withdraw in 1946. Mao's ultimate triumph in the Chinese Civil War of 1946–1950 would have been a triumph for Stalin were it not for the fact that Mao's popularity and control of China soon rendered him strong enough to oust the Soviets. The Russians eventually dismantled entire factories and relocated them to the Soviet Union. That which they could not transport they simply destroyed, not wishing China to become a stronger commercial nation.

been obliterated in a massive show of force that is immediately nicknamed "The Big Finale."

By 1:00 p.m. on the afternoon of Tuesday, August 14, as the people of Washington wait eagerly for the war's end, the city of Tokyo blazes once more.

★ ★ ★

Emperor Hirohito does not see the flames. He is cowering in his dank underground bunker, still clad in full-dress military uniform. But outside his Imperial Palace, rebellious junior officers of the Imperial Japanese Army are revolting. Their aim is to prevent the surrender of Japan by overthrowing Hirohito. But it is already too late.

Just three hours ago, Hirohito's agreement to the American terms of surrender was transmitted to the neutral governments of Sweden and Switzerland. They were instructed to forward news of the acceptance to the leaders of the United States, Great Britain, China, and the Soviet Union. Then, in an act unparalleled in the history of Japan, the emperor met with technicians from NHK, Japan's public radio network, who recorded him reading the letter of surrender. Two phonographic records of this speech are now hidden within his wife's personal safe in the Imperial Palace.*

The treasonous junior officers are led by Major Kenji Hatanaka and Lieutenant Colonel Jiro Shiizaki. They have controlled portions of the vast palace

---

*Nippon Hōçsōç Kyōçkai translates to Japan Broadcasting Corporation.

grounds since 4:00 p.m. yesterday. They have shot dead Lieutenant General Takeshi Mori, the commander of the palace guards, for his refusal to join the revolt.

Utilizing Mori's personal stamp, the two men created a false set of orders to fool seven Imperial Guard regiments, whose job it is to protect the emperor. The forged orders are designed to convince them to join the revolt. Soon, all communications between the Imperial Palace and the outside world are severed. Now Hatanaka and Shiizaki begin the process of searching the grounds for two precious targets: the emperor himself and the recordings of his surrender speech. The Imperial Palace and its gardens sprawl across a swath of central Tokyo a mile wide; there are countless places the emperor could be hiding. Hatanaka and Shiizaki are relentless. Though they haven't found what they're looking for, they have succeeded in disarming the palace police and have detained and interrogated eighteen staff members who, incredibly, do not tell the rebel officers where Hirohito is hiding.

Suddenly, there is darkness. The American bombings have cut off all power in Tokyo, and Hirohito's underground hideaway grows even more terrifying. He knows that leaving the utter blackness to venture out of the bunker could cost him his life. So he continues to cower.

Hirohito is completely severed from the world. The Imperial Palace's great stone walls, a haven for so long, have now become a prison. For the first time in his entire life, there is no one to pamper him, pander to him, or protect him. Like the Japanese soldiers who died in island caves across the Pacific, Hirohito can only hide and wait in his stone fortress, unsure if he will live to see the morning.

At 3:00 a.m., forces loyal to the emperor storm the palace. Officers Hatanaka and Shiizaki flee into the night, having never found Hirohito or the recordings. Within hours they will take their own lives rather than face the consequences of their actions.

At 7:21 a.m., less than fifteen minutes after Harry Truman has received the message of Japanese surrender in Washington, DC, the NHK radio network broadcasts a special message: the emperor will speak directly to his people at noon.

* * *

Harry Truman has just refreshed himself with a short swim in the White House pool. The time is shortly before 7:00 p.m. on Tuesday, August 14. The Oval Office is thirty-six feet long and twenty-nine feet wide, and every square inch is taken up by a scrum of journalists, klieg lights, and newsreel cameras.

Wearing a navy blue double-breasted suit and blue shirt, the president stands at his desk to alert the world: "I have received this afternoon, a message from the Japanese government," Truman begins, holding a copy of his speech in his right hand, "a full acceptance of the Potsdam Declaration which specifies the unconditional surrender of Japan."

Outside the White House, almost a half million Americans begin a massive street party in Washington. "This capital city . . . relaxed its worn nerves and celebrated the winning of the war with a screaming, drinking, paper-tearing, free-kissing demonstration which combined all the features of New Year's and Mardi Gras," *Yank* magazine will report.

Truman himself, accompanied by his wife, Bess, steps outside onto the White House lawn. "We want Truman," the crowds lining the black wrought-iron fence chant. "We want Truman."

The president responds by holding up the two-fingered V-for-Victory sign.

At long last, World War II is over.

✳　✳　✳

In Japan, a time of national mourning has begun. At noon on August 15, as Washington celebrates, Emperor Hirohito's radio address is broadcast to cities, hamlets, and villages throughout the country. Japanese soldiers abroad also hear the message via shortwave radio. The people have never before heard the emperor's voice, so they react with a mixture of curiosity and shock. They are confused, because the poor recording quality and the emperor's use of an archaic form of the Japanese language make him hard to understand. But eventually the message becomes clear.

"To our good and loyal subjects," the emperor starts in his high-pitched voice. "After pondering deeply the general trends of the world and the actual conditions obtaining in Our Empire today, we have decided to effect a settlement of the present situation by resorting to an extraordinary measure. . . .

"The war has lasted for nearly four years. Despite

the best that has been done by everyone—the gallant fighting of the military and naval forces, the diligence and assiduity of our servants of the State, and the devoted service of our one hundred million people—the war situation has developed not necessarily to Japan's advantage, while the general trends of the world have all turned against her interest."

Hirohito does not use the word "surrender." He merely states that his subjects must now "pave the way for a grand peace for all the generations to come by enduring the [unavoidable] and suffering what is unsufferable." To many, that is actually an enormous relief; their fathers, husbands, and sons might finally return home from the fighting. But other Japanese citizens are shamed and angry. Hirohito wraps up his address with words the Japanese never thought they would hear.

"Unite your total strength, to be devoted to construction for the future. Cultivate the ways of rectitude, foster nobility of spirit, and work with resolution—so that you may enhance the innate glory of the Imperial State and keep pace with the progress of the world."

★　★　★

All across Japan, the truth sinks in: defeat. Many of the emperor's subjects are so stunned at the sound of Hirohito's voice admitting surrender that they collapse to the ground in shock. Several hundred military men disembowel themselves rather than accept Hirohito's capitulation. A group of army and navy officers opt to make their suicides public, kneeling on the gravel in front of the Imperial Palace before placing pistols to their heads.

In some cases, the Japanese response takes the form of rage, as more than a dozen captured American fliers are taken from their POW cells on the island of Kyushu and executed with swords. It is due to war crimes like these that almost as soon as Hirohito's speech is concluded, military bureaucrats across Japan begin burning files and documents that could be used against them by American investigators.

And so it is that Japan, the once-mighty occupying power, will itself now be occupied. Not even the god-man Hirohito can prevent that. Will the Americans seek vengeance? Will the conquerors destroy the Japanese way of life?

No one is sure, nor does anyone know how the Japanese will respond to their subjugation.

What is apparent is that a new emperor will soon arrive.

All hail General Douglas MacArthur.

27

---•---

The supreme commander has arrived. General Douglas MacArthur's personal C-54 aircraft lands on a bumpy, treacherous airstrip. American warplanes have been bombing this airfield for weeks, and the shell craters buckling the runway in many places are still being repaired.

It is a hot and humid day as the general's transport taxis toward a hangar now decorated with an American flag. MacArthur surveys the scene through his small airplane window. He sees rows of newly arrived American B-29 bombers parked off the runway; a military brass band standing in formation, ready to strike up a march; and a column of official Japanese vehicles waiting to whisk him and his staff to their headquarters at the New Grand Hotel in Yokohama. Also present is a mob of two hundred photographers and journalists, most of them Japanese, poised to rush the plane.

In three short days the Japanese leadership will sign

the articles of surrender in Tokyo Bay, aboard the battleship USS *Missouri*. Dignitaries from all around the world will crowd the decks to witness the event, MacArthur prominently among them.

But history is also being made today in another way, and Douglas MacArthur is not sharing the moment with anyone.

Never before has Japan been profaned by a foreign conqueror's boot. As supreme commander of the Allied forces, MacArthur will not only lead the occupation forces that have already begun flooding into the country, he will also be the virtual dictator of Japan. He will control the media and Japanese politics. Unlike General George S. Patton, who is on the verge of being fired from a similar position in southern Germany, MacArthur will have unlimited power. Truman has firmly rebuked a Soviet request that one of their generals should serve as MacArthur's equal.*

MacArthur plans to implement drastic changes in the months to come: giving Japanese women the right to vote, influencing which generals are prosecuted for

---

* General Patton was openly critical of America's Soviet allies, believing the United States would be better served by continuing World War II until the Soviets were beaten back within their own borders. Ultimately, Patton's comments and actions, which favored his former Nazi enemies over the Soviets, led to his being removed from command of Third Army. He would die just before Christmas in 1945, after a fatal traffic collision on the day before he was due to return home to America and resign his commission. Some believe the accident was a revenge murder staged by the Soviets, a theory advanced in the book *Killing Patton*.

war crimes, and usurping Emperor Hirohito as the leader of the Japanese. Indeed, the general's style of governance will lead many Japanese to compare him with the shoguns, military warlords who ruled Japan from 1192 to 1867.

There is no guarantee MacArthur's transition to power will be smooth. A good number of Imperial Japanese Army troops still possess their weapons. As evidenced by Pearl Harbor, the art of deception is very much a part of the Japanese military culture. US intelligence officials know there is a very real chance the welcoming party awaiting MacArthur on the tarmac could be part of a clever trap to murder him.

Thus, the general's staff is jumpy as they line up to step off the plane. Each man wears a stiffly pressed khaki uniform, but no sidearm. Earlier in the flight, when MacArthur spotted them strapping on gun belts, he ordered the officers to cease. "Take them off," MacArthur commanded. "If they intend to kill us, sidearms will be useless. And nothing will impress them like a show of absolute fearlessness. If they don't know they're licked, this will convince them."

So, unarmed and unsure of the fate that awaits them, MacArthur's most trusted officers prepare to follow him down the ramp. Major General Courtney Whitney will describe the tense moment as a time when "the whole world was holding its breath."*

---

*Former British prime minister Winston Churchill will write of being shocked by MacArthur's arrival in Japan, surrounded not by a superior military fighting force but by a handful of senior

Until a week ago, this airfield was the home base of a Japanese Zero fighter squadron tasked with protecting Tokyo from American bombers. It was also a training field for kamikaze pilots. Right up until the very end of the war, thousands of civilians labored to build underground tunnels and hangars to repel the American invasion. Immediately after Emperor Hirohito's surrender broadcast, many of the fighter pilots rebelled, dropping leaflets on Tokyo urging the Japanese people to fight on. It is rumored that some of these fliers will take to the skies today to perform kamikaze flights. "My God," General Richard Sutherland has warned MacArthur, "the emperor is worshipped as a real god, yet they still tried to assassinate *him*. What kind of target does that make *you*?"

But MacArthur is undaunted, rising from his seat in the front row as the plane comes to a halt. He places his field marshal cap on his head and lights his corncob pipe, then moves to the back door of the plane. He does not take threats lightly, but his visits to Japan earlier in life schooled him in the ways of the Orient. Showing fear, or even the smallest sign of panic, will make MacArthur appear weak in the eyes of the Japanese. He has christened this aircraft *Bataan*, in defiant memory of the thousands of American and British soldiers slaughtered by the Japanese after the Philippines fell in 1942.

---

officers without so much as a pistol among them: "Of all the amazing deeds in the war, I regard General MacArthur's personal landing at Atsugi as the bravest of the lot."

MacArthur knows that the small group of American soldiers who arrived here yesterday and now stand ready to defend him would be powerless against the thirty thousand armed Japanese troops who have been ordered by their commanders to line the fifteen-mile route into Yokohama. These soldiers are armed with rifles and bayonets, but in a show of respect normally reserved only for the emperor, they do not feel themselves worthy of gazing directly upon MacArthur. Thus, they stand at attention with their backs to the road.

A blast of humid summer heat washes over MacArthur as he steps down the ramp. Spying the photographers, he does what he always does—vamps. The general dons his aviator sunglasses, draws on his pipe, and juts his chin forward. The band begins to play. It is just as MacArthur anticipated.

As long as there is a Japan, this moment will never be forgotten.

★   ★   ★

About a mile offshore, another strong American leader stands aboard the bridge of his flagship. Admiral William "Bull" Halsey and the United States Navy have beat MacArthur to Japan by three days. Halsey's USS *Missouri* prowls the waters of Sagami Bay, just south of Tokyo. A typhoon has passed through, leaving the water smooth, allowing the great gun barrels of the *Missouri* to aim level and true at the Japanese coast.

Halsey is sixty-two, a pugnacious career sailor whose brash tactical style is considered foolish by some but has earned him the deep respect of Douglas MacArthur. "His one thought was to close with the enemy and fight him to the death," MacArthur will write of Halsey in his autobiography. "No name rates higher in the annals of our country's naval history."

It has been a long war for Halsey, who was on board the aircraft carrier USS *Enterprise* at the time of the Pearl Harbor bombings. As commander of the navy's Third Fleet, he has played a vital role in almost every major naval engagement in the Pacific. It is a source of contention for Halsey and his boss, Admiral Chester Nimitz, that MacArthur and his army get much of the credit for victory in the Pacific. The distance from San Francisco to Tokyo is eight thousand miles and spans eight time zones; American naval brass well know that winning a war contested over such a vast swath of open ocean would have been impossible without the navy.

But finally, the navy is getting its due; President Truman has decided that the formal Japanese surrender will take place not on land but at sea. There are rumors in the fleet that the USS *South Dakota* has been chosen to be the site of the ceremony.

Now, in a massive show of force, almost three hundred battleships, destroyers, cruisers, light aircraft carriers, frigates, sloops, submarines, tenders, hospital ships, and minesweepers wait their turn to sail through the minefields guarding the entrance to Tokyo Bay. In addition to the American fleet, there are ships from the navies of Britain, Australia, and New Zealand. If the people of Japan have any doubt that they are defeated, they need only stand on the black sands of Sagami Bay and stare out to sea.

Among the many vessels, the most powerful is Halsey's flagship, the USS *Missouri*. Each of her sixteen-inch guns is sixty-seven feet in length, capable of launching a 2,700-pound armor-piercing shell twenty-three miles in less than fifty seconds. In addition, the "Mighty Mo" has twenty-five-inch guns with an accurate range of ten miles. She is a monster of a ship, almost as long as a football field, with a crew of two thousand and a top speed of thirty-three knots. The *Missouri*'s big guns have fired on Iwo Jima, Okinawa, the Philippines, and Japan itself. Six months ago, the ship endured a direct hit by kamikaze attack. She absorbed the blow without loss of life.*

There are also symbolic factors that add to *Missouri*'s stature: the slate-gray vessel is named for the home state of President Harry Truman. His daughter, Margaret, actually shattered the champagne bot-

---

*The plane struck the *Missouri* on the starboard side, just below the main deck. While cleaning up the wreckage, the crew of the *Missouri* came across the body of the kamikaze pilot, nineteen-year-old Setsuo Ishino. Believing that the young pilot had been carrying out his military obligation to the best of his ability, Captain William M. Callaghan of the *Missouri* ordered that he be given a burial at sea with full military honors. The body was draped in a Japanese flag sewn by members of the *Missouri*'s crew. After a funeral service and rifle volley, the crew saluted as Ishino's body was dropped into the deep.

tle across her bow when she was just twenty and he was still vice president, officially launching *Missouri* from the Brooklyn Navy Yard in January 1944. The Stars and Stripes that once flew over the US Capitol in Washington is securely stored on board, waiting to be hoisted this coming Sunday.* In addition, a second set of colors will be presented on board *Missouri*: the thirty-one-star American flag belonging to Commodore Matthew Perry, whose historic 1852 voyage to Japan opened Japanese ports to American trade.

Missouri is also the last battleship that the United States of America will ever build. So it is that shortly before steaming into Tokyo Bay, USS *South Dakota* is passed over for the special honor of hosting the Japanese surrender ceremony. Instead, it is to be the Mighty Mo.

Early on the morning of August 29, 1945, a Japanese harbor pilot boards the *Missouri* to help Halsey's crew navigate the minefields and channels of Tokyo Bay. The pilot helps Quartermaster Third Class Ed Kalanta steer the 44,560-ton *Missouri* from the conning tower on the main bridge. It was Kalanta who drove *Missouri* through the Panama Canal a year ago, sliding her into the narrow locks with just a foot to spare on either side. Now, Admiral Halsey is one floor below the main bridge as the twenty-year-old Kalanta and his Japanese adviser masterfully guide her into Tokyo Bay, en route to her appointment with destiny.

---

* The flag stored on the *Missouri* flew over the US Capitol when Pearl Harbor was bombed on December 7, 1941.

★ ★ ★

Missouri drops anchor at midmorning. Rehearsals soon begin for the surrender ceremony, as the ship's crew struggles to find space to fit the two hundred members of the press and dozens of dignitaries from around the world. History will take place on Sunday morning at 9:00 a.m. sharp. A call goes out to the crew, in search of the eight tallest sailors to serve as the greeting party when the Japanese surrender contingent comes on board. This is a subtle act of intimidation designed to remind the smaller diplomats of Japan that the power lies with America.

Throughout the days of rehearsals, even as the long line of Allied warships continues to snake into Tokyo Bay, *Missouri*'s mighty guns remain trained on Tokyo.

The war may be over, but the danger is not past.

★ ★ ★

General Douglas MacArthur steps past Admiral Halsey and takes his place at the microphone shortly after 9:00 a.m. on Sunday, September 2. He is dressed in a crisp khaki uniform, as are the other American admirals and generals. The eleven-member Japanese contingent is wearing military dress and even formal top hats and tails, but it is MacArthur's rationale that "we fought them in our khaki uniforms and we'll accept their surrender in our khaki uniforms."*

---

* None of the Japanese wanted to be there, fearing that the humiliation would stick to them personally. They were: Major General

The two thousand members of the USS *Missouri*'s crew, all in their dress whites, literally hang off gun turrets and other parts of the ship to witness this moment of history. The deck is packed with media, dignitaries, and weapons of war. The sky is gray on this storm-tossed morning and the mood somber.

"We are gathered here, representatives of the major warring powers, to conclude a solemn agreement whereby peace may be restored," MacArthur announces over the loudspeaker. "The issues involving divergent ideals and ideologies have been determined on the battlefields of the world, and hence are not for our discussion or debate."

The morning begins with the playing of a recording of "The Star-Spangled Banner." The thirty-one-star Commodore Perry flag from 1852 hangs in a frame affixed to the ship's superstructure, too flimsy to snap smartly in the wind. The same cannot be said, however, for the Stars and Stripes from the Capitol, which was run up the flagpole this morning. The Japanese contingent looks morose and seems to want to conclude the ceremony as quickly as possible. The generals among them have already suffered the disgrace of surrender-

---

Yatsuji Nagai (army), Katsuo Okazaki (foreign ministry), Rear Admiral Sadatoshi Tomioka (navy), Toshikazu Kase (foreign ministry), Lieutenant General Shuichi Miyazaki (army), Rear Admiral Ichiro Yokoyama (navy), Saburo Ota (foreign ministry), Captain Katsuo Shiba (navy), Colonel Kaziyi Sugita (army), Foreign Minister Mamoru Shigemitsu, and Chief of the Army General Staff General Yoshijiro Umezu.

ing their swords, and the diplomats had the Japanese flag removed from their official cars just this morning.

"As Supreme Commander for the Allied Powers, I announce it my firm purpose, in the tradition of the countries I represent, to proceed in the discharge of my responsibilities with justice and tolerance, while taking all necessary dispositions to insure that the terms of surrender are fully, promptly, and faithfully complied with."

MacArthur clutches a sheaf of notes. He stands tall as the Japanese tolerate his speech before the table on which the surrender will be signed.

"I now invite the representatives of the Emperor of Japan and the Japanese government and the Japanese Imperial General Headquarters to sign the Instrument of Surrender at the places indicated."

A coffee-stained, dark green cloth covers a folding table brought up this morning from the ship's galley when it became clear that the ceremonial mahogany table donated by the British for the surrender ceremony is too small. Two copies of the surrender agreement lie on the table, leather-bound for the Americans and canvas-coated for the Japanese. The surrender documents are printed on rare parchment that was found in a Manila basement.

The vanquished sign first, followed by the victors. Clicking camera shutters are the only sound as the crew and press eagerly capture the moment. The ceremony lasts twenty-three minutes and is broadcast around the world.

General Douglas MacArthur takes his seat at the

table in a simple wooden chair and patiently begins using a series of different fountain pens to affix his name twice. He hands one pen to Lieutenant General John "Skinny" Wainwright, his dear friend who spent the war in a Japanese POW camp after being captured during the fall of the Philippines. It is Wainwright whom MacArthur wanted denied the Medal of Honor after the fall of Corregidor, believing the Americans could have held out longer. But the sight of the skeletal Wainwright evokes the beatings, torture, and starvation to which he was subjected for three years as a prisoner of war and can leave no doubt of his courage.

Another ceremonial pen is handed to Lieutenant General Arthur Percival, the British general who also endured the horrors of a Japanese POW camp after the fall of Singapore. Like Wainwright, Percival was moved several times by the Japanese to prevent him from falling into Allied hands. By war's end, Percival and Wainwright were held at the same prison in Hsian, Manchuria. MacArthur has specifically asked these two bone-thin, malnourished survivors to stand immediately behind the surrender table, visible at all times to the Japanese party.*

The ceremony concluded, MacArthur rises to his

---

* Other ceremonial pens were distributed to the United States Military Academy at West Point; the United States Naval Academy in Annapolis, Maryland; and to his wife, Jean. MacArthur used the latter pen to write the "Arthur," in his last name, knowing she would treasure it because he shared the name with their son. There is a notable gap between "Mac" and "Arthur" in the general's signature on the surrender documents.

feet, stands ramrod straight, and announces to all in attendance that "these proceedings are closed."

As the Japanese are led back to the motor launch that will carry them to land, a massive formation of American aircraft flies overhead. Looking up, the diplomats receive a dramatic message: the Americans are now your masters.

28

———◆———

The war will never be over for Hideki Tojo.

The diminutive sixty-year-old former Japanese prime minister hides in plain sight, waiting patiently for American soldiers to arrest him for war crimes. He could try to make a run for it, but Tojo is a careful and thoughtful tactician, despite his reputation as a madman. Unlike the visages of the German Nazis now being smuggled into South America, there to live a life of apprehensive anonymity, Tojo's is one of the most well-known faces in the world. He is famous, he is wanted, and he is unmistakably Japanese. There is not a single place on earth he could hide.

So Tojo remains in his farmhouse on the outskirts of Tokyo, keeping a pistol close at all times. He has even had his physician paint a small black target on his chest, just to make sure that he will not miss when the time comes to put a bullet through his heart.

American soldiers and sailors have been pouring

into Japan by the thousands, disarming the Japanese military, spiking naval guns, and removing the propellers from airplanes. Thus begins the long, slow process of healing the great divide between America and Japan. In China, forty thousand United States Marines—many of whom landed on the bloody shores of Peleliu and survived those horrendous months of battle one year ago—are en route to the north, where they will serve garrison duty and accept the surrender of Japanese units that have not yet fallen to the Russians. Many Japanese forces in China have never before suffered defeat in battle; the act of laying down their arms and burning their regimental standards will be bitter and humiliating.

★   ★   ★

The war may be over, but there are still scores to settle. Arguably, both Japanese and American forces committed horrendous acts in the name of winning the war. General Curtis LeMay believes that if America had lost, his decision to firebomb Tokyo would most certainly have seen him indicted for war crimes. But it is the victor who metes out the final punishment. Just as the Nazi leadership is about to go on trial in Nuremberg, so too will Japan's generals and diplomats be held accountable for their acts of terror.

The encrypted messages the Imperial Guard headquarters sent to field units in August ordering the burning of all documentation pertaining to the treatment of prisoners of war, comfort women, chemical and biological warfare, and the illicit drug trade did not lead to the destruction of all evidence. Foreseeing the need for war crimes documentation as far back as 1942, MacArthur ordered the US Army's Allied Translator and Interpreter Section (ATIS) to comb captured documents for evidence of atrocities. By war's end on September 2, ATIS is in possession of more than 350,000 such files. Just one day later, using this information, ATIS commander Colonel Sidney Mashbir was able to confront Katsuo Okazaki of Japan's Ministry of Foreign Affairs with photographic proof that Japanese soldiers were ordered to burn and maim thousands of innocent Filipinos during the fall of Manila.

"And do you have the names of the soldiers responsible for these atrocities?" Okazaki asked, hoping to call Mashbir's bluff.

"You're damn right," the colonel replied angrily. "Depend on it: you will very shortly be called upon to turn them over to us for punishment."

There is no telling how many thousands of Japanese diplomats and soldiers will be forced to stand trial for war crimes ranging from murder and rape to mistreatment of prisoners of war. Strangely, however, the most heinous Japanese war criminal is completely ignored by Allied prosecutors. In fact, in the almost two weeks since the surrender was signed and the occupation began, General Hideki Tojo has yet to encounter a single American.

Day after day passes with no visit from the military police. There have been times when it seemed the Americans might not be coming at all.

But Tojo knows he is a special case: as the man who

led Japan into war against the United States, who personally oversaw every last detail of the Pearl Harbor bombing, and who happily encouraged his commanders to murder prisoners of war, he is far too notorious to escape indictment.

Execution will be another matter entirely, for he refuses to be taken alive.

Tojo does not have the courage to kneel on the floor, write his final death statement, and thrust a razor-sharp knife into his abdomen.

But a .32-caliber Colt automatic pistol is quicker and just as lethal.

☆   ☆   ☆

Incredibly, if not for two brash American journalists who knocked on Tojo's front door yesterday, the US Army might still be looking for him. To the great surprise of Murlin Spencer and Russell Brines of the Associated Press, Tojo was only too happy to grant them an exclusive interview. It was Tojo's last chance to tell his side of the story before killing himself. He reveled in the discussion, chain-smoking as the journalists peppered him with questions. No subject, with the exception of the coming war crimes trials, was off-limits.

"The shaven-headed one-time terror of Asia," the Americans wrote under a shared byline, "was willing to talk of many things . . . the mood ranging from steely-eyed impassivity to hearty laughter."

As Tojo knew it would be, the interview was published in newspapers around the world. Now, looking out his farmhouse window, Tojo sees that one of the journalists has returned, bringing along a photographer. They appear to be waiting for something to happen, for neither man is making any attempt to approach the house.

Sure enough, two American army vehicles soon come to a stop in front of the farmhouse. Tojo counts five soldiers who have come to take him away, each of them armed. One of them spots Tojo looking out the window, causing the group to move quickly toward the front door.

Tojo slides open the window and yells to the crowd: "I am Tojo!"

Tojo has little time. He closes the window, unbuttons his shirt, places his loaded .32-caliber Colt automatic to the black mark on his chest, and pulls the trigger.

With a resounding bang, a bullet is launched into Tojo's heart. Blood pours from the wound.

Every element of Tojo's suicide plan has been staged to absolute perfection.

Every element except one: the bullet almost completely missed his heart.

Hideki Tojo is not dead.

✳ ✳ ✳

Lieutenant John Wilpers hears the gunshot. The twenty-five-year-old army intelligence officer rushes up the steps and kicks open Tojo's front door. General Douglas MacArthur personally ordered the 308th Counterintelligence Corps to arrest Tojo this morning, and Wilpers plans on carrying out that order to the best of his ability.

To Lieutenant Wilpers, a dead Tojo just won't do.*

But the former prime minister certainly looks near death. He is splayed on a chair, his chest rising and falling faintly. Photographer Charlie Gorry, of the Associated Press, has followed Wilpers through the farmhouse door and begins taking pictures as Lieutenant Wilpers unholsters his sidearm and points it at Tojo, who has begun to apologize for taking so long to die. Taking possession of the dying man's .32, Wilpers immediately begins the desperate search for a doctor.

Orders are orders: Tojo must remain alive.

☆   ☆   ☆

Six days after Tojo's attempted suicide, on September 17, 1945, the young ensign from Brooklyn is terrified that a typhoon may sink his ship eight hundred miles southwest of Tokyo.

The USS *Oneida* has just arrived in Okinawa's Hagushi Bay after five days in Jinsen, Korea. But the approaching typhoon is chasing the ship back out to sea. There is every chance *Oneida* will survive the winds and rain if she remains in port here in Okinawa, but a similar storm just last week showed that it is better to be cautious.

Typhoon Ursula, as it was known, blasted through the Sea of Japan with winds registering more than

---

* Wilpers will be awarded the Bronze Star for his actions at Tojo's farmhouse on September 11, 1945. However, the army will lose his paperwork, so he will not physically receive the honor until he is ninety years old.

one hundred miles per hour. Aircraft transporting American prisoners of war homeward were caught in the deadly storm. Tragically, these men who had endured years of torture and starvation would never see America again; all nine hundred of them died when the storm forced thirty airplanes to crash into the Sea of Japan.*

Ursula is still fresh in the minds of *Oneida*'s crew as she powers away from Hagushi Bay as quickly as possible. A second typhoon, known as Ida, is also bearing down on the busy wartime port. The fast-attack transport will stand a better chance of avoiding damage if it can outrace the storms.

Ultimately, Ida will be even more deadly than Ursula. She is destined to slam hard into the Japanese mainland, there to be renamed Makurazaki. The city of Hiroshima, still a wasteland five weeks after the dropping of the atomic bomb, will be swamped by tidal waves and flooding. Three thousand more residents will die, six thousand more homes will be destroyed, and fifty thousand homes will be flooded. In any other time, this would be a catastrophe of global significance. But in the wake of the millions of lives lost from nations worldwide in the Pacific war and the more than a hundred thousand already dead from the atomic bombs, the typhoon damage will receive scant newspaper coverage.

The tall ensign from Brooklyn who recently graduated

---

* There were no survivors, making it the worst peacetime aviation disaster in history.

from the College of the Holy Cross, in Massachusetts, came aboard the *Oneida* ten months ago. As with the other sailors, he goes through the daily routines of life on board the ship: four-hour watch, regular meals in the officers' mess, and the utter off-duty boredom that defines life at sea. Soon, the *Oneida* will take part in the joyous exodus known as Operation Magic Carpet. Hundreds of US ships—even massive aircraft carriers—are clearing their decks for the thousands of soldiers, sailors, and marines who need a lift home. After enduring a brutal period of war, these men and women deserve nothing but the best, and the ensign knows it.

Back in Brooklyn, after months of uncertainty and countless prayers, the ensign's father and mother are waiting to see him walk through their front door. But that will not happen soon. There is still work to do in Japan.

He has been ordered ashore to help rebuild the defeated nation. On November 26, he will begin a six-month tour of duty at the Naval Communications Facility in Yokosuka, working for Radio Tokyo. It is the ideal job for a young man blessed with an easy wit and a way with words.

Whether or not he will be released from the navy after that or be forced to serve another year or two is unknown.

☆ ☆ ☆

It is 10:00 a.m. on September 27, 1945, as a nervous and preoccupied Emperor Hirohito steps out of his maroon 1930 Rolls-Royce at the entrance of the American embassy in Tokyo.* The emperor's war, like those of Tojo and the young ensign from Brooklyn, is not over. Hirohito is depressed, and his hands tremble. He suffers from severe jaundice that has deepened the sallow pallor of his skin. Last night he lay awake worrying he will have to stand next to Tojo in the prisoner's dock, listening to the sonorous tones of an American prosecutor listing his many war crimes.

Taking a deep breath, Hirohito momentarily calms his fears. Perhaps he won't hang, after all. His only hope is a direct appeal to General Douglas MacArthur, which is why the emperor has traveled to the American embassy this morning. Courage is everything right now, even if it is false.

The emperor could have saved himself days of worry by greeting MacArthur a week ago. Hirohito's Imperial Palace is just across the street from MacArthur's brand-new office headquarters in Tokyo's Dai-Ichi Seimei Building.† When he moved in, MacArthur gave the Dai-Ichi Life Insurance Company three days to vacate the imposing structure, then chose for himself a simple

------

* Maroon is the color reserved for imperial vehicles. Hirohito has long had a passion for the Rolls-Royce, and this is one of many he has owned.

† "Dai ichi" means "number one" in Japanese. In addition to its proximity to the Imperial Palace and the fact that it is one of the few prominent buildings in Tokyo still standing after the American bombings, this linguistic symbolism is a prime reason Douglas MacArthur chose this insurance office as the epicenter of America's almighty control of Japanese life and culture.

sixth-floor office that actually looks down onto the Imperial Palace.

While Hirohito can see MacArthur's office just by looking out the window, and MacArthur can just as easily see him, the emperor has waited for MacArthur to make the first move. But the general is cunning. Paying a call upon the emperor would have been seen as subservient. Better to have it the other way around.

MacArthur is a message sender—and this message says the emperor has no clothes.

MacArthur has designated that the meeting should take place at the American embassy, allowing the people of Tokyo plenty of opportunity to see the emperor's unmistakable Rolls making the shameful drive to MacArthur's residence. The emperor's journey from the Sakurada Gate of the Imperial Palace southward through the decimated streets of Tokyo has taken less than ten minutes. His imperial sedan has been followed by three black Mercedes loaded with members of the royal court, but the emperor pays little attention to them now.

Clad in a black waistcoat, top hat, and polished dress shoes, Hirohito steps through the American embassy's front door. He is unused to commoners touching his personal possessions and immediately recoils as two army officers salute him and then step forward to take his hat.

"You are very, very welcome, sir!" says a grinning MacArthur, striding into the room to break the ice. He wears his normal daily khaki uniform rather than formal wear, and has not even affixed his combat ribbons to the simple creased shirt. The general thrusts out his hand to greet the emperor, but Hirohito bows low at the same time, leaving MacArthur's open hand hovering awkwardly above the emperor's head. Hirohito continues to bow, finally extending his hand upward to clasp MacArthur's.

After a moment's hesitation, MacArthur invites Hirohito and his interpreter into a private room. The two men speak for forty minutes, during which the emperor apologizes for the war—an admission MacArthur actually downplays during their conversation.

This is the first of eleven meetings that will take place between MacArthur and Hirohito over the next several years, but it is the most important. For in this simple midmorning conversation, MacArthur makes it clear that he sees the emperor as vital to forging an alliance that will successfully rebuild Japan. Even though the emperor's admission of culpability makes him a Class A war criminal, MacArthur will do everything in his considerable power to make sure Hirohito never sees the inside of a jail cell—or feels the coarse braid of a hangman's noose around his throat.

✷ ✷ ✷

At meeting's end, MacArthur's personal photographer is shown into the room. It was Captain Gaetano Faillace who snapped the iconic image of the general wading ashore in the Philippines six months ago, and now he snaps another photo for the ages. Faillace actually takes three pictures of MacArthur and Hirohito standing side by side in front of a desk. In the first two, MacArthur's eyes are closed and Hirohito appears to be yawning. But the third image, the one that will forever remind the Japanese people that their emperor no longer rules Japan, is the keeper.

The six-foot MacArthur towers over Hirohito, looking dominant and unimpressed by the small man to his left. The emperor stands at stiff attention; MacArthur looks casual, hands on his hips and elbows sticking out from his sides like a random American tourist who has somehow stumbled into the emperor's inner sanctum.

Just to make sure the message is received loud and clear, MacArthur orders that the photos be released to the newspapers, so that all of Japan can see the towering *gaijin* who now rules their nation.

Predictably, the people of Japan are horrified.

Three months later, on January 1, 1946, at MacArthur's urging, Emperor Hirohito repudiates his divine status, admitting to the people of Japan that he is not a god.

Thus, the divine nature of the Japanese ruler is revealed as a fraud—but that admission comes far too late for millions of the dead scattered across Asia.

★　★　★

It is May 3, 1946. Formal war crimes indictments are being read at the International Military Tribunal for the Far East in a Tokyo courtroom; these "Tokyo Trials" will see a team of jurists hearing evidence against the accused war criminals. With the exception of Judge Radhabinod Pal of India, who considers the proceedings "formalized vengeance sought with arrogance by the Allied Powers upon a defeated Japan," the verdicts

General Douglas MacArthur and Emperor Hirohito, photographed together in MacArthur's office

against the accused will be authoritative. Seven men will be sentenced to death for Class A war crimes, sixteen others will be imprisoned for life, and two others will be imprisoned for shorter periods of time.*

---

*Twenty-five of the twenty-eight men charged as Class A war criminals in the Tokyo trials were convicted. In addition, Allied

Hideki Tojo is among those hearing the indictments. Thanks to the actions of Lieutenant John Wilpers, a doctor was quickly located after the former prime minister shot himself. However, this physician refused to treat Tojo, so the quick-thinking Wilpers was forced to find yet another doctor to save Tojo. After recovering in the hospital, Tojo has been living in solitary confinement in Tokyo's Sugamo Prison, under round-the-clock armed guard.

Now, as Tojo sits in the docket, a deranged Japanese civilian defendant hoping to plead insanity steps forward and slaps him twice on the back of the head. The prime minister finds this funny and smiles openly, despite the ominous nature of the proceedings.

There is another bizarre bit of humor that will shortly come into play—of which Tojo will be completely unaware. The war criminal wears false teeth, and during his time in prison he will come to require a new set of dentures. The United States will be only too happy to oblige. But unbeknownst to Tojo, the words "Remember Pearl Harbor" will be drilled into the false teeth in

---

prosecutors will hold tribunals against Japanese generals, diplomatic officials, soldiers, and camp guards at several other locations throughout Asia and the Pacific. The British were particularly vigilant in prosecuting those men who killed so many thousands in the construction of the Burma-Siam Railway. In addition to the 25 defendants convicted at the Tokyo trials, another 4,300 Japanese soldiers were found guilty of rape, abuse of POWs, and murder. One thousand of these men will be sentenced to death. The rest will be given life imprisonment, although many of these sentences will be commuted.

Morse code, ensuring that the Second World War will never really be over for Hideki Tojo—especially not late at night, when he lies alone in solitary confinement at Sugamo Prison, running his tongue along his new dentures, wondering about the curious bumps and divots studding the otherwise smooth porcelain surfaces.

29

The Second World War has been over for almost three years as Colonel Paul Tibbets steps into the Oval Office; the veteran pilot is among four men the president has spontaneously invited for a short visit. Tibbets, along with General Carl Spaatz, General Jimmy Doolittle, and Colonel Dave Shillen, made the short drive from the Pentagon together, whereupon they were ushered into the president's office without delay. They have no idea why they have been summoned.

Tibbets, the *Enola Gay* pilot, has been busy since World War II ended. He flew home from the Pacific to minor adulation but quickly withdrew from the public, preferring instead to focus on his failing marriage and the continuation of his aviation career.

Back in September 1945, with the war newly ended and American troops flooding into Japan, Tibbets was among the first pilots to fly into Tokyo with the occupation forces. Almost immediately upon being billeted at the Dai-Ichi building next to the Imperial Palace in downtown Tokyo, where Douglas MacArthur would also locate his headquarters, Tibbets received orders to transport a Japanese physicist to Hiroshima so that the man could study the A-bomb's aftermath. This would be the only time in his life that Tibbets would get a chance to visit the scene of *Enola Gay*'s destruction.

But fate intervened. The runway near Hiroshima was unsuitable for landing a large aircraft, so instead, Tibbets delivered Professor Masao Tsuzuki to Nagasaki and then spent three days there with a small group of crew he had flown with on *Enola Gay*. Tibbets and his fellow aviators were touched by the friendliness of the Japanese people, struggling to reconcile that new behavior with the "frenzied mobs that had been known to attack and kill downed American fliers."

Colonel Tibbets, bombardier Major Tom Ferebee, and navigator Captain Theodore "Dutch" Van Kirk slept along the waterfront, in an idyllic hotel with bamboo walls and a thatched roof. Tibbets could not help but note that the location was also the aiming point for the Nagasaki bomb. The quaint inn would not exist were it not for the heavy clouds that caused *Bockscar* to drop its payload miles off target.

The American officers are awed by Fat Man's destruction. "Block after block had been flattened, as if by a tornado.

"Strangely, however, I saw no signs of death. There were no bodies anywhere," Tibbets later wrote. "The brief visit left me with considerable respect for the people who had been our enemies such a short time before."

★ ★ ★

President Truman is not at his desk when Tibbets, Spaatz, Doolittle, and Shillen enter the Oval Office. The question of whether or not it was ethical to drop the atomic bombs still hangs over this hallowed room, as it will for decades to come. Strangely, just three chairs await the four air force officers. One man must remain standing.

The most powerful officer in the group is Spaatz, who has recently been selected the first chief of staff of the United States Air Force. In July 1945, it was Spaatz who requested a handwritten order authorizing the dropping of the atomic bomb. Protocol demands that the chair farthest to the right belongs to him.

Doolittle, whose flying career is perhaps the most legendary, led the 1942 bombing of Tokyo that became known as simply "the Doolittle Raid." As the second-highest-ranking of the group, the general will be seated to Spaatz's left, in the middle chair.

Colonel Shillen and Tibbets are of equal rank. It remains unclear which of them will sit and which will stand.

White House butler Alonzo Fields quickly takes charge.

"General Spaatz," Fields says, gesturing to a chair, "will you please be facing the desk?"

As expected, Spaatz takes the seat farthest to the right.

Tibbets remains standing. After almost fifteen years in the military, he knows better than to ask questions.

Following strict orders from the president, the White House butler shocks Tibbets by guiding him around to the opposite side of the presidential desk and gesturing to a chair facing the other three, right next to where Truman will sit.

A surprised Paul Tibbets takes a seat.

The men are served coffee as they await the president's arrival. Ten minutes later, Harry Truman walks in wearing a huge smile. The officers immediately rise.

"Sit down," Truman orders jovially, making everyone feel at ease.

Since taking office four years ago, the president has transformed himself from a piano-playing vice president into one of the world's great statesmen.

Which is not to say that the transition from war to peacetime has been easy. The tension between the United States and the Soviet Union that began in the waning days of World War II continues to escalate, as Russia relentlessly seeks to expand Communist influence around the world. The sense of power Truman felt in Potsdam back in 1945 when he informed Joseph Stalin that America possessed a superweapon has long since dimmed, and intelligence reports estimate it is only a matter of time before the Soviet Union develops an atomic bomb of its own.*

In addition to the troubles with Russia, Truman's

---

*The Soviet Union successfully exploded its first atomic weapon on August 29, 1949.

outspoken personality has alienated some voters here in America. Many point to the slowing economy as a sign that he is a poor leader. With his job approval ratings sometimes dropping below 40 percent, there is a widespread belief that Harry Truman will not run for reelection—and that he would lose in a landslide should he choose to.

There have, however, been some victories for Truman. His unilateral selection of Douglas MacArthur as supreme commander of the Allied powers in 1945 is popular. MacArthur has successfully transformed a former enemy into a burgeoning ally, rebuilding Japan from rubble and preventing it from embracing communism like so many of its Asian neighbors.

Privately, Truman now believes the appointment was a mistake. He no longer trusts the general's decision making, believing MacArthur's ego has turned Japan into his own personal fiefdom. But for now, Truman keeps his opinion to himself.

Still smiling, Truman begins the brief meeting by looking at the row of air force officers assembled across the desk.

"General Spaatz, I want to congratulate you on being the first chief of the air force," says the president.

"Thank you, sir," Spaatz replies. "It is a great honor, and I appreciate it."

Turning his gaze to Doolittle, Truman congratulates him on the legendary 1942 raid over Tokyo, which shocked the Japanese because heavy American bombers were launched from aircraft carriers—a feat once considered impossible. "That was a magnificent thing you pulled, flying off that carrier," Truman marvels.

"All in a day's work, Mr. President," replies the ever-confident Doolittle.

To Shillen, Truman shows that he is keeping abreast of postwar aviation technology. "Colonel Shillen, I want to congratulate you on having the foresight to recognize the potential in aerial refueling. We're gonna need it bad someday."

"Thank you very much, sir."

Finally, Harry Truman turns to face Colonel Paul Tibbets. The president says nothing at first, letting their shared moment form a connection.

For ten long seconds, the president does not speak.

"What do you think?" Truman finally asks.

"Mr. President," Tibbets replies, knowing full well what Harry Truman is talking about, "I think I did what I was told."

Truman slaps his hand down on the desk, rattling the legendary "The Buck Stops Here" placard placed there after the war.

"You're damn right you did. And I'm the guy who sent you."

★　★　★

More than eight months later, and twenty minutes before midnight in Tokyo's Sugamo Prison, Buddhist priest and prison chaplain Shinso Hanayama, the spiritual adviser to the seven Class A Japanese war criminals who will hang by the neck until dead tonight, shares a last moment with each man in the prison's Buddhist chapel. The date is December 22, 1948.

Two American chaplains will witness the executions, but Hanayama will not be allowed inside the death chamber. So as each man leaves the Buddhist ceremony, the priest says good-bye to mass murderers like General Hideki Tojo and former prime minister Koki Hirota.

A party of nine witnesses will be on hand to watch the war's final chapter unfold. A total of twenty executioners, guards, jailers, and legal officials will view the hangings. The loved ones of the condemned men have not been invited. Each of the observers in the chamber is under strict instructions not to display unseemly conduct or take photographs.

The execution order states that the hangings will take place as soon after midnight on December 23 as possible. The Sugamo Prison execution chamber is so small that there is only room for four nooses, so the war criminals must be hanged in two separate shifts. As the clock ticks toward twelve, each criminal is clothed in the uniform of an American army garbageman, devoid of any military insignia.

The men's legs are shackled, and waist belts are wrapped around their torsos. Each prisoner will be accompanied to the gallows by two American guards. The first group of four men is comprised of Generals Kenji Doihara, Iwane Matsui, Akira Muto, and Hideki Tojo.*

---

*General Kenji Doihara is the opium-addicted commander who led the invasion of Manchuria and the subsequent subjugation of

Leg irons clanking, the column of men is marched to the gallows and up the thirteen steps to the platform. The executioner stands at one end. His three assistants place a black hood over the head of each condemned man. Nooses are then lowered over the hoods and cinched snugly across their throats.

The process will be repeated for the second group to be hanged: General Seishiro Itagaki, Koki Hirota, and General Heitaro Kimura.*

The hangings take place twenty-nine minutes apart. The Buddhist priest, Shinso Hanayama, will write that he could hear the trapdoors swing open at 12:01 a.m. and again at 12:30 a.m.

Within ninety seconds of climbing the gallows, each man is swinging from a rope. The bodies are then removed and cremated, the ashes dispersed so that no memorial shrine might ever honor the men's lives.

In his last words, Tojo, the man most responsible for

---

the Chinese people; General Iwane Matsui is charged with leading the Rape of Nanking; General Akira Muto was responsible for inhumane activities in China, Sumatra, and the Philippines; and Hideki Tojo was the Japanese prime minister responsible for leading Japan into war.

*General Seishiro Itakagi was convicted on eight counts of war crimes, including inhumane treatment of prisoners of war. Former prime minister Koki Hirota was in power when Japan invaded China and was sentenced for the attack and subsequent proliferation of the war. General Heitaro Kimura was an assistant to Tojo and also went on to commands throughout Asia; he was charged with allowing the barbaric treatment of Allied POWs to proliferate.

the millions who died in the Pacific during World War II, says he is sorry.

The once arrogant and bloodthirsty prime minister is reduced to a broken man.

Thus, two days before Christmas, the Japanese brutalizers are no more, closing one of the most violent eras the world has ever known.*

---

*Like the bodies of the six other men executed on December 23, 1948, Tojo's body was cremated. Despite the best efforts of the Americans, his ashes were split between a Tokyo cemetery and the Yasukuni Shrine, a still-controversial memorial to the glorious Japanese war dead. Displays at the nearby Yushukan military museum espouse a revisionist history claiming that the United States was the racist aggressor in the Greater East Asia War, as the Pacific theater of the Second World War is known in Japan. Shortly before his sentence was carried out, Tojo gave his military ribbons to one of his American jailers.

30

The young ensign from Brooklyn looks at his brunette wife, who is holding their newborn son. The baby is big, more than ten pounds. The ensign has been back from the Pacific for more than two years and is now starting a new life: father and provider.

William James O'Reilly hopes his new son will follow in the tradition of his ancestors: hardworking Irish Catholics who value family and loyalty over money and material things. He and his bride of just over a year, Angela, are thrilled with their baby boy, whom they name Billy—William James O'Reilly Jr.

Bill and Angela married in New York City's Saint Patrick's Cathedral in 1948. She already had a good job as a physical therapist at Columbia Presbyterian Hospital, located on Manhattan's Upper West Side, and it is there where baby Billy is born. Ensign O'Reilly, with a college degree from Saint Francis College and military training at the College of the Holy Cross, is trying to decide on a career direction. Now, with the arrival of the baby, the urgency of that decision is more pronounced.

The newlywed couple lives in a small apartment just over the George Washington Bridge in northern New Jersey. Money is tight. Already the ensign is regretting leaving the navy, where there is security and direction. Unlike many of his peers, Bill O'Reilly Sr. loved his time in the service. He learned much during the occupation of Japan, the experience bringing him a measure of respect for the Japanese people, who, in his opinion, endured the occupation with discipline.

Soon, the ensign will move his wife and baby to the teeming New York City suburb of Levittown, on Long Island. Here, inexpensive housing is being built en masse and mortgages for veterans are favorable. The price for a Spartan two-bedroom home is eight thousand dollars. Both Bill and Angela will live there until they die.

⋆   ⋆   ⋆

My father was always nostalgic for the navy and fascinated by World War II. He firmly believed he would have been killed if MacArthur's land invasion had come to fruition; his ship, the USS *Oneida*, was set to ferry hundreds of marines close to the beaches of Japan. Only later did my father find out that thousands of Japanese kamikaze pilots were waiting to attack the US fleet. The carnage would have been devastating.

And so it is that Ensign O'Reilly, his wife, and their two children—my sister Janet arriving two years

Ensign William J. O'Reilly

later—built yet another traditional American family over the decades of the 1950s and 1960s. My dad never prospered in the marketplace, keeping his job as a low-level financial analyst for almost thirty years. As a child of the Great Depression, he valued a steady paycheck more than anything. Thus, he settled for a pedestrian job and allowed his vast talents for communication to go undeveloped.

Not usually introspective, my father was convinced of one certainty, which he shared with me on a few occasions—that his very existence, and therefore my life as well, was likely saved by a terrible bomb and a gut-wrenching presidential decision that is still being debated to this day.

But for the young ensign and his present-day son, there really is no debate, only a stark reality. Had the A-bombs not been used, you would very likely not be reading this book.

------◆------

Emperor **Michinomiya Hirohito** was stripped of all power by General Douglas MacArthur. However, the general felt that Hirohito was symbolically vital to healing the nation's postwar wounds. As such, MacArthur quietly decreed that Hirohito be absolved of all responsibility for war crimes. To maintain the ruse that the emperor was not directly involved in the war effort and its many atrocities, MacArthur and Hirohito collaborated to slant testimony of the war crimes defendants away from the emperor. In recent decades, revisionist historians in Japan have repudiated the notion that the emperor is *not* divine, suggesting that the wording of Hirohito's pronouncement was a vague gesture to placate the American occupiers.

"The occupation forces tried to sever the bond between the emperor and the Japanese people," reads a plaque at Tokyo's controversial Yasukuni Shrine and

Museum. "They widely advertised the new year statement as the 'emperor's declaration of humanity', but in
actuality the emperor had done no more than to announce a return to the principles stated in Emperor
Meiji's [1868] charter oath."

Hirohito made a point of boycotting the Yasukuni
Shrine, in the heart of Tokyo, after the war when he
learned that the ashes of Japanese war criminals had
secretly been enshrined there. In the four decades between the war's end and his death, Hirohito appeared
regularly in public, greeting foreign heads of state during their visits to Tokyo and traveling abroad to meet
with both Queen Elizabeth II of Great Britain and US
president Gerald Ford. In 1975, he famously had his
photograph taken with an entirely different head of
state, posing alongside Mickey Mouse during a visit
to Disneyland in California. Emperor Hirohito died on
January 7, 1989, at the age of eighty-seven, after reign-
ing for sixty-three years. He is said to have been buried
wearing a Mickey Mouse watch.

✶　✶　✶

Robert Oppenheimer became world famous once the
atomic bombs were dropped and details of the Manhattan Project were released to the public. He appeared
on the cover of both *Time* and *Life* magazines as the intellectual face of the dawning nuclear age. For a time,
Oppenheimer tried to return to the academic world, but
after realizing that his passion for teaching had waned,
he accepted a position as director of a think tank
known as the Institute for Advanced Study. He became

an advocate for nuclear arms control. The explosion of a new weapon known as the hydrogen bomb in 1952 ushered in the new age of thermonuclear weapons that explode with a force exponentially surpassing the Hiroshima and Nagasaki blasts. These new weapons actually require an atomic reaction to trigger the greater thermonuclear detonation, leading to the saying, "All nuclear weapons are atomic, but not all atomic weapons are nuclear."

Currently, nine nations possess the power to wage nuclear war: the United States, Russia, Israel, the United Kingdom, France, China, Pakistan, India, and North Korea. In all, it is estimated there are 16,300 nuclear weapons in existence.

Robert Oppenheimer's security clearance was suspended in 1953, then stripped altogether in 1954 after the FBI charged him with Communist associations. A later examination of declassified files would show that Oppenheimer never betrayed the United States and had resisted several attempts by the Russian KGB to recruit him as a spy. However, this revelation came long after Oppenheimer's death from throat cancer on February 18, 1967, at the age of sixty-two. His wife, Kitty, to whom he had remained married despite infidelities on his part, had his body cremated and his urn dropped into the sea just offshore from their beach home in the US Virgin Islands. The house was subsequently destroyed in a storm, leaving the urn's exact resting place a mystery—much like Robert Oppenheimer himself.

✳ ✳ ✳

The effects of the atomic bomb on **Hiroshima** and **Nagasaki** were felt for decades. Both cities have been rebuilt in remarkable fashion, with almost all buildings possessing the same concrete-and-steel constitution as those structures that survived the initial blasts. In Hiroshima, the legendary A-bomb Dome has become the most enduring symbol of the first atomic bomb. The T-shaped Aioi Bridge, which served as *Enola Gay*'s aiming point, survived the bombing and remained in place for several years afterward. However, structural damage caused by the A-bomb eventually took its toll, and the bridge was rebuilt.

The former Geibi Bank's Hiroshima location that survived the attack not only still exists but is open to the public free of charge. The building is unchanged in many ways, and the teller windows have been replaced in their original positions. Visitors are welcome to walk the nine steps up from the street and into the concrete-and-steel building to re-create **Akiko Takakura**'s fortuitous early arrival at work on the morning of August 6, 1945.

Nagasaki is less than four hours by bullet train to the southwest of Hiroshima. The rugged nature of the countryside is a subtle reminder that the Operation Olympic invasion would have required overcoming very formidable terrain. Nagasaki's bustling port and dockland are a popular port of call for cruise lines, cargo ships, and Japanese naval vessels. A large monument of polished stone two miles by streetcar from downtown Nagasaki (a stark contrast to the monument to the Hiroshima hypocenter, a small plaque located in an alley, with the words "Enola Gay" misspelled as "Enora Gay") marks the site of the A-bomb's hypocenter.

Like Hiroshima, Nagasaki does not define itself by the atomic bomb. But both cities are tourist sites because of the explosions. Their local monuments and museums detailing the bombs' damage are well worth a visit.

★ ★ ★

The father of the atomic age is **Albert Einstein**, whose famous 1905 equation, $E = mc^2$, explains how mass is transformed into energy, thus theoretically making possible a nuclear explosion. The German-born physicist was visiting the United States in 1933 when Adolf Hitler rose to power. He chose not to return home, due to the Third Reich's intolerance of Jews. At age sixty-one, Einstein was granted US citizenship in 1940. The year prior to that, he wrote a letter to President Franklin Roosevelt, alerting him to Nazi Germany's hopes of developing a nuclear weapon. This led to the formation of the Manhattan Project, beginning the race between the United States and Germany to develop the first atomic bomb.

Einstein, however, was not allowed to take part in the Manhattan Project. The FBI thought that Einstein's status as an avowed pacifist with liberal sympathies made him too great a security risk. FBI director J. Edgar Hoover maintained a secret file on Einstein but was never able to prove that the physicist had Communist ties. Many of Einstein's friends relocated to Los Alamos to take part in the project, and they made him well aware of its ongoing progress.

In 1947, Einstein was working with the Emergency Committee of Atomic Scientists, based in Princeton, New Jersey. As part of that group, he penned a letter that reads in part: "We scientists believe upon ample evidence that the time of decision is upon us—that what we do, or fail to do within the next few years will determine the fate of our civilization. . . .

"In the shadow of the atomic bomb, it has become apparent that all men are brothers. If we recognize this as truth, and act upon this recognition, mankind may go forward to a higher plane of human development. If the angry passions of a nationalistic world engulf us further, we are doomed."

Albert Einstein died in 1955 from an aortic aneurysm at the age of seventy-six. His body was cremated, but only after his brain had been removed without permission by a Princeton Hospital pathologist so that it might be studied for science.

* * *

Colonel Paul Tibbets was dogged by controversy about the Hiroshima bombing for the rest of his life. However, he never backed down from his belief that he had done the right thing. The *Enola Gay* itself became an unlikely lightning rod for controversy when the Smithsonian's National Air and Space Museum in Washington, DC, planned to refurbish it after many years of neglect and place it on public display to celebrate the fiftieth anniversary of the war's end. Workers spent two decades and more than three hundred thousand man-hours to restore the plane to its original condition. The tone of the exhibit was to have been apologetic, suggesting that America was wrong to have dropped the atomic bomb and that as few as thirty-one thousand American lives would have been lost in the first months of an invasion of Japan. Under pressure from veterans' groups, the exhibit was altered to allow visitors to come up with their own interpretation of the ethics of dropping the bomb. The *Enola Gay* is now displayed at the National Air and Space Museum's Steven F. Udvar-Hazy Center in Chantilly, Virginia.

Bockscar, the aircraft from which the second atomic bomb was dropped on Nagasaki, has also been lavishly restored. It is currently on display at the National Museum of the US Air Force at Wright-Patterson Air Force Base in Dayton, Ohio.

Both Colonel Tibbets of *Enola Gay* and **Major Chuck Sweeney** of *Bockscar* were promoted to general during their long military careers. Tibbets stayed in the air force and proved instrumental in pioneering the transition to jet-powered bomber flight. Sweeney left active duty after the Second World War but continued to fly in the Massachusetts Air National Guard. Sweeney died in Boston in 2004, at the age of eighty-four. Tibbets lived to be ninety-two years old and requested that he be cremated rather than buried, so that protesters might not make his grave site a rallying point for antinuclear demonstrations. His ashes were scattered over the English Channel, over which he had flown many times during World War II.

* * *

Mochitsura Hashimoto, commander of the *I-58* submarine that sank the *Indianapolis*, received word of the atomic bombings while still at sea. He and his crew thought the reports were just American propaganda. The submarine returned to port on August 15, just in time to learn of the Japanese surrender. Though the war was over, Hashimoto was promoted and given command of the destroyer *Yukikaze*, tasked with traveling to China to bring Japanese troops home. However, the United States Navy, still reeling from the *Indianapolis* tragedy, summoned Hashimoto to America to testify in the court-martial proceedings of Captain Charles McVay. Hashimoto appeared in court in Washington, DC, on December 11, 1945, and stated that there was nothing more McVay could have done to save his crew and that the captain was innocent of all charges. Despite this testimony, McVay was still found guilty. Hashimoto retired from the Japanese navy shortly after his return to his homeland in 1946; he later followed in his father's footsteps and became a Shinto priest. He died on October 25, 2000, at the age of ninety-one.

* * *

Jean Macarthur, wife of General Douglas MacArthur, lived to be 101 years old. She died in New York City of natural causes in 2000, some thirty-six years after her husband's passing. She was instrumental in the building of the MacArthur Memorial, a museum and research center in Norfolk, Virginia, serving as chair of the board during its development and cutting the opening ribbon at the age of ninety-one. In 1988, President Ronald Reagan presented Jean MacArthur with the Presidential Medal of Freedom. In 1994, during a visit to the United States, the emperor and empress of Japan paid a private visit to her New York apartment at the Waldorf Towers. She never remarried after the general's death, and was buried at his side in the rotunda of the MacArthur Memorial in Norfolk.

★ ★ ★

Arthur Macarthur IV, son of General Douglas MacArthur, is still alive, though his whereabouts have become an urban legend. At seventy-seven years of age, he no longer goes by his given name, preferring instead to be called David Jordan. After being paid a $650,000 settlement to move out of his rent-controlled apartment in Manhattan's Mayflower Hotel in 2014, he relocated to Greenwich Village, where he is known to play the piano and avoid all contact with those wishing to associate him with the MacArthur name.

★ ★ ★

Several future American presidents saw military service during World War II, among them naval officers **James Earl "Jimmy" Carter** and **George Herbert Walker Bush**.

Carter, as a midshipman at the United States Naval Academy, was considered to be an active-duty serviceman during the war. He entered Annapolis in 1943 and graduated with the class of 1946. If the war had not ended, Carter would most certainly have been sent to the Pacific with his classmates as part of the naval invasion that would have been launched against Japan. Carter later served on the USS *Mississippi*, a battleship that had seen extensive service in the Pacific theater. In 1948, he transitioned to submarines, where he served as one of the first group of sailors aboard nuclear submarines. Jimmy Carter was discharged from the navy in 1953.

George H. W. Bush, America's forty-first president, joined the navy in 1942 at the age of eighteen, earning his wings as a naval aviator before his nineteenth birthday. He was assigned to the Pacific theater of operations, where he would fly fifty-eight combat missions during the war. On September 2, 1944, exactly one year to the day before the Japanese surrender, he was forced to bail out when his Avenger dive bomber was hit by enemy flak. Bush parachuted to safety, spending four hours afloat on a life raft before being rescued by an American submarine. He resumed flight operations and was based on the aircraft carrier USS *San Jacinto*. In December 1944, after fifteen months of combat duty, he was reassigned to Naval Station Norfolk in Virginia, where he served as a flight instructor until his release from the navy upon the Japanese surrender in September 1945.

Both presidents Bush and Carter were asked by Bill O'Reilly to give their opinions about President Truman's decision to drop the A-bomb. Their letters are printed in this book for the first time, as is the opinion of President George W. Bush. Presidents Bill Clinton and Barack Obama declined to give their opinions of Truman's actions.

★ ★ ★

The relationship between Harry Truman and Douglas MacArthur did not have a happy ending. The last vestige of the war did not fade until April 28, 1952, when the American occupation of Japan was completed through a treaty signed in San Francisco and peace formally declared between the two nations. By then, **Douglas MacArthur**'s tenure as supreme commander for the Allied powers was long over. On June 25, 1950, the Communist state of North Korea invaded its neighbor to the south, and MacArthur was named commander of the United States and South Korean forces, charged with repelling the Communist advance. The general successfully launched one of history's greatest amphibious invasions in September 1950, sending waves of troops ashore far behind enemy lines at Incheon and recapturing the South Korean capital of Seoul. In October 1950, **President Harry Truman** flew to Wake Island in the Pacific to meet with MacArthur about the status of the Korean War and present him with the Distinguished Service Medal—MacArthur's fifth.

However, that meeting turned into a debacle. Truman was rankled that MacArthur delayed exiting from his plane for forty-five minutes, effectively keeping the president waiting. In addition, MacArthur treated the president like an equal, shaking his hand rather than offering a salute when they first met. Never a man to forget a slight or grandstanding behavior, Truman was deeply upset that MacArthur had publicly questioned the president's foreign policy in the Pacific as a strategy of "appeasement and defeatism"—a matter that was read into the official Congressional Record.

This behavior reinforced Truman's initial misgivings about MacArthur's ego, which he felt was out of control. The general did not return phone calls, thinking it beneath his position as "head of state." When asked to brief US State Department officials about the crisis in Korea, MacArthur's response was telling: "Why, as a sovereign, should I? President Truman doesn't do so, nor does the King of England or any other head of state."

The tide of the Korean War turned against MacArthur following the Wake Island meeting. Chinese forces joined the North Koreans to halt the American advance. In defiance of direct orders from Truman, MacArthur sought to expand the size of the war by pushing north into China to confront the invading Communists. On April 5, 1951, in direct contravention of the wishes of President Truman, MacArthur authorized a penetrating American strike into China. By this time, MacArthur's immense popularity made the decision to fire him a political liability, but Truman was unfazed. Calling a meeting of his top advisers on April 6, he broached the topic of dismissing the vaunted general. At stake was the question of whether or not civilian authorities had a say in military policy. It was clear that MacArthur planned to fight the war in Korea and

China on his terms, without heed to the authority of the president of the United States.*

The Joint Chiefs of Staff soon weighed in, favoring the dismissal of MacArthur for insubordination. On April 7, Truman wrote in his journal of the Joint Chiefs that "it is the unanimous opinion of all that MacArthur be relieved. All four so advise."

But on April 11, 1951, when Truman formally announced that he was relieving MacArthur of command, there was an enormous public outcry of support for the general. Truman's public opinion rating once again tanked. Nevertheless, at 8:00 p.m. Washington time on April 11, MacArthur was sacked. Truman had authorized his secretary of the army, Frank Pace Jr., to deliver the news, but Pace did not receive the order. Instead, MacArthur heard about his firing on the radio while eating lunch with his wife in Tokyo.

This marked the end of Douglas MacArthur's military career. He returned home a hero, feted by a parade in New York City viewed by more than seven million people that wound through nineteen miles of Manhattan streets. More than three thousand tons of paper were dropped from windows, balconies, and rooftops.

Meanwhile, there were calls for Truman to be impeached. His approval rating dipped to 22 percent, forcing him to decide against running for reelection in 1952.

---

* Truman's feelings about MacArthur's defiance are stated in a letter written by Truman and owned by Bill O'Reilly, which is reprinted in this book.

✮   ✮   ✮

Douglas MacArthur lived out the rest of his life in luxury, residing with his wife and son in a penthouse atop the Waldorf Astoria Hotel in New York City. In 1962, he gave his legendary "Duty, Honor, Country" speech at West Point, concluding with the words: "The shadows are lengthening for me. The twilight is here. My days of old have vanished, tone and tint. They have gone glimmering through the dreams of things that were. Their memory is one of wondrous beauty, watered by tears, and coaxed and caressed by the smiles of yesterday. I listen vainly, but with thirsty ears, for the witching melody of faint bugles blowing reveille, of far drums beating the long roll. In my dreams I hear again the crash of guns, the rattle of musketry, the strange, mournful mutter of the battlefield. But in the evening of my memory, always I come back to West Point. Always there echoes and re-echoes: Duty, Honor, Country. Today marks my final roll call with you, but I want you to know that when I cross the river my last conscious thoughts will be of The Corps, and The Corps, and The Corps. I bid you farewell."

Douglas MacArthur died on April 5, 1964, of primary biliary cirrhosis, a disease of unknown origin that destroys the bile ducts in the liver. He was eighty-four years old. Before burial, his body lay in state in the Capitol Rotunda, where an estimated 150,000 people waited in line to pay their respects.

☆   ☆   ☆

Harry Truman's habit of long daily walks and drinking healthy doses of branch water and bourbon resulted in a long and prosperous life. He died on December 26, 1972, at the age of eighty-eight; his wife, Bess, died ten years later. Both are buried at his presidential library in Independence, Missouri.

THE WHITE HOUSE
WASHINGTON

April 26, 1951

Dear Russ:

Your letter of the twelfth interested
me tremendously, and I also want to thank you
for sending me the original of Jacob Burck's
cartoon. I need not tell you that I am grateful for your favorable comments concerning the
replacement of General MacArthur and the speech
of explanation to the American people. It
seems to me that everyone who stops to think
should understand that under our constitutional
system military commanders are subordinate to
civil authority.

I am very glad that you wrote me, and
your prayerful wishes are especially appreciated.

Very sincerely yours,

Harry Truman

Mr. Russ Stewart,
General Manager,
Chicago Sun-Times,
211 West Wacker Drive,
Chicago 6,
Illinois.

JIMMY CARTER

This is an excerpt from "A Full Life." I haven't changed my mind.

"We… were again at sea about a year later, when we sat on deck and listened to President Truman's nasal voice announce over the loudspeaker that a formidable weapon had been dropped on Hiroshima and that he hoped this would convince the Japanese to surrender. All of us agreed with his decision, because it was generally believed that 500,000 Americans would have been lost in combat and many more Japanese killed if we had invaded the Japanese homeland and it was defended with suicidal commitment by Japanese troops on the ground. We were disappointed when we didn't return to port in time to join in the celebration when Japan surrendered just a few days later."

Sincerely,

Jimmy Carter

GEORGE BUSH

January 5, 2016

Dear Bill,

**In response to your question, I think Harry Truman
did the right thing. Thousands of Americans would
have died invading Japan. Maybe even me. My
squadron was training for the invasion and close to
shipping out again when Harry dropped the bomb.
So would I have done the same thing? I think so. At
that time, it was the right decision. Tough but right.**

I hope this helps. Happy New Year.

Sincerely,

G Bush

**Mr. Bill O'Reilly
Anchor
Fox News Channel
1211 Avenue of the Americas
17th Floor
New York, NY 10036-8795**

GEORGE W. BUSH

February 9, 2016

Mr. Bill O'Reilly
New York, New York

Dear Bill:

Thank you for writing about this consequential time in our
Nation's history, and thanks for asking my opinion.

When Harry Truman took office suddenly in the final months of
World War II, he said, "I felt like the moon, the stars, and the all
the planets had fallen on me." Yet the man from Missouri knew
how to make a hard decision and stick by it.

In the presidency, there are no do-overs. You have to do what
you believe is right and accept the consequences. Harry Truman
did just that. I admire his toughness, principle, and strategic
vision. He led with our country's best interests at heart, and he
didn't care much what the critics said.

As an American and the son of a World War II veteran, I
support his decision and am grateful.

Sincerely,

George W. Bush

SOURCES

A great deal of the joy in writing a work of history comes from the detective investigation required to flesh out an episode or a subject and make it rise up off the page. Travel, archival searches, governmental databases, websites, and the works of other authors are just a few of the resources that we rely upon. The authors wish to thank James Zobel at the MacArthur Memorial Foundation in Norfolk, Virginia, for his tireless help in tracking down obscure documents pertaining to the general and his life. Visitors to Norfolk are encouraged to pay this underappreciated museum a visit, for it offers an abundance of information about MacArthur's life as well as a vast number of his personal effects.

Head Archivist Dara Baker at the Naval War College was most helpful in tracking down the movements of Admiral Nimitz through the document known as the Nimitz Graybook. David Clark at the Harry S. Truman Library and Museum in Independence, Missouri, was also very helpful in finding some of the more obscure details of the late president's life. As with all presidential libraries, the Truman Library's website offers exhaustive detail about his presidency and lifelong habit of letter writing. The papers of a great number of lesser Truman administration officials can also be found there. Visit www.trumanli brary.org to have a look.

The US Naval Academy Museum in Annapolis, Maryland, should be a required stop for anyone with even a passing interest in history, showcasing the United States Navy—and so much more. The exhibits visitors can view include the spur belonging to John Wilkes Booth that caught on patriotic bunting as he leaped from the presidential box after shooting President Abraham Lincoln and the tomb of the legendary John Paul Jones. For this book, we were interested in the displays detailing the navy's impact on the Pacific war as well as a large number of artifacts, including the pen Admiral Chester Nimitz used to sign the Japanese surrender documents and a sword surrendered by the Japanese delegation to the Allies on the morning of September 2, 1945. Also on display at the Naval Academy Museum are a number of flags that have played prominent roles in American naval history, including the Stars and Stripes flown by Commodore Matthew Perry when he sailed into Tokyo Bay in 1853 and later displayed on board the USS *Missouri* on the morning of the Japanese surrender. The USNA museum is also in possession of the other American flag that flew aboard the *Missouri*, but it is not currently on display. Thank you to archivist Jim Cheevers for his assistance.

There is a fine Pearl Harbor display and film at the USNA museum, but for the greatest effect, readers are encouraged to visit the USS Arizona Memorial in Honolulu, Hawaii. In addition to looking around a detailed museum and watching a vivid film detailing the attack and its aftereffects, visitors can travel by boat to the spot in the harbor where the *Arizona* still rests. Many of the men who died when she exploded and sank that Sunday morning are still entombed inside the ship. Many of those who survived the attack have requested that upon their deaths, their ashes would be placed within the *Arizona* so that they might be laid to rest with their former shipmates.

On display nearby, positioned so that its guns symbolically protect the memorial and the men of the *Arizona*, is the USS *Missouri*. The Mighty Mo is a museum ship now, and visitors can come aboard to see the precise spot on which the Japanese surrender documents were signed.

The authors would also like to thank the Smithsonian's National Air and Space Museum in Washington, DC, and distinguished World War II writer and researcher Brian Sobel.

✫ ✫ ✫

What follows are other resources utilized in this writing. This list is by no means exhaustive but will provide

the readers with a road map to use in their own historical investigations.

Websites, Newspapers, and Archives: General Background Information

News Sources: *New York Times*, *Life* magazine, *Los Angeles Times*, the *Guardian*, *Washington Post*, *Spokane Daily Chronicle*, *Australian*, *Wall Street Journal*, *Times of India*, Associated Press, *U.S. News & World Report*, *New Yorker*, *Japan Times*, *New York Post*, *Chicago Tribune*, *Marine Corps Chevron*, Fox News, PBS, BBC.

Websites: Architect of the Capitol (www.aoc.gov); Office of the Clerk, US House of Representatives (www.clerk.house.gov); National Archives (www.archives.gov), especially dated February 26, 1945, entitled "Captured Japanese Instructions Regarding the Killing of POW"; Battle of Manila Online (www.battleofmanila.org); Congressional Medal of Honor Society (www.cmohs.org); Supreme Court of the United States (www.supremecourt.gov); FBI Records—The Vault (https://vault.fbi.gov); Office of the Historian (history.state.gov); Central Intelligence Agency (www.cia.gov); USS Indianapolis (www.ussindianapolis.org); Bulletin of the Atomic Scientists (www.thebulletin.org), especially Ellen Bradbury and Sandra Blakeslee, "The Harrowing Story of the Nagasaki Bombing Mission."

Archives: Franklin D. Roosevelt Presidential Library and Museum; United States National Archives; Princeton University Library, The Manhattan Project—US

Department of Energy; The George C. Marshall Foundation; US Department of State—Office of the Historian; Library of Congress—Carl Spaatz Papers; Congressional Record, V. 145, Pt. 8, May 24, 1999, to June 8, 1999; Congressional Record, V. 146, Pt. 15, October 6, 2000, to October 12, 2000; National Library of Australia—Trove (archives of the *Argus*); US Naval War College (especially the Nimitz Gray book); Harry S. Truman Library and Museum; Records of the United States Marine Corps; US Naval Institute *Naval History* Archive; US Army Center of Military History Combat Chronicles of US Army Divisions in World War II.

Peleliu

Adam Makos with Marcus Brotherton, *Voices of the Pacific*; E. B. Sledge, *With the Old Breed*; John C. McManus, *Grunts*; John Toland, *The Rising Sun: The Decline and Fall of the Japanese Empire, 1936–1945*; Major Frank O. Hough, USMC, *The Assault on Peleliu*.

MacArthur

Douglas MacArthur, *Reminiscences*; Samuel Eliot Morison, *History of United States Naval Operations in World War II*, vol. 13: *The Liberation of the Philippines—Luzon, Mindanao, the Visayas, 1944–1945*; Robert Ross Smith, *Triumph in the Philippines (United States Army in World War II: The War in the Pacific)*; Gavin Long, *MacArthur*.

Truman

Jon Taylor, *Harry Truman's Independence: The Center of the World*; Sean J. Savage, *Truman and the Democratic Party*; David M. Jordan, *FDR, Dewey, and the Election of 1944*; Jules Witcover, *No Way to Pick a President*; Margaret Truman, *Harry S. Truman*; Steven Lomazow and Eric Fettman, *FDR's Deadly Secret*; Leslie R. Groves, *Now It Can Be Told: The Story of the Manhattan Project*; Thomas Fleming, *Truman*; David McCullough, *Truman*; Margaret Truman, *Bess W. Truman*; Steve Neal, ed., *Eleanor and Harry: The Correspondence of Eleanor Roosevelt and Harry S. Truman*; J. Samuel Walker, *Prompt and Utter Destruction: Truman and the Use of Atomic Bombs Against Japan*.

Hirohito and Japan

Arne Markland, *Black Ships to Mushroom Clouds: A Story of Japan's Stormy Century 1853–1945*; Francis Pike, *Hirohito's War: The Pacific War, 1941–1945*; Herbert P. Bix, *Hirohito and the Making of Modern Japan*; Michael Kort, *The Columbia Guide to Hiroshima and the Bomb*; D. M. Giangreco, *Hell to Pay: Operation Downfall and the Invasion of Japan, 1945–1947*; Douglas J. MacEachin, *The Final Months of the War with Japan*; Tsuyoshi Hasegawa, ed., *The End of the Pacific War: Reappraisals*; Hutton Webster, *Rest Days: The Christian Sunday, the Jewish Sabbath, and Their Historical and Anthropological Prototypes*; Edward J. Drea, *In the Service of the Emperor: Essays on the Imperial Japanese Army*; Noriko Kawamura, *Emperor Hirohito and the Pacific War*; Gavan Daws, *Prisoners of the Japanese: POWs of World War II in the Pacific*; E. Bartlett Kerr, *Surrender and Survival: The Experience of American POWs in the Pacific, 1941–1945*; David M. Glantz, *Soviet Operational and Tactical Combat in Manchuria, 1945: "August Storm"*; Stephen Harding, *Last to Die: A Defeated Empire, a Forgotten Mission, and the Last American Killed in World War II*.

Air Corps

Robert Frank Futrell, *Ideas, Concepts, Doctrine: Basic Thinking in the United States Air Force, 1907–1960*; Samuel Russ Harris Jr., *B-29s Over Japan, 1944–1945: A Group Commander's Diary*; James G. Blight and Janet M. Lang, *The Fog of War: Lessons from the Life of Robert S. McNamara*; Edwin P. Hoyt, *Inferno: The Fire Bombing of Japan, March 9–August 15, 1945*; Graham M. Simons, *B-29: Superfortress: Giant Bomber of World War 2 and Korea*; Robert O. Harder, *The Three Musketeers of the Army Air Forces: From Hitler's Fortress Europa to Hiroshima and Nagasaki*; Eric Larrabee, *Commander in Chief: Franklin Delano Roosevelt, His Lieutenants and Their War*.

Trinity and Atomic Bombs

Everett M. Rogers and Nancy R. Bartlit, *Silent Voices of World War II*; Robert James Maddox, ed., *Hiroshima in History: The Myths of Revisionism*; Gar Alperovitz et al., *The Decision to Use the Atomic Bomb*; Robert Cowley, ed., *The Cold War: A Military History*; Richard Rhodes, *The Making of the Atomic Bomb*; Michael D. Gordin, *Five Days in August: How World War II Became a Nuclear War*; Robert Jay Lifton, *Death in Life: Survivors of Hiroshima*; John Hersey, *Hiroshima*; Paul Ham, *Hiroshima Nagasaki: The Real Story of the Atomic Bombings and Their Aftermath*; Al Christman, *Target Hiroshima: Deak Parsons and the Creation of the Atomic Bomb*; Charles Pellegrino, *To Hell and Back: The Last Train from Hiroshima*; Gerard DeGroot, *The Bomb: A Life*; Tsuyoshi Hasegawa, ed., *The End of the Pacific War: Reappraisals*; Dennis D. Wainstock, *The Decision to Drop the Atomic Bomb: Hiroshima and Nagasaki: August 1945*; Ray Monk, *Robert Oppenheimer: A Life Inside the Center*; Samuel Glasstone, ed., *The Effects of Nuclear Weapons*.

USS *Indianapolis* and US Navy

Richard F. Newcomb, *Abandon Ship!: The Saga of the U.S.S.* Indianapolis*, the Navy's Greatest Sea Disaster*; Doug Stanton, *In Harm's Way: The Sinking of the U.S.S.* Indianapolis *and the Extraordinary Story of Its Survivors*; Edwyn Gray, *Captains of War: They Fought Beneath the Sea*; Christopher Chant, *The Encyclopedia of Code Names of World War II*; Raymond B. Lech, *The Tragic Fate of the U.S.S.* Indianapolis*: The U.S. Navy's Worst Disaster at Sea*; Walter R.

Borneman, *The Admirals: Nimitz, Halsey, Leahy, and King—the Five-Star Admirals Who Won the War at Sea*; Kit Bonner and Carolyn Bonner, *USS* Missouri *at War.*

ACKNOWLEDGMENTS

The legendary *Killing* team made it happen once again: literary agent to the stars Eric Simonoff, astute and insightful publisher Steve Rubin, and Gillian Blake, the quiet editorial genius. My TV boss Roger Ailes deserves a big thank you, as does Makeda Wubneh, my imperturbable assistant of twenty years. Thanks, guys!

—BILL O'REILLY

Thanks for the friendship and professional inspiration of Eric Simonoff, Gillian Blake, and Steve Rubin. To Makeda Wubneh. To Devin, Connor, and Liam. To my wife, Calene, who is singularly awesome. And, of course, to the intrepid Bill O'Reilly.

—MARTIN DUGARD

ILLUSTRATION CREDITS

———◆———

INDEX

Page numbers in italics refer to illustrations.